VISION WORKS
Peter Hesse

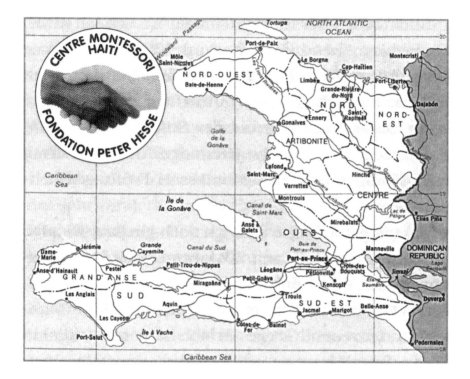

Peter Hesse

VISION WORKS!

**From vision to action
From Haiti
to ONE world
in diversity**

Wake-up calls for change

The "Deutsche Nationalbibliothek" lists this publication in the "Deutsche Nationalbibliografie". Detailed bibliographic data are available in the Internet at http://dnb.d-nb.de. *Detaillierte bibliografische Daten über dieses Buch sind im Internet über http://dnb.d-nb.de abrufbar.*

Peter Hesse – Vision works!
From vision to action.
From Haiti to ONE world in diversity.
Wake-up calls for change.

ISBN 978-3-9811650-2-9

Copyright © by Peter-Hesse-Stiftung

Photos by Peter Hesse (except when specially mentioned)
Symbols and models by Peter Hesse. All rights reserved.
Illustrations for management seminars by Jutta Schepers-Berger.
Cover design + graphic work for models by Martina Greene-Wallraf
Typesetting and printing by **druckpartner** GmbH, Essen, Germany
on FSC-certified paper

Mixed Sources
Product group from well-managed forests and other controlled sources
www.fsc.org   Cert no. IMO-COC-027827
© 1996 Forest Stewardship Council
FSC

All citations are in *Times Roman italics*,
some special ones are in *** Times Roman bold italics***

Published on 7 December 2008, the 25th anniversary of the
"Peter-Hesse-Foundation
SOLIDARITY IN PARTNERSHIP for ONE world in diversity"

2008 by Peter-Hesse-Stiftung, www.solidarity.org
Otto-Hahn-Str. 2 D-49699 Erkrath, Germany

German account: **Peter-Hesse-Stiftung**
No. 3156080, Commerzbank Düsseldorf. BLZ 300 400 00
IBAN: DE14 3004 0000 0315 6080 00, BIC: COBADEFFXXX

for Isa

Acknowledgments

I thank

Carol Guy-James Barratt from Trinidad,
the Montessori soul of the work for children,
for her enduring partnership in the Haiti project
and for her contributions to this book,

Susan Baller-Shepard, USA,
for her editing guidance, for transforming
German-English expressions into American-English
and for contributing the Reading Group Guide

Günter Kirsten, druckpartner, Essen, Germany,
for donating the typesetting of this book
as he donated all former brochures on the work
of the Peter-Hesse-Foundation.

Also by Peter Hesse

MANAGEMENT-SYSTEM
in "Management Enzyklopädie" – Ergänzungsband
1973 Verlag Moderne Industrie, München, Germany
*Please see reprint in www.solidarity.org, German section
in "Veröffentlichungen" ("publications")*

Management Bildungskonzept
in 4 Bildungsstufen:
Schule – Universität – Fortbildung – lebenslang
*Educational Management Concept
in 4 steps: school – academic – post graduate – lifelong*
1976 für "Deutsche Management Gesellschaft",
Komitee für Management-Bildung in Europa, Erkrath, Germany
*Please see reprint in www.solidarity.org, German section
in "Veröffentlichungen" ("publications")*

Von der Vision zur Wirklichkeit
Von Lernwegen zum Erfolg; von der Möglichkeit,
SINN-voll zu leben.
From Vision to Reality
On a learning path to success and the possibility to live with sense.
1999 Cogito Verlag, Kaarst-Büttgen, Germany
ISBN 3-00-4473-6

Unterwegs zu einem Jesus von heute
Nur wer die Herzen bewegt, bewegt die Welt
On the way to a Jesus of today
Only those, who move the heart of people, move the world.
(As editor and contributor in partnership with Clemens Wilken)
2003 Publik Forum Verlag, Oberursel, Germany
ISBN 3-88095-129-2

Solidarität, die ankommt!
Solidarity, which fulfils its purpose!
(As editor and contributor for the "Global Marshall Plan Initiative")
2006 Global Marshall Plan Foundation, Hamburg, Germany
ISBN 3-9809723-8-0

Content: **Page**

Forewords
– Why this book? (by the author) 13
– by André Roberfroid (AMI president)..............15
– Professor Dr. Winfried Pinger (Peter-Hesse-Foundation) .19

I. On a musical path to a wake-up call in Haiti...............21
– How it all started....................21
– Arriving in Haiti....................35
– The voodoo experience 37
– Haiti's wake-up call 41

II. Stumbling on a learning path in and for Haiti..........47
– Initial learning for action....................47
– Memories of a "Godfather"....................50
– The sewing machine initiative 52
– Forget western logical solutions! 54
– Business venture in Haiti....................58
– Miot's village: Ste. Suzanne 60
– A road for Ste. Suzanne....................62
– Seminars in project management....................66
– First country pre-school in Ste. Suzanne...................75
– Meeting Carol Guy-James....................77
– The need for a durable structure....................79
– The Port Margot failure....................87
– Problematic sponsorship for children...................94
– The Montessori vision 97
– Montessori teacher-training 98
– The search for students 108
– The "rest-avec" problem 112
– The start of a successful program...................113
– More basic learning 115

– The "harmonizing-vision" 118
– Montessori development in Haiti – an overview 122
– A Montessori pre-school child writing from Paris 128
– Problems with space and other deceptions....................133
– The building project...137
– Coincidence or higher purpose? 143
– The Brotherhood of the Coast on "La Tortue" 145
– "Facilitators in Partnership" – a micro-grant model 165
– 10-year celebration of Montessori in Haiti....................177

III. Journey inward and the search for "truth"............**182**
– From questioning reality to questioning myself.............182
– The key message..188
– The liberating message 191
– Bridging East and West..196
– The "color sermon"...198
– The Learning Spirals 200

IV. Reaching for global change as the path widens **205**
– My motivational background...205
– A new priority in German development politics 212
– The United Nations open up for civil society.................221
– The World Bank story...225
– World EXPO2000 HANOVER...226
– The failing vision to reform university...........................235
– The vision of a renewed United Nations 241

V. Researching guidelines for our world to heal **249**
– Terms and definitions 249
– Visions, goals and objectives..250
– The Millennium Development Goals (MDGs)................255
– "Heal-solving" 258
– Levels for visions...260

10

– The vision of a world in balance 263
– The Global Marshall Plan Initiative 266
– Enforceable rules for global business.......................274
– The 10 Global Compact Principles............................276
– Guidelines for "heal-solving" solidarity work...............279
– The difficulty of true partnership 283

VI. From Haiti to Africa – and onward **285**
– 43rd Haiti visit in February/March 2008 285
– Political obstacles from the macro-level....................289
– Montessori teacher-training manuals.........................290
– The visit of the AMI president in Haiti 294
– The importance of the first years of life....................306
– Montessori – the trainable method 315
– Reaching for Africa – and beyond............................317
– Early learning – a basic solution 324
– On a path to the future...326

Annex: Work in Haiti, facts and figures **329**
– Carol's article for the 20th anniversary of the Foundation.330
– Foundation policy / Guidelines for work...................336
– Some project details and facts from 1986 338
– Status of Foundation projects in 2008 348
– Foundation's financial overview 357
– Project evaluation by the World Bank in 2002.............361
– Reduced copy of the "harmonizing" letter.................370
– Curriculum vitae Peter Hesse 372
– Reading Group Guide (by Rev. Susan Baller-Shepard....377

Why this book?

Who might enjoy reading, who might benefit from reading this book?

Those, who seek a fulfilled, happy life which makes some deeper sense for themselves and for our world. In writing this book, I have those readers in mind, who believe in a possibility to combine rationality and spirituality, who use their minds, but accept spiritual guidance from a divine source. I also address readers, who – like me – are sometimes "constructively angry" and dissatisfied with our world sliding out of balance, who desire a sustainable integral development of humanity. I especially want to reach those, who want to give children a chance through good early education.

This book tells the story of a learning process in life in attempting to solve problems, to make **visions work**. It is also the story of a search for meaning in life. The search began through conventional, mostly conscious learning. Emotional experiences, intuition and initially unnoticed higher guidance later propelled the learning process. It became successful – supported by an awakening global consciousness and some mystical experience along the path.

The story started on a musical path to Haiti, continued from there over 25 years ago in a more serious way and ended up in an engagement for a better balanced world. The experience on the path from vision to action remained anchored in human development in Haiti, but reached far beyond in an integral way.

This path was, is and hopefully continues to be a challenge to maintain the inner motivation for needed change even in view of the deceptions created by some fellow humans on the way. Having been "marked" by a strong guiding word "DENNOCH" (anyway) in school, it was and is a challenge to truly follow this spirit which empowers the "DENNOCH". I am grateful to have been given the chance to follow that initially unconscious inner guidance throughout the learning process.

There are multitudes of comparable challenges in our today's world. Giving birth to a vision is an important first step and a fascinating exercise. Following the path to the realization of that vision, building that bridge from vision to reality, will frequently be paved with deceptions and even failures. To maintain "DENNOCH" needs energy. This necessity will be reinforced by the unspeakable divine energy which comes as a gift to those who are open to receive it.

Widened and deepened consciousness along the way suggests that sustainable development for a long-term survival of humanity on a cosmic scale today still exceeds the scope of human visions. The more we learn about our universe, the more we shall be able to truly act on a cosmic scale. The perspective of future potential possibilities is quite challenging. Today there is, however, enough to heal in our global village. We can and must develop realistic visions for concrete action here and now for our foreseeable future in our ONE world in diversity.

14

Foreword by André Roberfroid,
President Association Montessori Internationale – AMI

Another book on the meaning of life!
Another book on development!
Another book on education!
Most of us have read too many of these books, hoping to find, at last, some answers. And most of the time we ended frustrated and disillusioned.

This one is different. Yes it is related to development, to education and to the meaning of life, but it is not pretending to know the answers. It is telling the story of a humble, but determined quest for the questions. Peter Hesse is not a specialist in development or education; he does not claim to be a philosopher. Peter Hesse is a specialist in humanity!

The folly of the Nazi ideology, the horrors of war and the ultimate crime of the holocaust were the initial environment of Peter Hesse's young age. The deep scars of this period have marked his family. Experience, in his early days, has shown him that human beings are capable of the worst. And yet Peter Hesse chooses to believe that humanity is on a path of progress, that the reality of the worst does not prevent the likeliness of the best. An extraordinary lesson of optimism and trust in the future.

With such a background, Peter Hesse could have become an enlightened visionary, dreaming of a golden age in the distant future… and writing books about it!

But he decided to make "Vision Works". Rather than dreaming, Peter Hesse participated actively in the rebuilding of the society in post war Germany. As a successful businessman he learned to be pragmatic and concerned with results. The last fifty years in

Germany demonstrate that human beings can rise from the worst and flourish again.

The Peter Hesse who just wrote this book was shaped by this process, a process made of intense learning, hard work, strict organization and respect for fellow humans. This accomplished man had earned the right to enjoy his life. And so he did. His taste for dance and music took him to the Caribbean, precisely in Haiti, were he was hit by a strong wake up call.

As he writes "the direct confrontation with this living misery was too much for the inner balance of a well-to-do European holiday-maker". Just going back to continue to live in the comfort of wealthy Germany was simply not possible anymore. Something had to be done!

Many of us have experienced that kind of shock and the loud call for action that follows. Most will respond by giving some cash to a humanitarian agency and turn the page. Peter Hesse decided to get involved personally. As a businessman he wanted the action to be concrete, effective and profitable. But more importantly, and this is the key to understand this book, he wanted his action to be driven by people. All of us, in the development world, have claimed something similar. People's participation is a common cliché. Often it consists of asking people 'do you want my assistance?' and the answer being naturally positive, we proceed doing what we had previously decided. Peter Hesse started differently. Recognizing that he had no practical knowledge in development matters, he thought, quite rightly, that the golden rule for an effective assistance was to let people decide for themselves. But the second and equally important rule was that the results must be checked and assessed and one should be prepared to change course if and when needed.

The story of Peter Hesse in Haiti becomes a fascinating recollection of a practical path towards human development in one of the most difficult and challenging environment of this world. The cycle of action is quite simple: listen to people, decide what to do, observe carefully, assess the result and correct your action. Easy to say, but challenging to implement. It requires an open mind, able to listen intensely, it demands a capacity to decide and act quickly, it necessitates a frequent presence in the field for close observation and above all it needs an endless patience and ability to recognize failures.

Peter Hesse tells the story in simple words. He offers an opportunity for the reader to travel with him the long journey, made of trials and errors, towards a progressive discovery of human development. It is a long, difficult and often frustrating journey. We discover with the author that development is not about more, but about better. While reading the stories, it becomes clear to us, like it did for him, that education is the primary and the ultimate key without which nothing will succeed.

After a variety of initial experiences in Haiti the book takes us to an even more fascinating exploration. Continuing his path of trials and errors, Peter Hesse unveils another simple truth: as much as development is about human beings, education is about children. The energy that drives development is within the people, and similarly the energy that drives education is within the children. The child is the center and the actor of the education process, the adult is the guide and the service provider. The child achieves the best learning performance at a very young age. An effective learning environment should therefore be made available to the child as early as 3 years. This fact is obvious to any honest observer, and yet this book shows again that the obvious is not easily accepted. The commonly accepted false wisdom is too often that education from 3 to 6 years of age is a luxury to be reserved for the social elite or for the rich countries. The experience reported in this book demonstrates that it is not the case. Early childhood education is not only feasible in poor environment, but is the most productive investment.

In the slums of Haiti, at the end of the 20th century, Peter Hesse came to a conclusion exactly similar to that of Maria Montessori in the poor suburbs of Rome at the beginning of the century. This remarkable encounter did not happen out of theoretical readings, but as a result of an honest man struggling with reality and searching for effective way to bring a lasting change in a desperate situation. After one hundred years of implementation, mostly in the affluent countries, the method created by Maria Montessori is coming back where it started: to serve the most underprivileged children.

As the President of the Association Montessori Internationale, I can only express my immense gratitude to Peter Hesse and to all his friends in Haiti, for giving us this marvelous example. As Maria Montessori said many times, 'the child is the agent of change'. This book is a testimony to her vision.

André Roberfroid,
Carol Guy-James Barrett
and Peter Hesse
(from right to left)
in Liancourt, Haiti

Foreword by Professor Dr. Winfried Pinger

Peter Hesse is a pioneer and an example for all, who fight against extreme poverty and misery in the world. The reader of this book will meet the man Peter Hesse and his multiple activities. Many of those activities are in favour of those, who are relevant for our future: pre-school age children. The reader will also meet the politician Peter Hesse, the engaged campaigner for the renewal of international institutions and for better political framework conditions.

With his devoted long-term engagement for his Foundation's Montessori pre-school project in one of the most difficult countries of the world, Haiti, he has demonstrated what can be achieved by tenacious persistence and by permanently solving newly arising problems. His is an exemplary project, while too many projects – mainly those of the public development cooperation – have failed.

Development always boils down to human development. Peter Hesse knows this. Long before others he has learned from development mistakes of the past (including his own in Haiti). In many developing countries, development is not assured because of corrupt bureaucracies. The state must provide improved framework conditions and essential basic services – that is all he can do. The "trickle-down" effect, which is still programmed in the heads of many development politicians, has not happened. That concept has failed. Real development happens through people themselves. Therefore, development cannot be ordered from above or through regimentation. Development must come from below – from the people.

The poorest of the poor are capable of incredible achievements. All we have to do is to help them to improve their living conditions themselves. We must trust people. Peter Hesse shares this view with the Nobel Peace Prize winner Professor Yunus. With his "Partnerschafts-Helfer-Modell" (Facilitators in Partnership) he has successfully initiated a micro-grant model as an addendum to micro-credits.

What kind of development politic is successful or not, depends on our idea of man. If human beings in developing countries are only objects for state policy or production factors in economic calculations, development politics are doomed to fail. Successful is he, who counts on people. This is why this book is particularly valuable. It not only deals with development politics – but with people. It deals with trials and errors and with how one can learn from mistakes and thereby accomplish exemplary work. That describes Peter Hesse's work.

Professor Dr. Winfried Pinger*, former Member of German Parliament, former CDU spokesman for international development politics. Chairman of the Advisory Board of the Peter-Hesse-Foundation.

* I consider Professor Pinger to have been my mentor during all my learning years in development politics. He once came along to Haiti to see for himself (Photo). We share many ideas on development. During his 16 years as a member in Parliament he was an outstanding figure, but he remains the "Graue Eminenz" (gray eminence) of German development politics.

20

Chapter I:
On a musical path
to a wake-up call in Haiti

What does it take to wake a person up?

For me, it was a gradual process that started with a simple fall. I was on skis, like I had often been on skis, but with a simple fall, broke my right shoulder. Seven years later, in the warm weather of Haiti, instead of the bright cold of Switzerland, I began to wake up in the midst of a confrontation with a sad and challenging reality. It took an additional three years to put in place a structure, the "Peter-Hesse-Foundation SOLIDARITY IN PARTNERSHIP for ONE world in diversity", in December 1983. But what attracts a German Christmas vacationer to HAITI?

Well, originally – nothing did.

How it all started

I needed some pain to get started on the path. Waking up later involved costly mistakes and detours on our way to success. That fall on skis, in 1973, initiated the desire for change in me. Seductive Afro-Caribbean music in the West Indies paved the way, eventually, to Haiti. This waking up process took seven years , for me, a German manufacturer of artists' colors and management trainer, to notice and to awaken in Haiti. But even this detour had much earlier roots in totally different ways of adult life – subconsciously preceded by a turbulent childhood in crazy wartime (a Jewish grandmother on my father's side and a Nazi grandfather on my mother's side) – and equally problematic postwar circumstances. This life did not at all start halfway "normally".

After school, a mostly theoretical university training in business economics ("Betriebswirtschaftslehre – BWL") had first resulted in a very practical need: the acquisition of more useful management and marketing skills for a successful working life. Postgraduate training in the framework of Germany's organization of "Young Entrepreneurs" ("Junge Unternehmer – BJU") functioned as a "practical life university".

Many of us graduates realized that our formal university training was not sufficient for qualified managerial work. University had been much too theoretical and had neglected the "soft" human skills. An early educational activity and the engagement in the organization of young potential business owners led to a challenging career to become one the first management, marketing and creativity trainers in postwar Germany. All was set for a life-long concentration on management consulting and on business in general.

But from the beginning, there was always time for some recreational sport activities: sailing in summer and skiing during the short holiday period around Christmas. Those winter holidays became relevant for the start to future engagement in and for "ONE world in diversity".

Christmas, being a quiet, peaceful family feast in traditional Germany. Provided, one lives in well-settled economical conditions like in my case, one goes to midnight church on 24 December and visits extended family. Here, one eats a lot. If one does not have extended family, one eats a lot anyway. In my case, this was followed by a rush to a yearly changing skiing station in the alps in Austria or in Switzerland for some days of skiing. As an adult, this used to be my winter routine: a Christmas feast with my family, midnight church – and off to Austria or Switzerland on a late night train. Arriving in the Swiss skiing resort St. Moritz on 25 December rather early in the morning, quickly up the lift to the mountain top – in 1973 like in so many years before.

This year 1973 was, however, different. How was I to know that this 25 December would finally prove to be life-changing? Five minutes after arriving on top of the mountain in bright winter sunshine – just below the top of the gondola station:
– losing my balance as I caught a bad edge on skis,
– a simple fall after my first few meters of skiing,
– a painfully broken shoulder joint of the right arm – and total frustration.

In the resort hospital, the shining slopes in bright sunlight visible through the windows of the hospital room, the frustration hardened to an inner vow: This winter routine must change! My decision to quit skiing was mainly due to irrational anger about my hasty skiing movement in the very first moments of a potentially beautiful holiday period. The pain only reinforced the frustration. Anyway – the decision was made and it remained firm.

The alternative: no more late night trains to skiing resorts from next year on. After the initial family feast and Christmas-song singing in church late on 24 December – off to some warm Caribbean island for some days of less bone-breaking activities. This new concept for the next short Christmas holiday break in 1974/75, born out of frustration, was further reinforced during the year through a slow bone-healing process. This provided a good inner excuse for maintaining the Caribbean alternative alive and for some careful island choice. It was to be an island with enduring sun on the beach and water – instead of on the skiing slope. The island destination should not be too foreign, but with a touch of cultural adventure. Lazy sunbathing on some beach was never what I liked to compensate for my work life. It had to be some activity and I cannot deny a basic curiosity to learn something new about other cultures and other ways of life.

My first choice was an island in the Bahamas: lots of home-feeling through many fellow tourists – but with a touch of difference through dark-skinned locals and their music. Apart from some occasional Club Med summer holiday, this was to be my first mild cultural exposure to "something different". In the Club Med in various southern countries and in Africa, the only locals I had met were those serving me. This "something different" in the Bahamas became strong enough to create a lasting cultural imprint on my emotional system.

Musical vibrations have always "touched" me beyond what can be explained rationally. Is it an ancestral imprint? I do not know. My father was the southern German champion ballroom dancer as a student. It seems I have inherited some rhythmic sensitivity. I just know that I "feel" rhythmic music in a direct way in my body. It just "moves" me. Arriving on my chosen island between Christmas and New Year, the news of a local tradition somehow reached me – the news about "Bahamian Jankanoo". This strictly local mini-carnival, which was (and still is) celebrated only in the nights before the 26th of December and before New Year's Day, sounded fascinating. Further inquiries resulted in the wish to get a glimpse of this colorful local event.

I decided to get up before four o'clock in the early morning to get a first-hand impression on the first day of January 1975. To my amazement, almost none of the multitude of white tourists, who crowded the surrounding hotels, were up. The streets were full of "black" Bahamians, many of them parading in costumes made from colorful paper or bits of newspaper – all of them gently

24

swaying their bodies – or more precise: their hips – to a pounding drum, rattle and whistle tune. The rhythm intruded my stomach and created this warm euphoric feeling which I can still feel today – 33 years later.

I wanted to see and feel this trance like ritual from as close as possible. So I simply climbed on a tree which lined the street. A colorful rhythmic stream of Bahamians paraded directly below me. Their faces were shining in the dim light of some street lanterns and of first distant promises of a new day. They were too involved in their movements to speak or even laugh. It was a profound trancelike togetherness, which slowly moved the stream of bodies – occasionally interrupted by some individual outburst of joy like air bubbles in gently simmering water.

I was completely taken by fascination and almost forgot to film the stream of bodies from my tree position a few meters above the ground, when the dawning of the early morning provided enough light. It was as if it was not my body, clinging to the rather uncomfortable position, but that the collective aura of the gently swaying crowd had integrated me into their trance.

The first signs of daylight behind the horizon were soon bright enough to start filming the scene. My simple small "super 8" film camera could not register sound. But it still was a rhythmic revelation when I later viewed the film. The harmonious movements of the dancers made that rhythm visible and it vibrated in my memory. Later, it was possible to find a recording with Bahamian Jankenoo music to add sound to the film. It matched perfectly and reinforced the lasting memory.

I was particularly fascinated by the gentle dancing of a young Bahamian woman who carried the banner of her costumed group. Her swaying cool, movements created an enduring sensual imprint in my body and soul. I cannot explain this. It simply happened. Why it is especially this kind of Afro-Caribbean rhythm that "touches" me, I really cannot explain either. Here, in the Jankenoo night, it was not the first time that I listened to that kind of music, but it was the first time that this happened in such a dense lively atmosphere. I truly felt "in" this atmosphere. I was part of it.

When I later witnessed other Afro-Caribbean dancers, who seemed to have a comparable feeling in their bodies, my young banner-carrying Bahamian remained the swaying idol and lasting symbol of those harmonious rhythmic movements. Through watching and filming from my mental cloud in the tree, I had also re-discovered a passion which reactivated a student hobby: dancing. But unlike those early years, when we danced to traditional European music and "Rock-and-Roll", this new passion was even stronger and now firmly connected to Afro-Caribbean rhythms.

Back in Düsseldorf, Germany, I took up African drumming and dance lessons. The outcome was not very spectacular and certainly not comparable to my Bahamian memory: My own movements – although feeling good to me – were far too controlled and lacked the gentle ease of "my" Bahamian banner carrier. But the urge to be exposed to the real local musical atmosphere grew though the working year and resulted in next year's Caribbean Christmas holidays in a slightly less touristic West-Indian island: Ste Lucia.

In the following years, the passion grew further and led me to other Caribbean islands, gradually more local and "real" in their atmosphere. My musical taste became gradually more specific and selective. One musical search-line finally ended up in Trinidad, the home of steel bands and calypso. A second musical line led me to the French islands Martinique and Guadeloupe, the homes of "Cadence" (today called "Zouk"). Contrary to wild European imitations of Afro-Caribbean dancing, Cadence is much more gentle: It encourages released hip bones and allows the bodily senses to enjoy the rhythm and melody in dense quiet.

This may read as if my life during those years consisted only of different varieties of Caribbean music. Well, musically it did. This music, which moved me so much with its exhilarating rhythms, had become a real craze and addiction for me. This added up to my equally addictive work for our family business in Germany, Schmincke artists' colors – though on a different level.

Our family business enabled the fascinating combination of rational work with the values of quality production to serve the creative arts. The managerial work, which I also truly enjoyed, had become more and more intense with the rising responsibilities as the company's president from 1971. In working towards the company's 100-year jubilee in 1981, stress was added to the business.

The musical holidays in the West Indies, therefore, provided the perfect emotional and physical balance to the managerial work at home. But after seven years, they became unexpectedly relevant for a much more serious aspect of my life: my engagement in Haiti.

During the last relatively "normal" Christmas holidays in the French Island of Guadeloupe in 1979, my craving for the "real"

Afro-Caribbean music prompted two young local receptionists in my hotel in Guadeloupe to send me to Haiti. I had invited them to join me for a local dance near the hotel. Realizing that my passion for their music was real and not just a pretext to get into contact with some nice local ladies, they came along. After a wonderful Cadence-dancing evening they told me: "If you really want the best Cadence music, you must go to Haiti"!

Some problems in Haiti

Multiple problems: polluted water, child-labour and insufficient schools

Problem: hunger – a multifaced basic problem

Children in misery

30

Problem: insufficient possibilities of fruit conservation – here of mangos

Problems: hygiene and environment

31

More a solution than a problem: people replace technical solutions
– here in construction work

Up to then, Haiti had not at all been on my tourist agenda. Although I had totally lost all skeptical distance towards "strange" cultures, there were serious – and as I was bound to find out later: justified – reservations about Haiti. Too many bad stories of the ruling Haitian dictatorship of "Papa Doc" came across the Atlantic. Haiti was not really a place to spend some peaceful musical Christmas holidays. But after learning that some of my favorite Cadence bands, like Coupé Cloué, were from Haiti and regularly played there in a specific Hotel, "Le Lambi", I nevertheless decided to spend my next Christmas holidays there.

Haiti has also beautiful romantic sides – especially along the seashore.

Arriving in Haiti

Le Lambi was situated outside of the capital of Haiti, Port-au-Prince, beyond what Haitians call a "quartier populaire", a densely populated poor area. This part of the town, Carrefour, could be called a "slum", if there had not been the even worse agglomerations of tiny shags made from scrub iron and other debris. The Lambi hotel itself was a place with a rather bad reputation, as I was to find out later. It, however, offered what I had been looking for: a relatively clean room to sleep, some simple but very tasty local food – and most important: wonderful Cadence music almost every night. On a huge terrace built on pillars over the dirty waters of the seashore, the bands started playing around 10 o'clock in the evening and stopped between 1 or 2 o'clock in the night. It was a musical heaven in a surrounding hell.

In the evenings, the scarcely lit dance floor was crowded by tightly swaying local couples. Many of the often rather solid men had pistols casually and visibly tugged in their belts on their backs. They were obviously men who were somehow affiliated to the ruling regime and their infamous "Tontons Macoutes" (Duvalier's militia). These Haitians were able to pay the five dollars asked for at the gate. Single young women, some obviously on a more commercial look-out for men, others simply fans of the well-known Cadence bands, were listening to the music from outside. The loud music attracted people from the neighboring "quartier populaire", even when they could not afford the five dollars at the gate. There was no problem for a single man to find a dancing partner in this colorful situation. In my case, I only had to watch out not to get entangled with some of the ladies with "other interests". Even without being prudish, this other kind of holiday-making for single men was not, what I was looking for here in Haiti. I was simply addicted to Afro-Caribbean music and dancing. It was not too difficult to notice, which of the women outside the gate where out to meet a man for financial reasons. The "Lambi" was not a very refined environment. In a more sophisticated environment, I might not have been able to make such distinctions.

I was lucky to meet a gentle young Haitian woman, Paulette was her name, who came to listen to the music, as she said. I believed her, invited her into the Lambi's dance hall. I later felt that I had not been mistaken. My fascination to have arrived in my musical heaven had covered up all potential rational reserves and fears, anyway. This was, what I had been looking for: the feeling of being integrated in the home culture of my musical addiction – and in truly gentle female company. I felt like in a trance.

Paulette and I harmonized when we danced and even beyond. We became friends and some mutual trust developed. She responded very gently to my cultural curiosity. Perhaps inwardly she smiled about that crazy dancing tourist, but she accepted my curiosity and even introduced me to one particularly fascinating aspect of Haitian culture, voodoo. I would not have been able to witness a "real" voodoo ceremony as a tourist without such involvement. And though this is a different story, it is also related to my Haitian learning process and therefore shall be told here.

The voodoo experience

When my Cadence partner Paulette noticed that my interests did not stop at dancing and being in her company, she asked me whether I would like to be invited to a voodoo ceremony on the next evening. She was to be "involved" in the ceremony, as she said. I was, of course, curious and agreed without much hesitation. It became a memorable evening deep down in a slum-type section of Carrefour.

The path with no artificial lighting leading to a larger, but simple hut deep in the midst of the "quartier populaire" was an exciting adventure by itself. Never before had I dared to penetrate that deeply into the miserable "dark" side of this only partly beautiful country Haiti. The unlit path was dark – but Haiti has very dark sides in a social sense, too. Protected and guided by Paulette, however, I felt safe. In any case, my fascination was stronger than potential fear. Arriving at the temple hut, I was received most gently by the voodoo priestess, the "Mambo", and her well-educated son. He was put "in charge" to make me feel safe and well. Being the only white participant, this first true immersion into this traditional African spiritual culture in Haiti created a second imprint in my emotional system. It was not really comparable to my first rhythmic revelation in the tree over the Junkanoo night in the Bahamas. This here was even more "strange" to a traditional European. It was densely exciting. My emotions were intermixed with cultural curiosity.

The walls of the small temple were decorated with photographs of "Papa Doc", the Haitian dictator, as well as with paintings of Christian angels and saints, who all have their place in voodoo tradition, too. Originally used to camouflage African deities, angels and saints are now firmly integrated. The end-of-the-year voodoo ritual culminated in an ecstatic trance-inducing activity of some young women, including Paulette, around a big plastic pot. In this pot, branches of a bush with small leaves were rubbed in a mix of sea and coconut water in fast and rhythmic movements. The bush-smashing pot dance was in rhythmic harmony with the three sacred voodoo drums across from me behind a painted central pole. Their heads deep down in this rubbing action, one woman after the other fell into a trance, foam coming from their mouths and their bodies rolling on the floor around the central pole.

It was a scene of strange and exciting intensity, accompanied by wild movements of some other participants and stirred up by the most intense voodoo drumming. To my own amazement, I did not feel in any way mentally disturbed in my watching fascination. I could even take some photographs after discretely consulting with my "personal host", the Mambo's son. It was touching, however, to see "my" Cadence partner in her ecstatic trance rolling on the floor and seeing her being comforted by the Mambo. Later, the Mambo herself fell into a trance and was – in turn – comforted by other participants.

38

Voodoo Mambo in trance

The strangeness of the ritual created a respectful interest to learn more about this deeply moving tradition. In my view, my Cadence partner Paulette had now been fully transformed into my personal teacher in Haitian culture. Next day, when I met her again after her voodoo transformation, I asked her to escort me again to her Mambo in the daytime to bring a symbolic gift. This resulted in a deep and prolonged exchange with the very open and knowledgeable priestess on a variety of different global cultures, spiritual practices and world-views. The Mambo, although obviously fully integrated in her local, most simple environment, was certainly in no way "simple". This deep exchange and the evening ritual, which I had been allowed to witness, created a lasting respectful imprint in my mind. That meeting also resulted in an invitation by the Mambo to join the ritual again during my next year's post-Christmas visit. In my feeling, I had now truly arrived in Haiti.

Haiti's wake-up call

For all following 42 visits to Haiti I was, however, totally trans-formed by another new learning experience during this first Haiti visit in the end of December 1980. It needed a third cultural "happening", a true awakening of a different kind to finally pro-duce that change:

Having been celebrating my rhythmic dancing addiction during those first days in Haiti in December 1980 and having been cul-turally enriched by the voodoo experience, I euphorically walked the streets of Haiti on the following day. There, two young men approached me. One of them introduced himself as a "pastor" of a "Mission Globale" in Carrefour, the other one as a director of an orphanage and a school affiliated to this institution. Being used to rather creative begging approaches since my first days in Haiti, I was most skeptical. But this here felt different – I now felt different, too.

The two men told me that in the "Mission Globale" the children were hungry, that most of their orphans had to sleep on the bare floor and that the whole situation was desperate. It really sound-ed sad and did hurt emotionally in the heart of someone, who had just recently been spoiled by the fulfillment of his luxurious musical addictions and of exciting cultural learning. There was nothing important to do during this daytime break between danc-ing and another meeting with Paulette. So I followed the two men to their "Mission Globale".

It was shocking! All they had said was true! A totally run-down, flat stone building and a vast yard were crowded with small chil-dren in obviously desperate looking circumstances. It created a brutal awakening to a sad reality. I had rationally anticipated that reality during my first dancing days in Haiti. But – up to now –

it had not yet entered my stomach. It was obvious that I could not simply go on "having fun" in whatever way, but that "something had to be done" to help healing such misery. Rationally, I knew that I had earned my right to spend a Christmas holiday in a way which suited my musical addiction – but I still could not avoid to feel guilty. It was an inner wake-up call. Emotionally, I was shocked and touched. The direct confrontation with this living human misery was too much for the inner balance of a well-to-do European holiday maker – and it needed some (re-)action. Even though I unfortunately never had any children of my own, as I only married later in my life, I was simply moved by their misery. The stark contrast between the life I was living, and what I saw here moved me to action.

For safety reasons I did not carry much cash, but it was no problem to change some travelers' checks which I carried with me for unexpected emergencies. Well, this was an unexpected emergency! The few hundred US dollars, which I was able to donate to Mr. and Mrs. Platel, the responsible couple in the "Mission Globale", were nothing more than a drop in the bucket. This could only momentarily partly appease the situation – and my troubled mind. But it was not possible to simply returning to my "fun life" during the remaining few days in Haiti in this January 1981.

Even the gentle "relationship" with my cultural teacher and dancing partner, Paulette, changed after this cultural shock. She introduced me to her living reality in Carrefour and to other parts of Haiti around the capital. She helped me to obtain a realistic impression of the hard struggle for survival of her people. I planned to come back to Haiti during the next post-Christmas period in 1981 to bring some help to the desperate situation, I had just been confronted with.

What was and still is most touching in Haiti is the poverty of children, but at the same time the caring gentleness some older children show for their younger siblings.

Equally touching is the love the youngest children are receiving from their families.

Chapter II:
Stumbling
on a learning path in and for Haiti

At home in Germany, some friends, whom I had told about what had touched me in Haiti, helped collecting some money and we planned a first innocent support activity. None of us had any practical knowledge in development matters. We simply wanted to relieve the situation in this orphanage and – possibly – in some comparable situations. I believed that I could detect and choose such deplorable situations myself during my next year's stay in Haiti. There was no vision involved at that stage. Action was simply born out of need – my own inner need and the need, which I had witnessed.

Initial learning for action

Lucky circumstances in Germany initiated a new multidimensional learning process and proved very useful in somewhat limiting my innocent first mistakes while trying to help in Haiti:

Due to a recent engagement in German politics in the early seventies, I had met some "important" people at home. It had been a turbulent period not only in Germany. I also felt the need for change – but only through peaceful evolution at home. I simply did not like the radical revolutionary movements on the far "left". My passion was limited to my own group, the business community. There was no profound motivation involved to help disadvantaged people in the world. I simply fought for a better management education in Europe. That was all. After being drawn into German political life through this early passion for change in my own field, I had become a member of the conservative party: the Christian Democratic Union (CDU). This was the "normal" political home for a relatively conservative business person. Besides introducing marketing concepts to our traditional family business, I had become a management, marketing and creativity trainer – as mentioned in the introduction above. After having joined the CDU party, I had started to offer various kinds of seminars to the local members of "my" party. Project management had become one of my best-sold items as a management trainer. So – why not try to use this seminar in politics?!

PROJEKT-MANAGEMENT: 1. Über die Ziel r i c h t u n g einigen

2. Fördernde und hemmende Kräfte auf dem Weg zum Ziel analysieren
3. Detailziele und Planung (Rangliste) erarbeiten

4. Aufgaben und Kompetenzen durch Organisations-Matrix klären

5. DurchFÜHREN wie geplant

6. Soll-Ist-Kontrolle
und „feed-back"
mit neuen Ideen

7. Neues Ziel usw. (1.-6.)

© P. Hesse

PROJEKT-MANAGEMENT

The seminars were well accepted and soon gave me some "status" in the regional CDU. This resulted in being challenged to apply for candidacy for a CDU seat in the German Federal Parliament. A group of younger members in the party wanted some more dynamic personalities to represent them in parliament. They convinced me to accept this challenge and decided to actively manage and support my candidacy. My internal CDU opponent was a well-known, truly conservative and well-settled State Minister. He did win the final voting for being the local CDU candidate in the next election for federal parliament. But it was no shame to lose against him. It was an honorable narrow miss – and a very good learning experience in politics.

Having been involved somewhat more deeply in "politic matters" during the challenging period of the candidacy, I was now called to participate in various party circles and commissions, where I met the "important people". One particularly helpful VIP in this framework was Bernd Dreesmann, the secretary general of Germany's largest non-clerical aid organization, the "Deutsche Welthungerhilfe" – in Haiti today: "Agro-Action Allemande".

We were both members of a CDU "think tank" on global matters, even though I did not yet have any practical experience in the field. Bernd Dreesmann's organization was originally involved in Haiti under the name "FONd pour le DEVeloppement rural (FONDEV)". He was most helpful in limiting my initial mistakes in this new venture. He acquainted me to his Haitian counterpart and representative, a gentle expert in agrarian matters and the director of FONDEV, Miot Jean-Francois. We met in December 1981 as planned, and Miot became my friend and teacher in Haiti. This was the beginning of a never-ending learning path to become effective and to be efficient in "development matters".

Bernd Dreesmann rightly considered himself to be important for my early learning path in Haiti. He jokingly called himself a Godfather in his friendly notes, his memories, which I had asked him to contribute for this book.

Memories of a "Godfather" – *by Bernd Dreesmann*

It was in May 1981. A Peter Hesse from Erkrath near Düsseldorf had announced his visit. In our guest room, I met "a man in his best age", who immediately and without any detours started talking about his first visit in Haiti. I could feel his enthusiasm. He told me that he had been there for a short holiday as a musically interested tourist. This in itself was remarkable, since unlike the neighboring Dominican Republic or Martinique, Haiti was not one of those well-liked and frequently visited holiday destinations. On the contrary: The dictator, "Papa Doc", was an embodiment of tyranny and Haiti's surname "poorhouse of the western world" added to ward off tourists.

So Peter Hesse, obviously already the "DENNOCH type", who became widely known in development circles and beyond in the following years, had been in Haiti. And now he reported on his consternation about the poverty and misery, he had found there. Obviously it had been different from a normal sunny island holiday. Peter Hesse would not have been himself, if he had simply noticed his consternation and would have remained inactive. No! As a successful businessman, he knew that doing nothing creates nothing. The tourist Peter Hesse started to care. Cautiously and in small steps. He talked to local people, went into their poor quarters, which already then were in a dismal situation – with the exception of the bright white presidential palace. He started reflecting about what could be done. Even better: what he could do himself to at least relieve some of the poverty.

50

I read in his travel report that from the beginning he did not think of distributing charity, but of "help for self-help". I found this remarkable. Even more surprising was that he already had brought back an idea from Haiti, how he could help. He had seen people working on some junky old sewing machines to somewhat improve their living situation. So he knew what to do: What was needed were functioning sewing machines. 10 to 12 of them for a start – and fast.

Now he had arrived at the topic for which he wanted to see me. He wanted to donate the needed money to the "Deutsche Welthungerhilfe" (German Agro Action) and our office in Haiti should help in the distribution. This idea was basically in order, but not that easy to realize, since our guidelines asked for careful checking locally, whether his potential recipients were to be the right ones. Those careful "reserves", which were based on experience, must have looked to Peter Hesse, who was burning for action, as a critical example of "development bureaucracy". Our conversation went on. So I called "our man in Haiti", Miot Jean-Francois, and asked him to quickly evaluate the situation.

Then Peter Hesse come up with his second subject, the miserable condition of the children – badly nourished, shabby and with no chance to even receive a minimum of education. "I can not bear this", was his energetic conclusion. Later, he had a solution for this problem, too: "Montessori".

We finally agreed to cooperate actively. The rest is history. The sewing machines were predominantly well distributed with the help of our Miot Jean-Francois, and I offered Peter Hesse our qualified assistance, since the "Deutsche Welthungerhilfe" (in Haiti "FONDEV" at that time) was maintaining a vast program with a lot of expertise in Haiti.

Peter Hesse was learning fast. More trips to Haiti reinforced his view that he had to offer "help for self-help". Children became his "target group". And since the capable one is frequently also aided by luck, he found the right knowledgeable partner for the teacher-training of the "Peter-Hesse-Foundation" (created in 1983) in the person of Carol Guy-James from Trinidad. This became the basis for a comprehensive and very successful program.

As a member of the board of trustees of the Foundation, I had the chance to closely witnessing the exemplary growth of the Foundation's work over the years. – "Chapeau, chapeau, Peter Hesse!" Our first dialogue was one of the most effective ones in my 25 years as a Secretary General of the "Deutsche Welthungerhilfe".

The sewing machine initiative

Before the valuable linkage to the Haitian partner of the "Deutsche Welthungerhilfe" could be "activated" in December of 1981, I had made my first mistakes in trusting my western logical mind: Starting from the widely known idea that it would be better to give some fishing gear instead of fish, I thought that my rational mind was capable enough to structure some "help to let people help themselves". Having no practical experience in the field of poverty reduction in a different culture, it still seemed to me alright to buy some non-electric, foot-driven sewing machines and an initial stock of sewing material in Haiti for especially needy families. They, the families, would know best how to use such productive devices, I thought. They would be able to sew clothes for their children, I imagined, and also sell some of their production. Unfortunately, the idea proved to be too simple – though quite logic – to function in practice, as I had to learn in Haiti.

It was not difficult to see that we, the well-meaning people of the northern and western countries, were completely misled in believing that we could effectively help in collecting used

52

clothing "for the poor". The exception may be warm used clothes for winter disasters – and if distributed by reliable institutions. Under normal conditions, however, our clothes, even when truly arriving in a poor country, are damaging. They make a local production of clothing almost impossible. Only the importers of used clothes in those developing countries (and maybe some people in the following distribution chain) gain from such shipments. The used clothes in the open markets (see photo from Haiti below) make it almost impossible to locally compete. This, however, was not the only misconception in our sewing machine action.

Forget western logical solutions!

Why did the theoretically nice sewing machine concept, which my friends in Germany had helped me to develop and had even co-financed in a modest way, did not work out in practice, as we had believed? This was to become my first lesson on a learning path for "solidarity, which works" – or to be more precise here: "which does **not** work".

Before the second Haiti trip in December 1981, the money for twelve manual sewing machines and some initial sewing material was transferred to FONDEV. In Haiti, I immediately bought the machines and wanted to distribute them to some poor families – when Miot intervened. He warned me that there was a second reason – besides the dilemma of unfair competition to clothes production from cheap imports – why my concept was wrongly conceived: A relatively valuable item like a sewing machine would soon be sold by a poor family when there was need for cash for survival or for medicine to cure their children. The only decent solution would be, to give the machines to groups of people for training purposes, to local initiatives, which would exercise some social control over each other.

Luckily, I followed Miot's advice – at least for eleven of the twelve sewing machines. We gave eleven machines to four existing Haitian initiatives: to the Mission Globale from last year's first contact, to a citizens' self-help initiative "Conseil d'action communautaire" in Trou-du-Nord and to a Christian educational institution, the "Collège du St. Esprit" in Cap Haitien. In this school, young ladies were supposed to learn practical sewing skills among other household subjects with the help of only four old sewing machines for their 80 students. Five of our new machines where, therefore, most welcome here. Machine number eleven went to a group of women in the small village of Ste. Suzanne, in the mountains beyond Trou-du-Nord.

Ste. Suzanne, far up in the north of Haiti, was, where Miot originally came from. This village was to become an important locality for my future engagement in Haiti. In those four group initiatives, the machines served mainly to train machine-sewing for repairing clothes and occasionally for producing something for special needs. To compete directly with the cheap imported used clothes was no feasible option. Since my learning only started after the deciding and buying action – instead of preceding it – we at least could preserve part of the original idea. The nice machines were not totally wasted in this way.

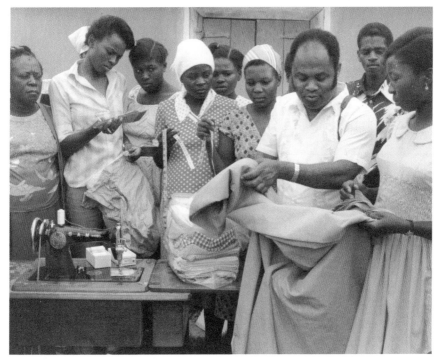

Handing over one machine in Ste. Suzanne with Miot

The choice of recipients for the sewing machines would have been difficult to make without inside knowledge. Miot's assistance was therefore most valuable. The fact that he favored recipients and places, where he had personal contacts or even relatives, was a normal Haitian procedure. Miot felt that it was quite alright to assist his own friends and relatives first. This was certainly not a totally objective procedure. As a newcomer in the field of practical solidarity "which works" I, however, convinced myself that this favourism could be relatively tolerated. To really be neutral and fair in targeting potential partners in development is only possible on the basis of deeper inside knowledge of the respective social structure. Learning to at least partly avoid local favourism took longer experience on the ground. Transparency as a social value and as a precondition for fair and best possible action must first be developed and internalized. In the beginning, I had to accept the risk of favourism as a mild version of corrupt behavior. But it was useful to become conscious that societies, like the ones in Haiti, traditionally practiced this kind of solidarity. It had derived from ancient traditional behavior where people naturally looked after their own group first.

Egocentrism and the related "tribocentrism" must eventually mutate towards an attitude and a behavior which considers our One world – if not even the universe – as "ONE in diversity". Worldwide solidarity, which extends beyond local or regional groups, must grow on the way to a needed global consciousness. Egocentric, tribal, group-oriented and even national consciousness must be overcome in favor of a true recognition of global and cosmic Oneness in diversity.

But let's get back to our sewing machines:

All of the four recipient groups were able to use the machines at least for training purposes during many years. So far – so good. But I had insisted to also try out my own original idea of one machine per family. This concept had, after all, been developed with best intentions together with my friends in Germany: With the assistance of my Cadence partner and voodoo friend, Paulette, we had found a particularly poor family with many children in Carrefour for the last machine – number twelve.

During my third Haiti visit in summer 1982, I revisited this poor family, only to find out that the machine had been sold for half its price. What Miot had predicted had precisely happened: A child had gotten ill and – since there was no other source of income – the family had sold the machine. It was a sad lesson, but not my last one.

The first reaction following my cultural learning and the wake-up call after Christmas in 1980 with the involvement in situations of human misery in the "Mission Globale" was to develop into an enduring learning process. How to better help people to help themselves, became a learning goal. In the beginning, the need to institutionalize the involvement, to create some enduring structure, did not yet become conscious. But being in Haiti took a serious turn, which was not planned – or even wanted. With time, Cadence music was reduced to occasional visits when special bands performed – still mostly at the hotel "Lambi". The initial holiday introduction to Haiti during my first visit had ended. Paulette later in 1981 had married a Haitian man, as I found out. I never saw her again. I became more and more involved in continuing my practical learning process in development questions.

Business venture in Haiti

As a business person, one of my first reflections on what could be useful in Haiti turned around business. Why not try to establish "something" economically useful and self-supporting in Haiti and at the same time be helpful? – As a manufacturer of artists' colors, a practical vision was to establish a small color-manufacturing plant in Haiti. This could be a development tool. At the same time it looked reasonable to produce some simple color lines for the very creative Haitian art market and eventually for the export to the USA. It sounded like a nice – and again basically logical – concept.

Productive initiatives, which are conceived and owned by the people themselves, are certainly one of the best ways to economically develop. Economic development is one condition also for social development in a country. This, however, requires political framework conditions with an independent justice system and a decently functioning state. This development truth was and still is widely accepted. But what I had to learn first, was that such economic initiatives must be truly wanted and conceived by the people who are to benefit. The local partners must at least be fully and truly involved themselves. Agreeing with some investment proposition is not enough.

At home in Germany, I knew a Senegalese, Mustapha Tall, the "owner" of the African hand in my Foundation's logo (the other hand is mine). He worked in the production section of our family's artists' color factory and agreed to join the project. Mustapha was willing to practice "African solidarity" with his Haitian brothers.

58

In Haiti, I found a potential local partner who was producing simple house paint for protective exterior needs. This provided a suitable technical framework. But the project was not my potential Haitian partner's own initiative. So he did not make any effort to help in solving the local stumbling blocks due to bureaucratic and administrative problems. Training some Haitians would have been necessary and many needed substances for a decent quality paint would have to be imported. Such problems can be solved, but they normally (at least on such a small scale) need support by a local initiative. To develop in a sustainable way, such an initiative must in practice be grounded in local motivation. Again, it was my western idea, born out of the basically logical and sound presumption that Haiti would certainly benefit from their own local production.

For my own learning process it was still a worth-while venture because it allowed me to realistically learn about problems in the field of the Haitian mentality. Glimpses into the procedures of Haitian public administration in business matters added to the learning process. My learning in Haiti had started on many levels, but proved most necessary to limit further mistakes. And there were more to come. Dancing to Cadence music – still playing a modest role during my second stay in Haiti after Christmas in 1981 – had faded away during the next trips in 1982 and unfortunately was reduced to almost zero in the course of the now 43 visits to Haiti.

One vital lesson, which I had to learn very quickly, was to be more skeptical about my own "good ideas" – even though they might have been theoretically sound and logical. During the two next visits to Haiti (visits no. 3 and 4) in summer and again after Christmas in 1982, Miot took me along in his FONDEV jeep on his project visits. He especially took me to Ste. Suzanne, in the north of Haiti. There, FONDEV maintained a larger agricultural project. During those long trips around deep holes in the pavement, over dirt roads and through small rivers, I stressed his patience to an almost unacceptable degree. Endless questions were raised. Multiple ideas on what could be done and how to help needy people in Haiti in a correct and effective way were born. This systematic learning finally resulted in guidelines, which still serve as a useful framework for my own actions. Later, these guidelines became part of the more formalized work in Haiti. They are quoted in the annex.

Miot's village: Ste. Suzanne

Miot's visits to Ste. Suzanne induced major lines of action for the whole Haiti engagement. To find out what the villagers needed most, Miot suggested to invite the natural authorities of Ste. Suzanne for discussions under the huge tree in the center square of the village. Those natural authorities were a group of "elders", including Miot's aunt and the Catholic priest (in whose house I was given a bed during my visits in Ste. Suzanne).

Due to his family ties and his important local FONDEV project, Miot was well respected in Ste. Suzanne. The FONDEV project was an agricultural "centre de ramassage", a big house for collecting and storing agricultural products. Miot was presiding the meetings and translated my French questions into Creole. It was quite fascinating to witness, how local ideas and initiatives developed when they were induced by direct questions. Ideas popped up and were discarded again when it became clear that needed preconditions for their realization were not existing. I remember one of the elders suggesting to initiate the making of straw hats which could be sold. But who would handle the selling of the potential hats – and where could they be sold? Was there really a market? The idea was quickly discarded again by the villagers themselves, when practical marketing problems came up. One other idea was, however, received well:

Miot's aunt, a strong and obviously "important" female member of the village community, suggested to be given a refrigerator to store perishable goods belonging to the villagers. She opted to organize a fair village use of a large gas-powered unit. Everybody liked the idea. So I agreed to pay for it and Miot organized the purchase. Later we found out that Miot's aunt used the refrigerator mainly for her own needs. Nobody had pursued the original idea to create and save some income for the running expenses for the relatively expensive gas containers. Not even Miot's aunt herself. That refrigerator, therefore, became useless for the community and Miot even had to help paying to maintain its function – for his aunt.

Such "cases" happen frequently in Haiti (and probably elsewhere) when a potential problem solution is not born out of a sustainable local initiative, involving personal sacrifice and some transparent planning. The failed color-manufacturing business

61

venture mentioned above was an other example for the need for local motivation and engagement. Witnessing also some much larger cases of bad investments in development situations in Haiti strengthened my own motivation to learn how to do it in a better way. My own newly developed guidelines and further learning helped to slowly avoid costly mistakes. But my amazement about what can go wrong in development reality never stopped in those 28 years – by now at the end of 2008.

A road for Ste. Suzanne

A serious problem of the village came up during the discussions under our tree: the miserable condition of the rough mountain path, which led from the valley to Ste. Suzanne. Every tropical rain had up to now made the existing "road" up the mountain impassable even for vehicles with four-wheel drive. When the idea came up to improve the road condition, Miot reacted enthusiastically. His FONDEV project had suffered from the miserable road as much as the whole village. – But how to organize such a venture? There was not enough money in sight to simply have the road repairs done by professionals. Miot suggested that FONDEV could provide the material like cement and some basic technical know-how, if the villagers would find a way to organize themselves to do the work.

In such cases it helps to investigate local traditions and "natural" ways to solve problems. In Haiti, there is a local tradition for neighborhood action called "coumbite". Farmers help each other periodically when needed. "Coumbite" is one of the rare examples of village solidarity through teamwork beyond family ties. In such rotating activities, the men of the village work together during daytime. Traditional drumming rhythms and some rhythmic singing boost up the working spirit. After a day's work, the women provide food for the working men as well as "clairin", the first strong result of a sugarcane distilling process, later to be refined to become rum.

"Coumbite" is very special. Here the women "only" provide the food in the evening for the working men. This may create the wrong impression that men work more than women in Haiti. My observation is suggesting a completely different picture: Nothing in Haiti would function at all, if there were not those strong and enduring women. Women carry the main burden for survival. The whole informal economy is dominated by women. Visibly this is true in the markets, where women dominate in every way. Men in Haiti are, of course, also active in various creative ways, but mainly: men talk! This talking is mostly highly creative and sounds "important".

Creativity is one of the outstanding qualities one can witness in Haiti in beautiful perfection in men and in women. It is a general quality – which I found most admirable. Of course, one has to watch out, not to fall into the trap of believing every creative story – like in the above case of the refrigerator for Miot's aunt. I do not want to generalize too much, but in my observation, women in Haiti are most certainly not the weaker sex, when it comes to taking action.

Having found out about the tradition of "coumbite", it looked quite promising to use the existing farmers' tradition for the larger task of road building in Ste. Suzanne. In discussing this, the idea was basically well-accepted, but there were doubts among the villagers around the tree, whether they could handle this more demanding organizational task. Transferring a mountain path into a real road could certainly not be completed in one day as a "coumbite". That realization created a suggestion, which I first discreetly made to Miot. He immediately jumped on what I whispered in his ear and asked the villagers what they thought about "it". – The idea caught on:

Road "construction coumbite"

Seminars in project management

In Germany, one of my best-selling seminars as a trainer was a two-day course in simple project management. The seminar was specially designed for various professionals with no specific management experience. That same seminar also had been useful in my local political work in Germany. There it was supposed to help party activists to pursue political campaigns in a planned and organized way. The seminar treated the development and internalizing of concrete objectives on the basis of a vague goal, supported by simple planning and an organizational matrix. The local road problem and its solution in Ste. Suzanne looked precisely like a case for professional project management to be tried. A potential added value was Miot's interest in increasing the organizational capabilities of his local country partners. Under the village tree Miot publicly confirmed his willingness to support the activity of the motivated community. FONDEV was to provide food for the two-day seminar, which he suggested to be held during my next visit in December of 1982. Miot also suggested to help the village to organize a representative group of villagers to be invited. The idea was unanimously welcomed and – back in Germany – I worked on a further simplified adapted version of my German project management seminar.

This became a most challenging venture, far from being perfectly adapted to the local culture initially – but still basically successful and more so after further adjustments. The process followed the simple pattern of my "management circle", which I had developed in the early years as a trainer from the (only seemingly) linear management functions "goal-setting – planning – organizing – leading and controlling".

SUGGESTIONs FOR ONE WORLD DEVELOPMENT

1994
for 3.95

II. To facilitate development – including alleviation of poverty, productive action and social integration:

Project MANAGEMENT

A tool to reach goals

Any conscious process starts with more or less precise goals, more or less precise ideas of what I/we want to achieve, to get done, to obtain. Those goals may come from totally different origins. In this process intuition and rational do not need to be contradictions. Intuition through inner/ higher guidance and conscious systematic use of the rational mind can blend in to facilitate successful and meaningful problem-solutions. The process also adapts itself to various cultural frameworks.

The simple PROJECT MANAGEMENT-process, suggested hereafter, shall help groups of people working together to reach a goal of whatever type to get there. The process, which can be taught/trained in 2–3 day seminars is a result of many years of professional management-training-activity. The process has been boiled down to essential basic management steps and adapted to project-needs where formal learning is uncommon (s. reverse for history of the process). Anybody with management practice should be able to lead this process.

Training seminar for groups
to reach a common goal in time through planned and organized group activity

First (1/2) day:
MANAGEMENT-SYSTEM:
The management-functions of the circular-model – setting objectives / planning / organizing / leading / controlling - as well as the ever-needed central functions analysing / DECIDING / communicating should be discussed in groups which are used to abstract thinking. The whole system should be seen as interdependant in itself and with the surrounding human and environmental factors which influence it and which are being influenced by the management-system.

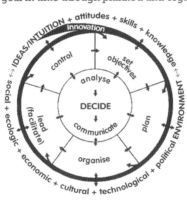

In groups with little or no abstract training, but which are used to think and act in a concrete way, the first (1/2) day should be used to informally discuss and to deepen the common understanding and reveal existing problem-solving approaches/ideas:

– what problem is to be solved
– what are the existing social and hierarchical structures influencing the process
– what are the usual decision-procedures
– what are (if existing) the traditional ways of group cooperation/group-work
– what are the relevant „taboos" to be observed

Introduction of the poster
P.1 – goal(s).
In groups with learning experience and project-practice, every group-member should be asked individually to formulate on paper as precise as possible the goal to be reached. This will most likely reveal different goals in detail. At the end of the first (1/2) day all group members should have reached a common understanding of the goal to be reached through the process.

P1 goal(s)

The poster **P.1 – goal(s)** has proven to be understood even by illiterate, totally untrained participants.

In groups with no or little learning-experience the group leader should try to reach a common understanding of the necessity and the content of one problem solving goal by free discussion and – if possible – through active role playing by the participants.

The posters P.1 – P.6 may be obtained on request (free for NGOs in developing countries) from the Peter-Hesse-Foundation

67

SUGGESTION for a 2–3 day seminar		Basic PROJECT MANAGEMENT
A	1st day	**B**
For professional project-management of all kinds		Simplified version e.g. for rural – and village-projects
P.7. Management system using the example of a team of 3 friends planning and organizing the climb of a mountain. All Management-functions should be systematically treated and discussed. Modern leadership may well be explained through this model.		Informal discussion of the problem to be solved by the project etc. – without trying to ask for abstract analogies – but remaining concrete to share and reveal existing problem-solving approaches/ideas
P.1 – goals Reach consensus on goal through group		Trainer seeks to find out group-goal and helps to define it
P.2 – influences Systematic Force-field-analysis	**2nd day morning**	Discretely structured informal discussion on strengths and weaknesses
P.3 – objectives Precise definitions worked out by group	**afternoon**	Trainer helps to define precise objectives which are acceptable to group
P.4 – plan Including precise dates – possibly overlapping	**3rd day**	More emphasis on order of activities than on precise dates
P.5 – matrix Introducing more than one symbol		Matrix-organisation using one symbol only
P.6 – plan + matrix Combining P.4 + P.5 in group-work		Combining and explaining P.4 and P.5 for use during project duration

Leadership and **control** treated with reference and respect to local culture.   Peter-Hesse-Foundation

At the end of the first two-day seminar, the villagers decided to discuss "the subject" amongst themselves. As I found out later, they soon started to repair the road in using the planning form connected with the suggested matrix during the following months. This was motivating, since the main purpose of the seminar, the road building, worked out well.

The seminar participants in Ste. Suzanne, however, asked that the workshop should be repeated one year later to work on those suggested management tools, which were not yet clearly understood in the first two days. The planning and the simple matrix organization had been well applied in the seminar exercises and in the following practical work. To build understanding among the seminar participants for a sequence of needed activities, for a simple plan for the work on the road, was relatively easy. Even the matrix was well understood as a tool for the visualization of needed tasks and people to be involved in each task. The central managerial functions "analyzing – deciding – communicating" were relatively well understood, too. But they also had to be treated in a very practical "down-to-earth" way in the seminar. In a very concrete way, we discussed the problem of the slippery road when it was raining and how the road should look after the repairs. How to decide and communicate amongst each other about who would be involved in which kind of work on the road, was much easier than could be expected in view of the relatively big task.

What proved to be problematic, was the full understanding of the way from the "goal" to the concrete "objectives" (through a "force field analysis" which looks at inner and outer strengths and weaknesses). This had even been difficult for some trained academic minds in my own home country. Of course, I did not even try to explain the complete structure of a professional "force field analysis" in the Ste. Suzanne village seminar – but only used some practical examples of existing strengths and weaknesses in the projected road building process. Provided it was very "concrete" and connected to the "real" work, even the partly illiterate villagers were able to follow, to understand and to reproduce the right examples in our practical seminar simulations. The villagers still wanted the seminar to be repeated.

The comprehension of the managerial functions "leadership and control" is very much depending on culture and tradition, which I, of course, had to keep in mind. This subject had to be treated with the utmost care in the Haiti seminars. I had to watch out not to create problems with underlying social structures, which were not always transparent. Therefore, when touching the managerial functions "leadership and control", I simply referred to the existing village leadership. I did not even try to make any assumptions in this delicate matter. The villagers themselves knew best, who had which "rank" in their community, who owned the "power of decision". It would not have been appropriate to discuss this part of the process in Ste. Suzanne, without first obtaining full knowledge about the human relationships which existed between the villagers. It is vital to first develop a feeling for cultural and traditional procedures in a country which is so emotionally driven. But to get a feeling for those difficulties is in itself valuable learning.

What did not work at all in the first seminar in Ste. Suzanne, was the use of the little figurines in the poster illustrations from my German seminars. These drawings were considered "devils" and were not accepted as symbols for humans. After replacing the little "devils" in the poster illustrations with little black figures for further seminars in Haiti, I had to learn another lesson: People in Haiti simply refused to be "painted in black" (in the true sense of the expression). They are not black, they are brown, I was clearly told. The third replacement version of the "devils", pictured here below, was, however, well-excepted in later seminars in Haiti. I had to learn to be more careful to use any analogy to my European experiences in this different cultural situation.

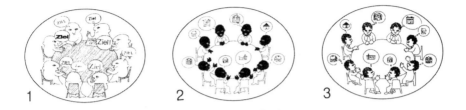

The whole seminar venture, though far from being a perfect tool for solving key problems in Haiti in the beginning, at least proved to be useful for the road project – and to get a feeling for the local culture. It taught me a practical lesson on how people in Haiti are learning: concrete, immediate, without any analogies or abstractions. I do not know how much of what I tried to "teach" in my seminars created any lasting effect (beyond the repaired road in Ste. Suzanne). It, however, opened my own eyes for the lack of early "learning to learn" in this culture and it created a motivation for my future engagement in the field of education in this country. The seminars in Ste. Suzanne also resulted in a particularly nice final "happening":

When I was asked at the end of the second seminar, what the village could do to thank me for offering the seminars, I asked them to organize a village dance with my beloved Haitian music. This was warmly welcomed: The village managed to find a small generator to create some electricity and two huge old trumpet-shaped loudspeakers. In the evening after the end of the second day, they set up a table for the elders and myself in the village square – and they played "my" Cadence music. The ice fully broke when I asked the dominating female village chief for a dance. It became a memorable evening – certainly in my memory.

71

More project management seminars were given in various situations and on various levels: for delegates from foreign NGOs and from the Haitian state in 1982 and again in 1983, for a self-help initiative of Père Cico in Kenskoff in 1983, for a group of public primary school directors in 1983, for students and city-representatives in the University in Cap Haitien in 1984.

One additional projected management seminar proved to be most bizarre and provided additional learning about what strange things can happen, seen from a rational mind: A well-known international agency had heard that some German was active in the field of management training in Haiti. So they invited me to lead one larger seminar. We, Miot and I, accepted and a decorative addition of academic names were added to my two-day concept in a heavily enlarged program to be given at a precise time and place some time later. I especially changed my travel agenda from Germany to come to this "event" which looked challenging to me. Miot picked me up at the airport and we headed to the designated place well in time for the start of the program. Getting there, we, however, had to discover that the whole clearly planned program was a "paper tiger".

There was nothing "real" behind the heavy program book, which I kept for future reference in case someone would doubt that such irrationalities can happen. We never found out, why nothing was happening. Nobody ever informed us – before or after that time. But it further opened my eyes to be watchful concerning international organizations in Haiti. I had never imagined that a renowned international organization would allow such bad management. Without knowing this for a fact, we believed that a request for funding for the enlarged program was submitted to the organization's home office, which was either refused or – if being honored – the funds misused (to put it mildly).

When working on a grassroots level in situations like in Haiti, one inevitably witnesses bad and failing solutions. Such mismanagement involves a lot of public money, not even to think of possible criminal misuse of funds, of corruption. Such waste and misuse of funds may be created and caused on both sides: in the recipient and in the donating countries. Human beings, even those in leading positions in renowned institutions, are clearly not automatically behaving as they should in the interest of the common good – and not even in the interest of their own organization.

**Corruption is not an exclusive domain
of failing states.
Transparency should be an essential value
to be enforced by law and
to be powerfully controlled
– nationally and also internationally.**

Other problems are simply created by faulty concepts or bad decisions. This does even happen to renowned and basically valuable institutions. I witnessed such misconception, when I started my work in Haiti:

UNICEF, certainly an institution with most valuable goals, had installed a nice-sounding three-year project in creating a large number of pre-schools in Haiti. Schools were built, teachers trained in rapid courses. Unfortunately, this was done by using a didactical system, in which all children were taught the same subjects per day. In a training manual, developed in the University of the West Indies in Jamaica, every workday of the year had one subject assigned to it. All children, therefore, had to learn the same thing per day – regardless of their learning differences. This made the preceding teacher-training look relatively easy. One page per day is an easy rule to follow. The fact, however, that no child learns at the same speed and in the same way made this didactical system doomed to fail. And to train teachers for this delicate age group of 3 to 6 would need more time in any case. UNICEF simply used a bad concept. But that was not the only reason for failure. At the end of the program, most of the schools fell down anyway, due to the lack of assured continuing financing. International money and beautiful local energy were wasted through misconception – as I see it.

Later, UNICEF had obviously learned their lesson, but they did not immediately heal the two major mistakes: teacher-centered didactics and unsecured financial sustainability. Instead of trying to improve what was not working well, UNICEF dropped their concept of institutional pre-schools for children from age 3 to 6. They simply switched their working emphasis to early childhood care for the very first 3 years of life. This would have been a beautiful addition to a better conceived child-centered pre-school system, which indeed would be wonderful for Haiti. All six years before arriving at the usual primary school age are equally vital for the best possible holistic growth of a child. For anyone dealing with human development, this truth is known and accepted today. Who else, but a special UN organization like UNICEF should actively align behind that truth? There is ample scientific and practical experience today to know, how to do the work in the best possible way.

For me, the UNICEF pre-school venture in Haiti was a warning and a learning experience for what became the focus of my engagement in Haiti: pre-school for needy children. UNICEF's failure (as I see it) further sensitized my consciousness in this field and therefore provided valuable learning.

This "case" also provided more insights into the harmful international procedure of project-financing for (normally) only three years. Sustainable development needs more time. If there is no real assurance of continuation of an initiative after the end of the initial project, many well-meaning ventures are doomed to fail. This can be witnessed all over the world. For me that meant that I had to solve this problem in some way. It was not acceptable to start something without thinking of the future – even more so since the money involved was to be my own. In view of the UNICEF pre-school activities in Haiti, the long-term aspect became even more present in my mind.

First country pre-school in Ste. Suzanne

Discussions with the village elders in Ste. Suzanne in 1981 led to the above-mentioned seminars on project management. But they resulted also in the villagers' plea to "do something" for their children. I had no idea what this could be in reality. Therefore, after further meetings, we innocently created a simple "Kindergarten" for 40 of the weakest and least "developed" children of Ste. Suzanne. Not knowing how to select the most needy children, I asked UNICEF for help (and thereby learned, how their own pre-school program was supposed to work). A UNICEF delegate came to Ste. Suzanne and – together with the village elders – helped to select the most needy children following some formal criteria like weight and size in relation to age. UNICEF also invited a young lady from Ste. Suzanne, who had been selected by the local priest, to their crash course on how to organize an informal pre-school. To me this sounded quite good. At this time, I did not yet have the full "insight" into the weaknesses of a teacher-centered method. After all, my own memories of a school in Germany included teachers, who treated all of us children alike. I simply did not know any better way – before meeting Carol.

First country pre-school in Ste. Suzanne

Countryside in the north of Haiti

Meeting Carol Guy-James

Having been "bitten" by Caribbean rhythms some years earlier, our German traditional carnival had lost its attraction for me. As a German in the Rhineland, one can either participate in local traditions or get away during those crazy days. I certainly liked a crazy break from serious managerial work. Getting away, however, attracted me most. The logical solution for a lover of Afro-Caribbean music was to spend this nice crazy period where the best Caribbean carnival music is at home: in Trinidad.

I had discovered Trinidad to be the most fascinating place in the world during the carnival-season. For me, carnival in Trinidad meant to indulge in my favorite rhythms like real "pan" (steel band) music for a few days and thereby totally forget all obligations or other "serious business". Haiti had already become too burdened with serious occupations and left no space for my musical addiction. This increased the relevance for a short carnival holiday in Trinidad to let go of all worries for a few days. In Trinidad, "playing mas" means: diving into a different reality. To participate, one simply contacts one of the many costume groups, "carnival bands", buys one of their costumes through the net and then tries to find a room to sleep (the most difficult part).

In February 1982, the theme of "my" carnival band was "butterflies". One of the fascinating carnival creatures in this band was Carol Guy-James. Carol's wing colors were beautiful and her movements reminded me of "my" Bahamian banner carrier eight years before. I took a photograph of her and managed to get her address in promising to send her the photograph – which I did. She was in the final stage of her Montessori teacher-training in London – and I visited London later during the year.

It was easy to make this visit look necessary to me (and to her), since my family business was trying to strengthen our distribution in England. After so many years, I truly do not remember, to what extent this London visit was really necessary for my work – or whether I simply wanted to meet Carol. I still hesitate to believe today that this urge to meet her had any deeper meaning in a spiritual sense, but that it was simply due to Carol's impression on my emotional structure. However, looking back today, there was more to it than simple attraction. Carol changed the whole structure of my Haiti engagement – and thereby my life.

In London we talked about carnival and I planned to participate, to "play mas" in her carnival band next year, in February 1983. But we also talked about my first experiences in Haiti – especially concerning the new Kindergarten pre-school in Ste. Suzanne. This sounded interesting to her Montessori mind. It was the beginning of our MONTESSORI vision. It started as a tempting idea. But the seed was planted and a real vision grew from here.

The need for a durable structure

It took only two years of engagement in Haiti and four visits from the initial post-Christmas holidays in December 1980 to realize that sustainable change in Haiti needs time. But how much time? I did not know – and I still do not know even today, in 2008. But one of the immediate and certain results of my intensive learning process in Haiti was the recognition of the need for some kind of durable structure in Germany and in Haiti.

Back in Germany in January 1983, it was easy to find out, what kind of structure was legally possible and what might make sense in my case. I simply wanted to successfully contribute to a "real" and sustainable development in Haiti (or elsewhere in the world). The normal solution for small initiatives like mine was to form an association (in German: "Verein"). If a "Verein" was to be a legally registered association, there were a number of regulations to be followed. The most relevant one was to form a group of at least seven people who would agree to share the same formal purpose and to agree to some rules on needed decisions. We were nine people to initiate the very first humble sewing machine action after my return from Haiti in January 1981. It, however, proved to be difficult to assemble all of them under one "permanent hat" of a legal association. While I was still investigating, who could be my future six partners to form a German "Verein", carnival time had come up. Carol was back in Trinidad and we did participate – "play mas" – in the same carnival band in February 1983, as planned the year before in London. It was quite a colorful event.

Steelband music and Calypso occupied my body, mind and emotions during the two carnival days, but we also used our remaining time in Trinidad to further discuss and plan to co-operate in
Haiti. Carol was fully convinced that her Montessori studies
would be very useful and valuable in the framework of our small
first pre-school project in Haiti. It was, however, obvious from
the beginning that such venture might take more time to succeed

than just an occasional visit. This reinforced my intention to search for a feasible durable structure of my Haiti engagement. I became more than ever convinced that it would have to continue – and possibly together with Carol.

While still struggling with the problem to find the six needed German partners for the creation of a legal association, a friend put me on the right track: "Why not create a foundation?" I had no idea what that implied. Foundations in my mind were huge institutions created by very wealthy people or by big business. There were very renowned foundations like the Ford Foundation, the Krupp Foundation or the Bertelsmann Foundation, all very wealthy and with a lot of people working for them. They represented a different category of organization – ways beyond my possibilities. But since I was deeply motivated to create "something" durable, I still investigated what could reasonably be done. A new vision was born.

A personal friend was working in the state's official supervising agency ("Stiftungsaufsicht") which is responsible for foundations in my part of Germany. I made an appointment with him and was quite surprised to learn that I was wrong in my belief that all foundations must be "big". In 1983 – contrary to now, 25 years later – it was still rather complicated to overcome all bureaucratic hurdles to create a foundation, but it was possible. I was informed that an amount of "only" DM 100,000 would be the legal minimum capital for a new foundation. I, however, was also told that the bureaucratic machinery would rather prefer to become active, if the founding capital would at least be DM 200,000. That sounded like a lot of money to me, but my motivation had recently been reinforced after coming back from carnival in Trinidad. So I started the founding procedure in March 1983.

It took me full nine months to develop the needed structure and to get it officially accepted. Finally, on 7 December 1983, the "Peter-Hesse-Stiftung" (Peter-Hesse-Foundation) was officially registered. The controlling state institutions allowed me to invest the DM 200,000 (very roughly US $ 100,000.– later enlarged by an anonymous donator and by my sister, Dr. Ariane Hesse, to DM 210,000) in our family business, H. Schmincke & Co. There, I also established the first formal address of my new Foundation. After some detours during the following years, this founding address (§ I. of the Foundation's by-laws) is now again the formal seat of the Foundation. (The full original German by-laws are cited in the Foundation's homepage: www.solidarity.org/de/satzung.pdf). The key legal requirement of any foundation is its purpose:

§ II. 2: "Zweck der Stiftung" – Purpose of the Foundation:

"The purpose of the Foundation is help for needy people in developing countries, especially as survival-help for children and – wherever possible – as help to self-help; also (with never more than one third of all spending) the promotion of tolerance and understanding between people in developing countries and in Europe, especially in cultural fields."

This somewhat complicated formulation corresponded to my "state of mind" at the time of the Foundation's creation in 1983. Today, 25 years later, I would formulate the Foundation's purpose wider in scope. This is roughly what would correspond to my state of mind now: "The purpose of the Foundation is to first learn and then contribute to heal our unbalanced world order and to help to solve global problems in our ONE world in diversity – with special emphasis on providing children a chance."

One might consider the wording of a formal foundation purpose to be something like a basic vision – at the moment of its formulation. Since, however, it is most difficult to change the original text of a German legal foundation, I might as well live with the limitations of my own original wording. Visions develop with learning. My visions certainly have changed over the years. This process will probably never end in an active life. After new learning and at a given moment in life, a vision is the beginning of a mixed rational, emotional and spiritual process towards action for a living reality.

Not having had any experience, although being helped in basic structural questions in 1983, I originally did not think a lot about the name of my Foundation. All I knew and saw around me indicated that a foundation carries the name of the founder. That certainly tickles the founder's pride, but it is not the best solution for future acquisition of funds, as I found out later. Some neutral name with a meaning – like "Menschen für Menschen" ("People for people") would have been much more effective for future growth. "Menschen für Menschen", a foundation which was created during that same time-period by a famous German actor, is probably benefiting from that better name – apart from the public attention, which a famous actor will get anyway. I was, however, happy that my durable structure had finally materialized and that it provided the needed basis for my own serious professional "development in development". It also provided a better starting position for Carol's engagement in Haiti in the forthcoming years.

Carol had suggested to come along with me to Haiti next time to work with the Montessori method with children of our Ste. Suzanne project. So in December 1983, she simply packed a few pieces of Montessori didactical material into her suitcase and brought them along to Ste. Suzanne. This became a memorable experience.

The first attempts with the Montessori material and "our" children were fantastic. Even I could see it. The children reacted wonderfully. They obviously and easily learned what the didactical material was to enable them to do. To me it was a revelation. Carol was not surprised. She had anticipated this functioning of the Montessori method, but her motivation to "somehow continue" in this direction grew. Maria Montessori's soul must have smiled down from her "other dimension", since what was happening with these country children in Haiti was Maria Montessori's purpose. The children learned through the handling of the didactical material – with Carol acting "only" as a gentle professional facilitator. Believing, however, that our Ste. Suzanne village teacher could master the Montessori material in a proper way after some individual instructions only, was an error. The Haitian culture was too different from accepting that a teacher might "only" have to facilitate a child's work. From her own childhood experience, our Ste. Suzanne teacher was used to be rough and "bossy" with the children.

I documented parts of this first testing with a small camera (the film is now available on DVD). The testing of the Montessori method in Ste. Suzanne created long discussions between Carol, Miot and me. It became clear to us that we could not simply stop here and accept that rough aspect of Haitian culture. That "culture" was not truly indigenous from Haiti or the former African homeland of the Haitians. It had only been adopted from the former European masters. It was our own old-world culture. We also realized in our discussions following the stimulating Montessori experience in Ste. Suzanne that we could not limit our activity to only one village. We had to think about some wider scale for our engagement.

The successful Montessori experiments with the children in Ste. Suzanne themselves were inspiring. Carol's basic consent to help to try implementing Montessori for disfavored children in Haiti gave this aspect of our Haiti engagement a special priority. But I had also started other small projects outside of Ste. Suzanne, mostly guided by Miot's knowledge and experience. Later on, those side projects were all brought to an end, when the Montessori teacher-training reached a definite and successful larger stage. One initial side project shall, however, be described here for one particular reason: It provided more inside views on what can go wrong in development efforts, even if such activities look well-conceived and even if such actions are based on a local initiative. Other small initial projects were ended after the first five years in Haiti to concentrate on the Montessori project.

The Port Margo failure

Already in July 1982, my Haitian friend and teacher, Miot Jean-Francois, had taken me to another place in the north of Haiti, Port Margot. There he knew of a child project which asked for assistance. The local Baptist pastor, Clorin Calixte, had managed to start building a rather large, flat house with five rooms with the help of his church community. The house was to become a home and school for up to 100 poor children from Port Margot, 40 of them being orphans. Such numbers and reported facts may not always be correct as we had reason to suspect, but the existing initiative still looked trustworthy enough to Miot and myself. It was especially convincing that the house was already partly finished. We considered this to be proof of a local initiative. Therefore, we started to invest part of our funds in Port Margot. FONDEV was also willing to contribute and Miot agreed to participate in a new local mini-financing concept, which included a micro-credit portion.

Negotiations in Port Margot

I was encouraged by Professor Yunus' success story with his Micro-Credit Grameen Bank in Bangladesh, which had started about eight years earlier and which had become well-known in Germany's "development circles". But we did not follow Professor Yunus' successful Bangladesh model in Port Margot. To follow the Grameen Bank procedures would have required cultural adaptation – and mainly prolonged presence in Port Margot. Here, we were quite dependant on the co-operation of and with pastor Calixte. He was also the one to know, who in his community was most in need. We, therefore, asked him to select the twenty most needy families in his area and started a yearly sponsorship program for their deprived children with US $ 205 (then DM 500) per family. Included in this amount was a micro-credit portion for each family. I had found donators in Germany for the sponsorship program, who would receive yearly reports and photographs of "their" children. They had accepted to pay DM 500 per year for this Port Margot project.

The key idea was to combine direct modest financial support with a micro-credit portion. As much as they were capable of working in some way, all twenty families were supposed to invest the credited amount in a reasonable way. Five of the poor families pastor Calixte had chosen were physically in too bad a shape to be asked to try some income-creating activity. They were to be given the full $ 205 in monthly payments by pastor Calixte. Seven families had their own productive ideas, on how to invest the small credit. Eight families did not know, what to do productively. Therefore, we suggested an income-creating activity to those eight families, which was not suggested by the eight families themselves. That was a conceptional mistake, as we were to find out one year later.

In this case, the productive idea was not based on some concept from my northern mind, but on Miot's culturally adapted idea: He suggested that the eight families should use their credit to process locally growing cacao beans to produce chocolate. Without the possibility of further processing the cacao beans, they had to sell them to traders at a very low price. To make the processing technically possible, we agreed to provide a small cacao bean mill. This device could be used by the families, who did not come up with their own productive idea. Pastor Calixte agreed to "supervise" the functioning of this mini-project.

Miot and I went back to Port Margot every year to meet the recipients of our small initial credits and donations and to document the results. At our visit in December 1983, it became clear that the cacao-initiative had failed. The project was simply not initiated by the people themselves. They also did not have the needed minimal management skills in this environment. So from 1984 on, the eight families, who had been involved in this mini-project, were asked to use their yearly credit in their own preferred way. This worked out much better, as we should find out later. The group of eight managed to economically "develop themselves" in the same modest way as the seven families, who knew how to invest their money from the beginning. All fifteen families would eventually have been able to repay their credits, if asked to do so. Their credits were, however, for the time being further extended and the program was gradually enlarged to include more families.

One observation in this process reminded me of Professor Yunus' Grameen bank experience in Bangladesh: There, it proved most effective to grant micro-credits to groups of women. In our small micro-credit model in Port Margot, we addressed the "families". In looking, who really is active in these (in a northern/western sense) less conventional families, the women clearly dominated.

Even though our small micro-credit program lacked a more thorough adaptation to the local possibilities, it was not totally in vain. To me it became obvious that even a basically great idea to provide micro-credit for productive self-help initiatives needs more than good intentions. It needs professional management. Only through periodic visits, we could not handle such a program in Haiti in a fully sufficient way. It was valuable learning.

In December 1984 and in July 1985, we created a further self-help initiative in Port Margot for the whole village: a garden project, which involved agricultural learning provided by FONDEV. We were convinced that the engagement in Port Margot was at least partly successful – until the unfortunate forced ending of the whole program in December 1986.

In December 1985, the situation in Port Margot took a serious turn, which almost ended in a dramatically dangerous way one year later: After discussing all procedures in Port Margot with pastor Calixte, he approached me in the presence of Miot to ask for direct support for himself: "You have done enough for Port Margot. I now need support for myself to continue building my own house!" We knew that pastor Calixte was paid by his church and that he already used members of his community, who benefited from our support, for his personal building work. Besides, from the beginning of our engagement in Port Margot we had paid him a justified "supervising fee". Therefore, I refused to honor his additional direct request. This immediately changed his behavior towards us. All gentle priestly attitude was blown away.

At the next firmly projected visit in summer 1996, pastor Calixte had left Port Margot with his whole family for a holiday in the USA. He had not informed us about his absence, so we came as agreed before. We continued to discuss details of a previously planned garden project in Port Margot with some villagers and those local farmers, who had been involved in the former conceptual discussions. This garden project had been developed together with pastor Calixte and his community to produce food and thereby obtain some sustainability for the children's home. There was even a financial participation of the German Ministry for Development involved. The ministry had agreed to finance the needed gardening instruments as well as other needed materials and the teaching participation of an agricultural professional to teach suitable skills in the village. In addition, a learning- and voluntary working-participation of the local villagers had been firmly agreed upon in December 1985.

In December 1986, Miot and I went back to Port Margot, hoping that our project work there would peacefully continue. That proved to be a misjudgment of pastor Calixte's willingness to continue working with us. His anger about our refusal to honor his personal needs in a more substantial way and the fact that we had continued working in his community, while he was on vacation in the USA, culminated. He openly and loudly proclaimed that we now should pay salaries to those farmers who were to learn and participate in the garden project. This totally conflicted with the original concept, as it was clearly and openly agreed upon before. The new request, however, provoked emotional heat waves among the villagers and a spontaneous aggressiveness against Miot and myself, when we expressed our view. In the presence of many of his followers, pastor Calixte not only insulted us verbally. He shouted that we exploited the people in Port Margot – which culminated in the statement that I was responsible for the death of a child in one of our recipient project families. I was supposed to have "eaten the child" – a common Haitian accusation deriving from voodoo!

The atmosphere became more and more dense. Pastor Calixte's followers drew a close circle around us and threatened us with their gestures. I got quite confused because I always knew them to be peaceful. Miot, however, who knew the quickly changing temper of his people, realized the danger. He made up some appeasing suggestion to avoid direct physical confrontation. This allowed us to quickly leave Port Margot – not to ever come back. It was the first and only time that I was directly in physical danger in Haiti – after five years of supporting the community and especially the children of Port Margot.

Later I realized that we had made several serious mistakes in Port Margot: Miot and I did not respect the cultural tradition to pay for the goodwill of pastor Calixte. We did not honor his own culturally "normal" interests. We also brought in too many of our own concepts in the financial support program and we depended too much on the one local authority, pastor Calixte. The whole Port Margot initiative was the personal project of pastor Calixte. His community simply followed him. It became evident again that sustainable development needs to build on the initiatives of those who are willing to develop themselves. Local leaders are, of course, most important, but even on that micro-level, peoples' motivated participation is vital.

Following the subsidiarity principle, help should always be addressed to the smallest possible entity. This was and still is one of our Foundation's original guidelines. Usually local leaders are far more reliable than distant "higher" ones, but here, in Port Margot, even this very useful principle failed to be successful. Later, we were informed that pastor Calixte had found other financing sources among Christian communities in the USA and that he did get ample support to finish his own house.

One additional sad side-effect of this development in Port Margot was that I had to cancel a public grant for Port Margot from the German Ministry for Development, which we had managed to obtain for the following year. The ministry agreed that this cancellation was correct in view of threatening personal misuse of funds in the project.

In the beginning of our engagement in Port Margot and later in this project, Miot and I did not always make the best decisions and we did not invest the needed time to develop the system successfully from bottom-up. But when the program had to be ended in 1996 as reported above, all families, who had been involved in our small micro-credit program, had used their credits productively. Since we now could not continue working in Port Margot any more, their debts were cancelled by us.

Was this small credit program a failure? Not totally, I believe. It depended too much on the relationship with the local authority, pastor Calixte, who had "selected" those who were benefiting. A better conceived initial phase, truly based on those families only, who wanted to engage in productive activities, I believe, would have been better, could have been sustainable. That would have meant to follow the subsidiarity principle truly down to the individual needy beneficiaries. Micro-credit certainly is a most valuable development tool. Such a program must, however, be conceived and organized in a humble way from bottom-up, taking all cultural and psychological variations into account. All needs learning first. What can be retained, however, is:

**Micro-credit
– but only if properly conceived and organized –
is one outstanding "development instrument"
to fight poverty.**

Problematic sponsorship for children

One aspect of the finally disrupted program in Port Margot was less visible at first sight, but remains a permanent problem in many development ventures around the world: It is not only difficult, but mostly impossible to make a fair and just selection of the people, who shall be the beneficiaries of the program. If such a program is in favor of one person, there always will be someone else left out. It is specially tempting for the "help industry" to look for sponsors for a poor child. Photos of poor children touch people's hearts. That positive human reaction is being exploited by advertisers. Unfortunately, potential donators like to sponsor a specific person, "their" child. Using children's pictures to motivate sponsors works much better than to acquire funds for non-specific programs which avoid exclusion. The "help industry" is well aware of this dilemma and one can now observe a trend to some more truthful advertising. There are still photos of children to attract donors, but in reading, what the collecting organization really wants to do with the acquired funds, the "better way" clearly shines through in a more or less refined way.

Again, the dilemma is evident: If the donation for a specific child is really reaching this one child only, others around that child are being left out. Even if the child's family benefits from the donation and even if many such "cases" exist in the same environment, there will be others left out. Therefore, good sponsor-seeking organizations are telling their sponsors that their money will be used for the respective community of the child. Mostly this involves some schools. In cases were the donator does not only pay school fees for his or her child, the advertisement with an individual child is misleading. Supporting a whole school or even a whole community would certainly be the better way, but: If "good" organizations advertise without using pictures of individual children, they reach less sponsors. The dilemma is difficult to avoid: Either the program is executed as advertised for one person only and others around that person will get nothing or the organization acts in a "better way". But in this case, the advertising, the acquisition statement, is incorrect. Such advertisements should not pretend that a specific child will benefit from a given donation. There is no real solution for this problem outside of the growing consciousness of those responsible in the "help industry" and of donors who avoid the dilemma by preferring best possible programs.

The big question behind the dilemma between honest acquisition of funds and best possible reality is even more problematic: It is more than doubtful, whether any aid program, inflicted on the daily life of needy people (even in a positive way), is really desirable for true human development. Fighting the reasons behind poverty and misery can rarely be achieved through some healing programs. Behind poverty and misery, there are often structural and political problems far beyond the reach of any targeted program. Conscious and well-governed states are the precondition for sustainable development. In our globalised world, some structural problems can, however, only be solved globally. One of the major stumbling blocks for a world in balance, for peaceful, fair and sustainable, for "real" development are egoistic rules and regulations of some powerful states and some even more powerful small groups in those states.

The world needs a renewed, fair world order. We are far away from getting near such "good" global order. This is, however, a subject in itself, which will be treated later here. To shortly summarize already here my view, as it condensed after prolonged learning, after many mistakes and after receiving guidance from a "different dimension", here in the shortest possible form:

**For humanity to survive in peace
we must first develop
a global (or even cosmic) consciousness
towards oneness of all in diversity
and then promote the
political creation of a legally binding,
fair and sustainable global order
for a world in balance
in the spirit of compassion and solidarity.**

To "attack" global problems may mostly be out of the direct reach of individual civil society institutions like us. But such problems become visible for an open, unblocked mind. And: Civil society as a whole is not at all powerless in global questions – at least not in the long run. It "only" needs some better cooperation and working together amongst each other, with the media – and constructive engagement in politics.

Unfortunately, those, who are officially involved in setting the structure of our one world, are very often far away from the reality "down at the bottom". To be a representative of a given political structure like a state, means mostly a comfortable life. This is particularly visible in our international institutions, especially the United Nations. Such country representatives almost exclusively come from their countries' powerful "elite" circles. Their international lifestyle is far "above" that of their own countries' population. Why should they desire a change? It does need a higher (and deeper) motivation to want a change, when it does not directly concern your own life. It may even be more comfortable to be surrounded by less well-off people. They provide you with more and cheaper services. But we are getting away here now from first describing the reality, in which our newly established small Foundation had to tackle micro-problems in Haiti.

The Montessori vision

The Montessori experience with children in "our" first Kindergarten in Ste. Suzanne in December 1983 had been promisingly positive. Carol had basically agreed to give a few years of her professional life for what became our Montessori vision. It clearly was the first priority wish of the village population in Ste. Suzanne to ask us to "do something" for their children to make us feel useful and legitimately engaged in this field. Of course, it was helpful that the formal goal of the newly established German Peter-Hesse-Foundation also put children in the foreground. The practical experience in my seminars on project management demonstrated that learning in Haiti was still done in a very unrefined way. It was just as in Europe about two generations ago. The UNICEF early-learning model, which had been unsuccessfully tried in Haiti, encouraged us also to go on with our "Montessori experiment". A child-centered approach simply looked like the right way to tackle one of Haiti's major educational problems: insufficient in quantity, authoritarian teacher-centered in quality and without financial sustainability.

The state did not show any enduring interest in early education – otherwise they would at least have made an effort to continue with the UNICEF pre-schools after the termination of this international initiative. The didactic concept of that international project was basically not very different from what people in Haiti were used to. A teacher in front, children doing what the teacher asked them to do – mostly in a purely repetitive way. So why not continuing the UNICEF way? It would still have been better than to let the initiative fail totally.

The priority and usefulness of early learning was not yet recognized in the early years of our engagement in Haiti. The state was politically in a bad shape – and had other worries. But for us, there was no reason, why we should not continue to do in the best possible way, what looked like being in accordance with an essential basic need of the population: help for their children. Once this basic line of action was found, Montessori looked like the best possible path to walk. We felt encouraged to go on.

Montessori teacher-training

In December 1984, Miot Jean-Francois, backed by his FONDEV organization, was again most helpful in planning what we considered and hoped to be a breakthrough activity: a two-week workshop for educators in Haiti. Together, we managed to identify 40 educators from the private sector who had already some experience with work for children. All of them, almost all women, came from civil society initiatives, predominantly carried by the various churches that are active in Haiti. We invited them to one week of theory in Port-au-Prince and a second week of practice in Ste. Suzanne with "our" children.

A gentle former Minister of Education made it possible to use a suitable room in the Education Ministry in Port-au-Prince for the first theoretical part of the program.

FONDEV made a big effort to create an environment in Ste. Suzanne which could be accepted even by those of the 40 candidates who normally lived in more comfortable city situations. Aided by FONDEV, the villagers in Ste. Suzanne even constructed improvised showers in the village square. Big, old oil drums were positioned on two wooden frames serving as shower cabins, protected by plastic curtains. The main problem was the water itself. There is no well or running water in Ste. Suzanne. All had to be carried manually from a small river below the village.

But all started well. The motivated group of 40 were instructed by Carol in the open air and practiced with the children in a small house, which we rented for the week.

101

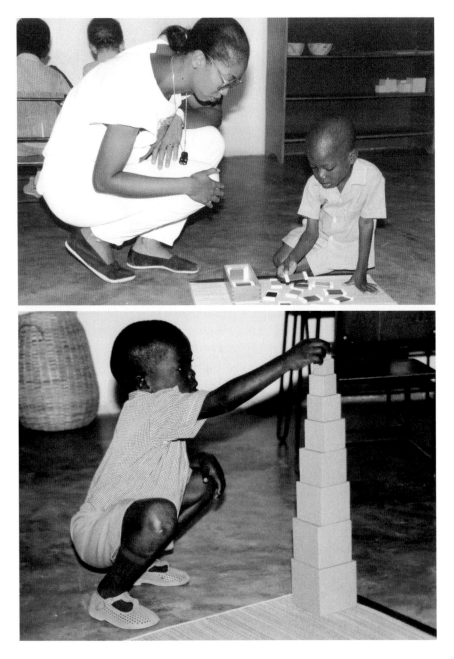

A few Haitian dignitaries and people affiliated with FONDEV were taking part in the Montessori practice as observers. Everybody, including myself, was very impressed, how well the seminar seemed to function. A few days later, the water drums and shower cabins were dismantled again and everybody left Ste. Suzanne for their regular occupations. The Montessori seminar participants – although expressing great satisfaction – went back to their traditional educational activity. Most of them continued teaching from above or from up-front, as we found out later. Not much visible alterations in behavior. No child-centered Montessori spirit. With the exception of a few participants, who started questioning their traditional methods, not much of a change. Even in the pre-school in Ste. Suzanne nothing changed in the behavior towards the children. The young teacher from the village had, of course, also participated in the workshop. We, Carol and I – still staying in Ste. Suzanne for a few days – were frustrated. We wondered what could have gone wrong in the two-week Montessori work-shop.

The conclusion was simple: A two week workshop is simply too short to change grown behavior. All our participants had grown up in Haiti under the same teacher-centered old didactical concept, which Haiti – after all – had inherited from ancient European ways of teaching. Haitians had freed themselves from slavery and, therefore, from direct European influence almost 200 years ago. They, however, had not freed themselves from our bad behavioral examples in the educational field. The old teacher-centered way had remained the normality in the world for another 100 years. It dawned on our consciousness, how radical Maria Montessori had changed the way to teach and learn. In concluding our frustrated reflections we realized that we could either forget quality early childhood education in Haiti – or fully engage ourselves in a long-term commitment. How long this commitment would finally have to be, was not clear to us. Otherwise we might perhaps have given up right then and there.

Carol made the biggest – and most daring – commitment, which cannot be praised enough. She agreed to establish herself in Haiti for at least two more years. Those two years became more than 20 years. Only now, in 2008, Montessori in Haiti has finally reached a "point of no return". We could now leave Haiti – and Montessori would continue to grow – slowly, but certainly. To keep up the needed didactical quality may be a different question. The need for good quality necessitates some more organizational investment for a truly sustainable future of this wonderful child-centered methodology in Haiti. – But first let us look on what happened after our decision not to give up.

Precondition to start a prolonged engagement was Carol's willingness and high motivation in 1985 to continue in Haiti with limited resources, provided by the newly established Peter-Hesse-Foundation from Germany. Several aspects had to be considered and respected in realizing our vision to introduce child-centered Montessori pre-school didactics for less fortunate children in Haiti:

- We had to be legally "embedded" in some formal structure with our teaching program.
- We needed a suitable place – if possible away from the capital city of Haiti.
- We had to find suitable candidates to be trained as Montessori pre-school teachers.
- Carol needed a decent and yet affordable home for her teaching work.
- The language question had to be decided: French, the "official" language – or Creole, the "native" language.

104

Besides solving problems in the other projects like in Port Margot and in Ste. Suzanne, the next Haiti visits in December 1985 and in July/August 1986 were dedicated to the preparation of the first full year Montessori teacher training program. From the beginning it was clear that we were to act outside any official state structure. We had, however, at least to be "legally ok" and observe local customs, like e. g. school periods. Since the Haitian school year of 9 months usually starts in September or at the latest in October, we just had to follow this custom. We therefore envisaged to start the first teaching year in the beginning of October 1986.

Since the German Peter-Hesse-Foundation was not yet formally registered in Haiti, we searched for a suitable legal partner. FONDEV had cooperated from the very beginning and was helpful with advice, but could not fully be engaged in the needed way. The education sector was not covered by their policy at home in Germany. FONDEV's Miot Jean-Francois advised us not to concentrate all activities in the capital Port-au-Prince as most other international initiatives in Haiti do. From his own working experience he knew that life for Haitians in the countryside was sometimes even more miserable than for the poor in the capital. We followed his advice and looked around in the north, where our FONDEV friend had good connections. The second most important town in Haiti is Cap Haitien in the north. Here we found solutions for the two first essential necessities: a legal umbrella and a school room.

There was a small private university in Cap Haitien, the "Université Roi Henri Christophe", presided by Dr. Louis Noisin. He suggested that the newly created "CENTRE MONTESSORI D'HAITI", as we named our initiative, could be formally integrated in his potential "faculté des sciences de l'éducation en formation". Dr. Noisin simply created this new educational university branch for us. Since this gave us some formal backing and sounded good, I, of course, gladly accepted. Dr. Noisin invited me to give a speech on my seminar in project management (in French) in front of his students and town dignitaries. Thus, we were "introduced" in Cap Haitien, but what was even more important: Dr. Noisin also suggested to look for potential candidates for our first yearly Montessori training in the north of Haiti.

A modest, but potentially suitable room to establish the first "training center" was found – free of charge – in the large Christian multipurpose school "Collège du St. Esprit". Their section for "Hauswirtschaft" (housekeeping) had received 5 of the 12 sewing machines which were part of my first attempt to help in Haiti in 1981. The responsible Episcopal pastor Père Bruno even suggested to ask his wife to be our first student. The room which we were given was an old canteen. While I settled open questions with Père Bruno and Dr. Noisin, Carol threw out all the rubble which had accumulated in the canteen. She cleaned and painted the inside. I painted our new name outside: CENTRE MONTESSORI D'HAITI. We felt in a pioneer-mood. The start of the new venture looked promising.

In summer 1986, it was no problem to find a living-place for Carol in Cap Haitien: a small, but well-situated rental house. The next question to be solved was the language question. This proved to be a delicate problem which is still creating some discussions today. Since the official language in Haiti is French, all higher education is supposed to be in French. Hardly anybody in the less fortunate majority in Haiti does, however, speak enough French to be able to successfully study – or even teach – in French. Those with a minimum of schooling do understand some French, but do not feel safe enough to express themselves in this culturally demanding language. Since in our vision we did not aim at the "elite" in Haiti, but wanted to provide a better starting chance in life for deprived children, French was no feasible option. We inevitably had to predominantly train suitable candidates from "simple" surroundings to become Montessori preschool teachers. Even if we would be able to find a few candidates with sufficient knowledge in French, they would most likely not want to stay and teach in the countryside, but run away to a "better" situation as soon as they had a chance. For Carol and myself it was therefore soon clear that our teaching language had to be Creole to achieve the goal of our vision: good quality preschool for children in deprived situations.

The director of the "Université Roi Henri Christophe" did not like our language decision, but we remained firm in this question. Even though the Haitien "elite" always speaks French in formal situations, they all (or at least most of them) speak Creole amongst themselves. Carol, being from an English speaking country, had to learn to express herself in Haiti anyway. The initial teaching had to be translated in any case – at least during the first years, until she had learned enough Creole – and then French as well. For my initial speech at the university, my modest French was sufficient. In all other situations up to that point in Haiti, Miot had been helpful to translate my French into Creole. Since he had studied in the German-speaking part of Switzerland, we were also able to communicate in German, when my French was not sufficient.

The search for students

Back in Europe after the eighth trip to Haiti in July/August 1986, the only remaining question was: Who would be our first students? Carol had stayed in Port-au-Prince as a house guest of Miot Jean-Francois for the rest of the summer, working on the preparation of her first yearly teaching program in Cap Haitien. Carol had also used this period to give a three-week intensive Montessori seminar for the best students of the "École normale de jardinières d'enfants". This used to be the only existing training institution for pre-school teachers in Haiti. The main reason for integrating their "elite students" was to appease the directress of the monopolistic traditional training institution, who was not at all amused to see some qualified competition developing in the form of the CENTRE MONTESSORI D'HAITI for deprived people in Haiti. The teaching in the existing traditional institution was strictly teacher-centered. The directress literally sat on an elevated podium and gave her lectures from that elevated position. Questions were only allowed occasionally and in a very structured way.

Our integrating appeasement strategy worked well. This "special cooperation" with the only existing establishment proved to be valuable later on – but did not solve our main problem: the search for the right candidates for our new yearly training program in Cap Haitien.

Dr. Noisin, the director of the "Université Roi Henri Christophe", had clearly reaffirmed his willingness in summer 1986 to search

108

and present us young motivated candidates from the north of Haiti for our first year training program. We had trusted him in this question and had agreed on the needed qualifications of potential students. Academic preconditions for potential students were not required. They would have been strictly theoretical anyway, since there are hardly any possibilities to acquire such credentials in the Haitian countryside. Therefore, we did not even try to ask Dr. Noisin to search for candidates who had been through any kind of advanced education. A "good heart", positive motivation and – if possible – some kind of experience with children was considered more important by us. Discussing this in detail with Dr. Noisin had given us "a good feeling" that he would keep his promise to help us in our search for candidates.

Haitians in the countryside have very limited possibilities even below academic subjects to acquire some useful skills beyond the traditional farming on scarce and overexploited land. Jobs are very rare and the basic motivation to learn "something useful" is strong. Learning is relatively expensive in Haiti. A "boss", a traditional craftsman who accepts a student, is paid for his teaching. Perspectives in life are very dim in the Haitian countryside. Learning is a luxury. In view of our planned training program, knowing this had been reassuring for Carol and myself. We could count on many potential candidates for our training.

When Carol and I arrived in Cap Haitien in the first days of October 1986 – well prepared to begin the first training year and expecting to be able to interview possible candidates – nothing had happened. We were frustrated. The room in the "Collège du St. Esprit" was ready – but the only student, who was there to start working, was Madame Bruno, the school director's wife. It would have been easy for Dr. Noisin to find young men and women already in some way positively engaged for children or for their community in the north of Haiti. Exercising caution when dealing with promises, even when they were given with the best intentions, was something which I certainly had to learn in Haiti. This realization did, however, not help us in this moment. We needed to act.

One good aspect of Haiti always was – and still is – the great capability to improvise! Planning or any kind of rational forethought are not deeply rooted in the Haitian culture – but the improvising skills of the Haitians are remarkable. So we had to adjust to this cultural strength – and further improve our own improvising skills. Since Haitian culture is an oral culture (verbal and non-verbal through body language), direct communication works very well. Information transmits fast from person to person. This includes all the "normal" distortions of such forms of communication which are the object of numerous jokes and the reason for frequent misinformation. We, however, could capitalize on the positive aspects of this oral culture to find the suitable medium easily available: the local radio.

In 1986, Cap Haitien had four local radio stations. All but one were very small and admirably simple – and efficient. Radio receivers of all sizes, run on batteries, are widely spread and almost permanently listened to all over Haiti. All "relevant" information is transmitted in this way – even personal messages. All four stations, which can be received in the north of Haiti, were easily accessible in or around Cap Haitien. I simply drove to one after another – just one day before the training was supposed to begin. The result was overwhelming. After a short explanation of our problem, one station after the other immediately interrupted their music and/or regular information flow and put me on the air in my French with a German accent. In all cases they added some explanation in Creole. The largest of the four local stations first made a recording, which was then passed on the air in their programmed news section and was repeated several times during the whole day.

The next day, our potential training site was overcrowded by young Haitians, predominantly women, who all wanted to take advantage of this unexpected possibility to participate in "some" training. I was completely overwhelmed – and lost. Haitians can be very convincing if they want something. The possibility to learn "something" for free is rare and valuable – therefore it is wanted. Carol used all her female and Caribbean intuition to "select" the most promising 30 candidates. The situation was saved. And another lesson was learned in Haiti.

The remaining work to start the training was easy to accomplish: A "real" Montessori pre-school for training purposes opened parallel to the start of the first yearly teacher-training. With the help of Père Bruno we quickly found 25 deprived pre-school age children. Pre-school took place in the morning, teacher-training in the afternoon in that same room of the CENTRE MONTESSORI D'HAITI in the "Collège du St. Ésprit" under Carol's direction.

Every morning some of the afternoon students were "on duty" for practical training with the children.

The small group of "elite students" from Port-au-Prince joined that practical training a little later for a few weeks. Some of those "elite students" even became friends and were helpful in our future work. One later on became an assistant trainer, another one helped Carol in her translation needs. The system had started to work – and progressed well.

The "rest-avec" problem

It was not only the possibility to learn "something useful", which attracted some really motivated young people to apply for our training. The possibility of working with and for deprived children also played an important role for many candidates. Like almost everywhere in the world, children in Haiti are loved and treasured, even though the extreme poverty forces many parents to give away some of their children to other, slightly less poor families. There, they are often exploited as "rest-avec" children – in many cases as cheap labor. "Rest-avec" ("to stay with…") is a name which clearly sounds more positive than it is. The problem is well-known in Haiti. It is estimated that over 300.000 children live in such often slave-like situations. They are the poorest of the poor – especially the girls. Rarely do they get a chance to go to a school and the "rest-avec" girls are quite often an easy prey for male members of the host families.

Much later, in the context of the planned bicentennial celebration of Haiti's liberation from slavery, I had a chance to discuss this matter with President Aristide. He told me that about every third person in Haiti is somehow involved in this recognized problem, which makes it most difficult – he told me – to do anything to heal that situation.

As long as we are engaged in this country, the "rest-avec" children will remain a problem, which we must try to tackle with our limited possibilities. These children must not be deprived of their basic human right to learn – and thereby develop freely. Fortunately, there are other NGOs who have especially taken up the challenge to try to heal the "rest-avec" problem. It will have to be solved on a country scale – or even globally, since the children's miserable fate does not only exist in Haiti. The least we can do, however, is to remind the world tirelessly of this shame for humanity to hopefully find a solution in a better balanced world in the future. For us it was painful not to be able to heal this problem in Haiti except in some few cases in the framework of our Montessori projects.

The start of a successful program

When in October 1986 the first full academic year (nine-month) Montessori teacher training course had finally and successfully started in the "Collège du St. Esprit" in Cap Haitien under Carol's personal leadership and teaching, it was the beginning of a success story. But it was also a time to review the whole Haiti engagement. First failures were now balanced by some successes. Not all attempts – whether successful or not – are reported here, since this would not necessarily serve one purpose of this book: *the encouragement of visionaries.*
Not all miserable situations can be healed by visionaries – and certainly not from the outside – but to tackle visible problems in a visionary process is often possible and worth the effort.

In those first five years, I – later Carol and I – were experiencing an alternating *"Wechselbad"* (German expression for alternately being dipped in hot and cold water, i. e. mixed emotions) of euphoric hope and deep frustration. It was never purely rational, but always involved big emotions. It involved, however, always valuable learning, too. Carol found her field of engagement in successful teaching, but she also had to suffer very sad moments. We could not – and we did not – expect people to be grateful for our engagement, but what Carol had to witness was sometimes hard to bear. Students, who did not succeed in the final exams at the end of the nine-month period, blamed Carol for their failure. This resulted in a number of nasty insults and even aggressions. Gifts of poisoned food and punctured car tires are such examples. With the exception of the one dangerous situation in Port Margot in December 1986 reported above, I had never been personally attacked. But Carol had to suffer often.

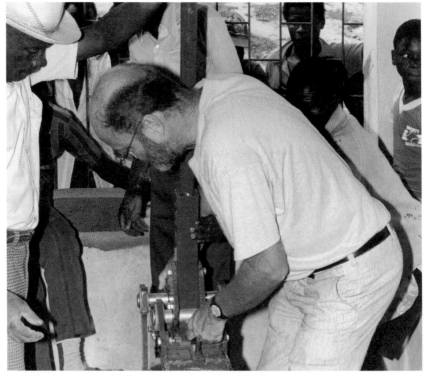

Building stones manufacturing attempt in Ste. Suzanne

More basic learning

Apart from the one-year Montessori teacher-training courses, Ste. Suzanne remained in the focus of our attention in an almost desperate attempt to help making the initiatives in this mountain village self-sustainable. Here I lost money. Since it was my own money, this might be tolerable and even considered as the cost of learning, but it took me a while to accept this internally. Besides of what was already described above (the case of the gas-powered refrigerator), we started to bring garden terracing-techniques from other comparable development situations, tried to introduce solar-cooking, built a house for the Ste. Suzanne Kindergarten, introduced clay brick building stones and roof tiles, using successful examples from African experiences.

All of those basically valuable initiatives finally did not succeed, since – apart from the foundation of the first Ste. Suzanne Kindergarten – nothing was truly initiated and carried by the people of this village. This underlines one of my first general lessons from the field of action:

Nobody, nothing can BE developed.
All must develop from the inside out, and
all development must be owned by those developing.

We had been drawn in to several self-help projects through the gentle advice of our FONDEV friend Miot Jean-Francois. Some were taken over later by larger organizations, others had to be ended for reasons beyond our control. We always remained open for occasional small emergency needs, but basically started to concentrate on what looked more and more promising for an inner long-term development in Haiti: MONTESSORI. There was enough to be learned and to be further improved around this central endeavor.

115

One incident, which would be almost funny if it had not been so sad, was the reaction of people in Haitian "elite" circles to our Montessori engagement for less favorite populations: In the early eighties, there was only one good, but very expensive Montessori pre-school in Haiti. It is understandable that those who earn money from being in a monopoly situation do not like new competitors – in this case: us. Carol's work was systematically talked down and discredited in a sad way. I had openly declared that the purpose of our activity in Haiti was to help the majority population, who lived in less favorable situations – in accordance with the German foundation's formal goals and with Carols and my inner motivations. This was enough to be denounced by a representative of the "luxury" pre-school on Haitian public TV as a communist. – For an active member of Germany's relatively conservative party, the Christian Democrats (CDU), this was a joke. The political climate in Haiti at that time was such that everybody, who was engaged in favor of the disfavored, was put in a far left corner. Even though such discrediting attempts were not directly dangerous, they still created a climate of mistrust, which is neither helpful nor motivating.

In the meantime (by now in 2008), critics have been silenced by the facts they cannot deny: The Montessori pre-school system has gained a good reputation and is well excepted in Haiti. There are many MONTESSORI signs everywhere in the streets of Port-au-Prince – even were they do not belong. "MONTESSORI" outside is no guaranty for Montessori inside. For many years we tried to negotiate a system of formal binding quality control with the changing Ministers of Education. We got friendly reactions for this proposition – but nothing concrete followed. The subject lacked public (and financial) interest. As a small Non-Governmental Organization (NGO) we were powerless. Private agreements are impossible to monitor and will not even be negotiated by those institutions who are concerned. As long as we cannot constructively cooperate with a stable government of Haiti in this question, everybody can call their money-making Kindergarten a Montessori pre-school. This is certainly not desirable – but beyond our possibilities to intervene. It does, however, clearly show that the Montessori method has made an impact in Haiti's society.

The "harmonizing-vision"

In the very beginning in Haiti, when I first discovered the value of Maria Montessori's didactics for early childhood development, I talked about Early Childhood Education in my political circles in Germany. In my view, the reality in Haiti and also in Africa was rather sad. Whatever happened for children before their school age of six was concentrated in the larger cities and of very insufficient quality. It, however, proved to be difficult to suggest Montessori as a well suited didactical model to "give children a starting chance in life" (as I usually simplify my appeals) for educational reforms on a wider scale. In political discussions people were skeptical when I mentioned Montessori as one suitable method.

Any particular method often created acceptance problems in politics. This was independent of the method itself. Only when there was personal experience or deeper knowledge concerning a specific method, there was acceptance among important opinion leaders. Sometimes, when someone knew Montessori from their own experience, mainly through their children, there was positive resonance. Other people had positive Waldorf school experiences. In the USA, "High-Scope" had their followers. High-Scope is a didactical system, which leans heavily on Montessori, as the founder of High-Scope himself admitted in a private discussion, but created its own "brand" for marketing reasons. Those three (and later some more) child-centered initiatives all fought for change. All wanted to replace traditional teacher-centered methods with something better – with their respective child-centered didactics. Unfortunately however, all good systems fight their own political battles. That gave birth to a new vision:

good child-centered early childhood educational systems working together to gain political recognition. Still remaining skeptical myself, whether this vision could work, I started a process to at least give it a chance. (See page 370/371 – letter of 15.11.1990)

The fact that learning begins with birth, or even before started to be recognized by the educational world, but not yet in some systematic form. This became evident at the "World Conference on Education for All" in 1990. In most competing quality concepts, pre-school started around the age of three. So why not get together and argue together as one group for more political support?

I found relatively easy acceptance for the general principle that children and not teachers must be "in the center", because children are individually differing, but equally valuable personalities. Good didactical systems simply cannot treat children as if they were all learning at the same speed. Good teaching must follow the children's differentiated learning. This was widely accepted in political discussions even among people who are not engaged in educational questions. To increase political "impact" in arguing for educational change, for better educational quality, I wanted to bring representatives of at least the best known child-centered didactical systems together to form a unified platform for change. It was an early rational vision in the early beginning of my own widening consciousness. This vision of a united action may have been naïve. I tried it anyway.

"The World Conference on Education for All" in Jomtien in March 1990 was organized by UNESCO, UNICEF, UNDP and the World Bank. I tried to get invited to the conference – in vain. State representatives and the international community did, however, follow a good direction in Jomtien. The Education for All

("EfA") goals were not yet decided, but Early Childhood was already being looked at – although not yet very seriously. Five years later, during the "UN Mid-Decade Review Education for All" in 1995 in Amman, Jordan, Early Childhood Development was reinforced. By that time, it had also become easier for the engaged civil society to participate in UN conferences. I again made an effort to be invited – and finally was allowed to join the conference in Jordan. I participated as the only NGO from Germany – but we were an engaged group of international Early Childhood activists working and arguing together with some success.

Five years earlier, in 1990, the time had not been ripe for serious cooperation between the official representatives of states and the international community with the engaged civil society. Inside the international organizations and inside the civil society, true cooperation was also slow to develop. I, therefore, had tried to speed this up a little in those circles who were involved in improving the quality of Early Childhood Development and Education ("ECDE").

In November 1990, I approached the three UN EfA-organizing bodies and the World Bank with a two-page proposal (see copy of the original pages in the annex) to help to bring together "didactical specialists for early childhood education" with the (naïve) goal: *"Optimizing didactical material as much as international consensus can be reached"*. The final goal was to initiate good quality pre-school projects in those One-world countries (in 1990 we still called them '3rd world countries') who would be willing to participate. – Nobody in those great UN organizations responded to this suggestion. When I directly approached representatives of the three main educational groups, it became quite evident that my vision was truly naïve.

Nobody wanted to give up their supreme feelings of being the best. In the case of Montessori it was not clear to me at that time that there was no fully homogenous Montessori structure, but several somehow competing fractions. The followers of Rudolf Steiner's anthroposophy responded with basic sympathy and some Waldorf school teachers even joined an "INITIATIVE PRE-SCHOOL EDUCATION for children in ONE world" which I started two years later in 1992 (please see pdf pages in www.solidarity.org/en/one – "Early Childhood Education" under "ONE world concepts"). Following my suggestions to cooperate with the other systems, however, did not catch on with the Waldorf schools I contacted. "High-Scope" did at least seem interested in the beginning. They invited me to come to their headquarters where the whole managerial group carefully listened to the suggestions – with poker faces and no positive reaction either.

Well, it had been worth trying. Finding out that group interests are difficult to overcome for one united political purpose was not really a surprise to me, but hopefully at a later date, the engagement for all children may still bring people together in a growing One-world consciousness. In Haiti, our option was simply to continue building on what had been started.

The Montessori development in Haiti
– an overview

Here is a short summary of the Montessori development since our first training year in 1986/87:

Well over 700 young Haitians (predominantly women) have been trained in one-year (nine-month) courses. About half of them were what we call "project students", which means that they did not pay a tuition fee. The other half were "private" students. They paid a full tuition fee, which was adjusted to comparable training offers in Haiti – but always much cheaper than Montessori training in the USA or somewhere else in the world. Carefully chosen "project students" always had and still have priority. With the years and with growing experience, we became more and more selective and even started to ask for a small inscription fee as a "motivation filter".

Soon after Carol had started the yearly training in 1986, information in Haiti traveled quickly that there was this new possibility to learn a profession, which could be used in various ways to create an income. We were soon more and more crowded with demands for training. Many Haitians, who applied for free training, invented some project for deprived children. Haitians can be very creative and convincing in inventing stories, as I mentioned before. It took us a few years to develop a feeling for recognizing who really was concerned about poor children and who just wanted to freely benefit from our offer. To shortly summarize the 21 years of training and their results, I just want to give the general picture first.

Over 50 Montessori pre-schools for predominantly deprived children, what we call "our" project schools, resulted directly from our training of "project students". In reality, such schools are not "our" schools. Only during the first years we maintained our own training pre-school for the needed practical training of our teacher-students with children in a Montessori pre-school class. Later, we had the possibility to offer practical training in project pre-schools. All project pre-schools belong to various Haitian groups or organizations. Those are church groups, parents' initiatives or Non-Governmental-Organizations (NGOs). A list of all project schools which resulted from this work is in the annex of this book.

Teacher-students have to organize their own living and food. We merely pay for the training of the accepted teachers. Those, who are successful and obtain a teacher or a director/directress diploma, receive one complete set of Montessori didactical material as a donation. Most of those didactical Montessori materials are purchased by us from the Dutch quality manufacturer "Nienhuis-Montessori". In addition, successful students or their sending projects receive some financial help in various individual ways to open up bottlenecks for new schools or classes to get started. Those initial contributions as "help to help themselves" never cover the total cost for opening a pre-school. Sometimes we pay for the wood for the local manufacturing of adequate furniture, sometimes for the material to cover the roof. Only in the beginning did we also pay a part of some modest salaries in the most needy situations.

All partner initiatives had and have to provide some proof of their true engagement. Besides the fact that we cannot afford more than initial help, this very restrictive method of "only" helping to get started and to open initial bottlenecks has proven to be one of the open secrets of our system's success. In this way, running expenses for project pre-schools remain very low. We never build a complete school for our partners. They set up what they can afford, which is mostly very simple. There is rarely running water or electricity. Parents of the children often have to be directly engaged, for example in doing repair work in the buildings. But there is no compromise for the didactical child-centered quality of the teaching.

Since we normally do not pay any salaries, the trained teachers have to be supported in various unconventional ways by those, who own the project schools. Teachers usually get some modest salary from paying parents, but not all parents can pay what amounts to about one US dollar per month. In most cases, parents are asked to pay a tiny school fee for the participation of their children, since this is according to local culture. In Haiti, anything totally free is not considered valuable. In reality, however, many of the parents cannot afford even the smallest tuition fee. In those cases children are accepted anyway. The usually highly motivated teachers and their supporting groups are proud of their achievements and get permanent confirmation through the good development of their children. The system supports itself in all simplicity through quality, ownership – and pride of accomplishment.

But what about the "private" students?

We do not even always know what they are doing after getting their diplomas as Montessori directors/directresses, teachers or assistants. Some open up Montessori pre-schools for children whose parents are more fortunate, others get paid jobs in such money-earning schools, some others manage to go abroad. We have no possibility of interfering in whatever way with our former "private" students. Unfortunately, we also have no control over the Montessori quality in such private schools. In view of the many MONTESSORI signs in Port-au-Prince (there are less outside the capital), we strongly doubt that they can really all be considered quality pre-schools. Only recently we regained hope that we have found a way of supporting the quality of all pre-schools through Carol's new Montessori training manual in French, "Atelier Montessori", published by the Peter-Hesse-Foundation in 2007 (please see descriptions of these teacher-training manuals in the VI. chapter of this book, "From Haiti to Africa – and onward" – pages 290-293).

Project pre-schools receive the new training manual at a strongly reduced price, private schools will have to pay the full price of EUR 59 (about US $ 85 in 2008). Only in exceptional cases we will fully donate those valuable books to project students or project pre-schools. We certainly cannot and do not intend to "make money" on those manuals. Carol's work and the production cost of those books could never been even halfway recovered in reality. The reason why we are so restrictive is simple – and has already been mentioned before in another context: What is given for free, is not considered valuable in Haiti!

To maintain the quality of Montessori didactics of at least "our" partners' project pre-schools is one of our main concerns. In relatively peaceful years between various political turbulences, Carol used to invite "our" former project students to training camps during the long summer vacations in Haiti. Usually this took place in one of our partner schools – modestly supported by the Foundation. Summer camps in a simple form do not only serve to permanently retrain quality aspects, but are also used for the production of new, locally adapted Montessori teaching material, for example for language teaching. This also furthers bonding between teachers and gives them the moral support for their not always easy situation. During all those turbulent years which we witnessed in Haiti since the beginning of our engagement, the

Montessori pre-school system has slowly, but steadily grown and established itself as a successful and well-recognized model.

But there were setbacks as well to be witnessed. A few schools became victims of political change. In one case, the school's initiating teacher, who had been one of our rare male project students, decided that he wanted to earn money as a "private" Montessori pre-school. He had started as a "project school" for deprived children with a group of parents who wanted this school. He simply stole all the didactical material and opened up a "private" school in a different region of Haiti.

In the case of our very first Kindergarten in Ste. Suzanne, which had been transformed to a Montessori pre-school, the system failed because we had not yet fully learned our lesson of the first years: In Ste. Suzanne, where the villagers had led the way to our work for children ("something for the children" had been their wish), the support had not been growing out of their own local initiative. Later we had to learn what cannot be repeated often enough: Local initiative is a "must" for success. We, Miot and I, came here in 1981 to start that first Kindergarten merely on the basis of the general request under the village tree. But this generated not enough motivation to endure. Looking back, Ste. Suzanne was a relatively costly, but valuable learning occasion on how development does not work in a sustainable way.

In general it can be said that wherever personal motivation and initiative had grown "from below" (like in about 65 % of all cases), the Montessori pre-schools developed in a very good way. The best schools continue to grow rapidly from inside out. They need more and more trained teachers. They will continue successfully – like the whole Montessori system in Haiti.

Carol on the way to a distant Montessori project pre-school in the mountains

Problems, which are directly connected to the success, are normal – and have to be solved. Some deceptions are also normal – and have to be "digested" in the learning process. Uplifting and encouraging are the stories of some of the children from our early pre-schools in Haiti. Here is a nice example.

A Montessori pre-school child, Anais Exil, writing from Paris

I had spent my first pre-school year in a traditional Haitian establishment with overloaded classes, when the Montessori pre-school opened its doors in our area. Later, we moved but I still didn't have to change pre-school.

There was an open house day, and since my parents lived close by, they visited the school, and, surprise, they were flabbergasted by the décor, the order, the material, and everything. They enrolled me. I stayed four years in this school.

My most beautiful memories are linked to this school. Indeed, I say "school", but it was more like a family than a school. There was no barrier between the children. Big children and small children were side by side. We did the same lessons at different levels. Each student teacher had to prepare practical tasks, a song, a poem, a story, or a lesson on a given subject. Like this, the children learned many things.

I loved the practical life exercises because of the coffee grinding device, the pouring exercises, to serve the others, or to clean the dishes…. I adored the sensorial material because of the pink tower, the color boxes (arranging the colors to form a rainbow), and the sound boxes….The mathematics for the golden pearls and the spindle boxes. The reading material for its illustrated alphabet, the sandpaper letters, and also for its secret bags.

The material serves also as an instrument to get on-board a language, writing, mathematics, sciences, music, geography, art, and history. It's an incomparable opening to the human universe and its environment.

What I have retained from those four years is to know, learn, and apply, and to be able to wait one's turn; mainly to respect others, and not to disturb them. For example, one looks at one child to do a lesson several times, even when you would really like to work with this material yourself. One has to wait until the other child is finished and has returned the material back to its place. And mainly, one may only help the other child, if the other child wishes it.

This method is strongly based on observation, it encourages the child to touch, to discover by himself; the child is autonomous, free to move around, explore by himself....Afterwards comes the phase of application, this is good, one can restart alone if one has made an error until one has finished the exercise well. The material is self-corrective and since one has the possibility to do the exercise as often as one wishes, one masters it and one will never forget it again.

This school is part of my most valuable memories. Additionally, during the embargo, during the Coup d' État in Haiti in 1991, I spent one year sleeping in the school. The reason is there were not many possibilities for transport, as gasoline was scarce. The gasoline was also very expensive. Due to the Coup, my parents had the choice to take me back from the school, to place me somewhere else near them, or to let me stay at the school. Well, they have given me the choice, and I choose to live at the school. I didn't miss my parents, I could manipulate the materials as I desired, and to read as many books as I wished, this compensated. I learned to observe, to appreciate these things, the good things. During my stay in this school, I devoured the books, books for learning to read, but for me, they were storybooks. Storytellers were brought in who familiarized us with the stories of the country. I adored it!

129

Still today, my best friends are those from this school. Some are considered like brothers and sisters. Firm ties remain between us. We maintain permanent and cordial contact.

I will never forget the Christmas celebrations since Mister Peter Hesse not only limited himself to financing the school, but invested himself. Once he disguised himself as Father Christmas and distributed gifts to all of us. For the Easter holidays, one of the teachers disguised herself as the Easter Bunny with a basket full of eggs. The children were to look for the eggs that the Easter Bunny's helper had hidden in the courtyard. And, it was comparable in Carnival in February, and during the children's festival in June.

What are also unforgettable are the field trips. After each field trip, the children had to write about what they had seen, to make a book together with the photos which were taken. Sometimes we made a recipe, and all the children participated in the cooking: some set the tables, others served, some cleared the table, and finally some cleaned the dishes and put them away.

I still remember the paintings on the walls of the school. All the children participated. And, each time one came to the school, or if one left again, the drawings reminded us that they were our works. There were also paintings on the calabashes. Each child had decorated his calabash. This was pretty and very motivating. Indeed all these activities were made to motivate us and to enhance our self-worth. Like me, the other children must have kept a pleasant memory of the school, of Mister Peter Hesse, of Carol, of the teachers, of the student teachers, the materials, the décor, where everything was well arranged in its place.

The only shadow on that picture was the closure of this school. I felt badly about this separation. And it later proved difficult to me to function in other universes than that school where I spent four mar-

velous years. It should continue to provide another image of school. A school made by solid learning, of human warmth, comprehension, and cooperation. It should continue to give children a well-ordered education, where learning is a real pleasure.

From this experience, I have retained the taste for reading, for the style of learning with rigor and method. I read fast and with comprehension. I am also very observant. And, this I owe to this method. I can only congratulate these people to have made available this type of learning.

Many parents were afraid that their children may become individualists and egoists, because of this method rooted in individual learning. This fear has proven to be ungrounded, since there is nothing more helpful and generous than a Montessori child. Since the child has learned from a very early age to help others, this is something one cannot take away easily. Therefore, inevitably, one utilizes this in one's daily life also.

What else can one say but to wish a long life to Mister Peter Hesse, to Carol Guy-James Barratt, and to the project! A lively thank you to these people who knew how to guide my first steps in life!

Anais is the daughter of Lolotte, one of our early teacher students and one of our most valuable partners in Haiti. Her daughter Anais was a pre-school student in the first Montessori pre-school, which we set up mainly as a training facility for student teachers. At the same time it was in this small school, where we attempted to include the first years of Montessori primary school in the system. This attempt failed simply due to the fact that we were lacking resources and personal capacity to proceed on that path, due to the increasing demand for Montessori pre-schools. Today, one of our remaining dreams is to extend our successful pre-school system to Montessori primary school in Haiti.

Problems with space and other deceptions

In October 1986, we were overwhelmed by the demand for training. It, however, quickly became clear during that first year that it would be almost impossible on the long run to find enough potentially successful candidates in the north – far away from the country's capital Port-au-Prince. Only a few of our first local students had the potential for maintaining a Montessori pre-school in sufficient quality. Potentially good candidates were mostly unwilling to leave Port-au-Prince. Haiti suffers from a worldwide trend to the capital cities and we had to take this into account to reach our goal. We certainly did not like the necessary decision which we had to take in view of the need for quality:

After our first year in Cap Haitien we had to move to Port-au-Prince. A suitable rental house was found halfway between "downtown" Port-au-Prince and the somewhat more peaceful "upper town" Pétionville. There we stayed for a few years, lived and taught in that small house.

The demand, however, grew further and we needed a larger place. Buying a piece of land was an early option (later leading to new problems), but building a house or even renting a bigger place was too expensive for us. One solution for the space problem was to rent the flat roof on top of an office building. The bishop of the Episcopal church in Pétionville had his office in a suitable one-story building with a flat roof. We made "a deal" with the bishop to use that empty space on his roof for building two interconnected training rooms and a tiny kitchen apartment for Carol. The bishop gave us written permission – including a guaranty for five years with a "promise" of prolongation.

With financial aid of the German Government we managed to erect the walls and a roof over that available space. I literally brought a folding door in my baggage for the separation of the working space to obtain two rooms. This allowed us to offer two parallel classes, but to also use the rooms as one for larger events. The space was dusty and noisy, water had to be bought and stored on the roof in drums, electricity was only temporarily available (like all over Haiti) – but we were able to continue our training as needed in two parallel classes – until the five years were over.

Then, after the fifth year, the bishop thought that he might be able to use the new rooms on his roof as living quarters for his occasional visitors. This presented a serious problem.

Legally we had no more right, and a "promise" for prolongation did not count much – not even from a bishop (which I found amazing). Being thrown out of the place, which we had been building to service some of the country's educational needs, was only one of the many deceptions which Haiti presents to people who come to render service. But in this case it was particularly hurting, since our "partner" was the bishop of that same church we had worked with in Cap Haitien in the beginning, the "Collège du St. Esprit" of the Episcopal church. In Cap Haitien, our initial partner, Père Bruno, had been most helpful – what could not be said of his superior, the bishop.

We had to move again – this time to a small rental place with only one training room, but with running water and a tiny room for Carol to sleep. This was not far from our first rented house directly next to the main road from downtown Port-au-Prince to Pétionville. The new rented place was well positioned to be reached by our students – but it only allowed one single class. It was too small.

Other deceptions originated from inside of our own system: Though it took us longer then originally expected, we finally managed to train eight Montessori teacher-trainers. After a short working period with us, most of them decided that they could earn more in other frameworks. Some went abroad or opened their own independent training centers – with unfortunately lower quality standards – for paying students. Up to now, only two of "our" trainers remained faithful to our commitment for self-help development. These are Naomie Joseph, who runs our affiliated training center in Port-au-Prince after many years on our payroll as a trainer and Heliana Charles, who is responsible for our "mobile training center".

With Naomie we have a working contract, which allows her to accept more paying students with a fixed percentage of free "project students". For the moment, this is a good compromise in Port-au-Prince. The mobile training serves faraway places. It is fully paid by us for predominantly "project students" and proves to be a good solution to fulfill needs for more good teachers in places far from Port-au-Prince. Now, in 2008, it operates for the second year in the deep south, in Jérémie. Before, Heliana had worked for two years high in the mountains in Kenskoff – and even earlier once again in Cap Haitien, where it all had started.

This mobile training is particularly useful for re-training less qualified students from former courses, but it also serves to prepare those young ladies being already engaged by our project partners without having been trained properly. It is a solution for the quality problem, which developed in practice with the growth of the whole system.

The building project

When we realized after a few years that we would finally need our own training site in or near Port-au-Prince, we again looked for a piece of land, which could be affordable. After having been kicked out by the Episcopal bishop from "our" top flour on his office, it became ever more urgent to find a solution for our space problem. There was a growing demand for training, which we could not satisfy. Finally, in 1997, we found a suitable lot of land, the size of a football field – affordable and well-connected for potential students to be reached. We bought the land and properly fenced it in to avoid misuse of uncontrolled settlements.

In Haiti, it is legally very difficult to chase wild settlers away, once they have established themselves on a piece of land. Youngsters around that area discovered that our land had the perfect size for their football games – which also helped to keep wild settlers away. A building concept was conceived "correctly" by way of a bidding process, and the winning concept was harmonized with the professionals of our potential building partner, the "Deutsche Welthungerhilfe – DWHH", in Haiti: *Agro Action Allemande.*

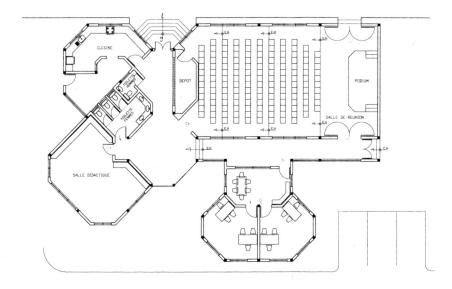

Without the cooperation of a strong partner we could not have handled the administrative side of such a building project – and certainly could not have financed it alone anyway. Luckily, the concept also appealed to the "Deutsche Welthungerhilfe", since they also have some need for occasional training space in their predominantly agricultural projects.

In our concept, the structure would at least partly have financially supported itself. There is a need in Port-au-Prince for an affordable training space for up to roughly one hundred people. After carefully formulating a project proposal for co-financing through the German Ministry for Development or the European Union with the professional help of the experienced "Deutsche Welthungerhilfe", it all looked very promising. Unfortunately, however, Haiti was not really in the focus of Germany's development priorities and certainly even less in the field of education. The European Union had become so "reserved" and choosy in their participation that the whole project had to be "put on ice" for better times. Our German partners were equally sad and frustrated about that development – but they could do nothing about it either.

But an even worse deception was yet to come:
For some years, there was intensive football-playing on our land. Once we had to repair the fence and re-erect our sign of ownership. But all looked safe. When in 2005 Carol went once again to check the fence around our piece of land, she saw that someone else had built a solid wall around our terrain and deposited a building container on the field.

Carol immediately came back with a "justice of peace" to document that strange development. It was, however, up to now impossible to find out who had re-sold our property to whom. All we learned was that the land had indeed been resold or simply taken, altogether illegally, but nevertheless. Due to insecurity and public disorder in Haiti during the recent years we had no chance to find out anything. Nobody bothered. We had involved a lawyer who later never responded to our request for information – not to speak of legal action. We do have all papers proving our ownership, but that does not mean much in the Haiti of the past years. The "case" is not yet closed, but the outlook is very vague – and the deception is mixed with amazement that such a situation can happen in our seemingly civilized world.

Only recently I found out, where we could at least get some information who might be involved in this strange matter ("strange" only in the view of a German, who is used to a functioning legal system). There is a land register which even some professional land sellers hide before their customers to avoid formal registration, eventually enabling them to resell the land. Perhaps we have been falling into this legal trap, when we first bought our piece of land – even though through a notary with all correct procedures, as we were clearly told.

So many deceptions may hurt the motivation. Yes – they do. But in view of the wonderful positive effect on deprived children of what we started over 25 years ago in Haiti, such de-motivation can be overcome. The above report by Anais Exil, one of the first children in our own training pre-school after our move to Port-au-Prince, is enlightening and motivating:
She reports her memories in a very sweet and loving way. She is now successfully studying in Avignon, France. And she is not an isolated case. Unfortunately, we have not systematically followed

up what happened to "our" children over the years. In the beginning, we simply did not anticipate to be engaged in Haiti for so many years. One simple truth is, however, stronger than all our setbacks and deceptions:

There is ample evidence that Maria Montessori is right to assume that the first six years in life are of the utmost importance for a fulfilled life. We, of course, have no way to positively influence what happens in the equally important very first three years before children reach pre-school at an age of 2 1/2 to 3. In his fascinating book "Radical Knowing", the author, Christian de Quincey, pleads strongly and convincingly for small children to be kept close and tight to a parent's body as much as possible early in life. In poor situations like in Haiti, this plead is traditionally followed much better than in our "civilized" world. I have, therefore, included this "radical knowledge" in my own "learning spiral" later in this book (at the end of the third main chapter).
Recently, the "Association Montessori Internationale – AMI" has extended their work also to the very first three years in the life of a child. Luckily, the political world has also started to recognize the utmost importance of early learning. There is hope for the future of human development, if such knowledge becomes "mainstream".

Today it is common knowledge – at least among all people in education – that all six or seven first years set the path for life. It is beyond our influence what happens to "our" children in Haiti when they reach primary school age. We only know that "our" children are always considered the very best students in primary school. Many parents in Haiti ask us to continue with Montessori primary schools. This would be highly desirable, but our possibilities are (at the moment) too limited to seriously extend our Montessori work to the age group of six to twelve. Since our engagement in Haiti started through a listening and learning process, it was not a carefully pre-planned project, but developed during the first years with some detours. I today believe that some kind of higher purpose, some good guidance was leading our way to give deprived children a better starting chance in life. What looks like having started as a coincidence has gradually developed to be a vision which works. Other comparable initiatives have failed. This leads to the question, what is driving us?

Coincidence or higher purpose?

How would I know any answer to this question? Believing in the usefulness of rationality and in visions, I am frequently tempted to create my visions "the rational way". This does, however, not always produce the desired results. But visions which did not work are often more interesting than immediate success. Such experiences provide valuable learning – and allow improved visions which do work. There was no lack of conceptional mistakes (and some deceiving behavior of partners) on our way to reach our visions. There were, however, always moments to recharge the positive "motivation batteries". Those moments were – and still are – not necessarily spectacular. Bright and gentle eyes of children provide such moments. Pre-school children, who manage successfully to finish one of their learning tasks with the self-explaining Montessori material, are proud of their achievements. This is largely compensating for deceptions. But beyond these moments of "enlightenment" from the eyes of children, there are also some more success stories, which should not be forgotten.

Success in Haiti usually began with a personal coincidence or in totally disconnected, unplanned circumstances – as if life was part of an invisible plan beyond our own control. With all my "management mind", which favored precise objectives and conscious planning, I became skeptical about my own rationality. Too many coincidences simply happened. Where they really coincidences? Or did everything happen because it was fitting a larger plan?

It was not only the skiing accident in 1973 that started to change my life. My favorite sport in summer, sailing, was also participating in creating change. Sailing was leading to a successful side project in Haiti as will be shown in the next chapter. Yet in whatever way our successful cases started, they all needed to be sustained by deeper motivation *and* in using the rational mind. Looking back today, spiritual guidance, in my humble experience, is never commanding any specific action. I am always free and I feel, that I am even supposed to decide for myself on the right action. Later, this led me to the conclusion that spiritual guidance and using one's rational mind are not contradictory. There is no "middle-way" which seems to be the best combination of both types of "influences". It is some integrative "ensemble" (togetherness) or in German: "MITEINANDER" of mind and spirit which leads to success.

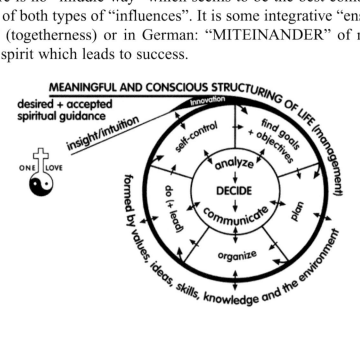

The Brotherhood of the Coast on "La Tortue"

Whether it was just a coincidence or some kind of unnoticed higher guidance, I certainly did not reflect on that question at the time, when my summer sailing passion became relevant in Haiti in the mid-eighties. Later, when reflecting about these questions, I was surprised myself when I realized what created the link between my sailing-hobby and serious work for deprived children – and for other side projects in that area of Haiti. Here is that story:

In the 17ᵗʰ century, the small turtle-shaped island in the north of Haiti, La Tortue, was the home of some wild people. They were not pirates as it is widely believed, but a colorful mixture of Europeans, especially French as well as escaped slaves, pursuing a rather aggressive profession: robbing the enemies of the French king. Some lived on La Tortue under a French Governor and chased – "legally" in the name of the French king – mainly Spanish ships returning with stolen treasures from South and Central America. Others lived on the coast of Haiti's mainland, hunting pigs. Those pigs had been imported by the original Spanish settlers and had proliferated there. The "Brothers of the Coast", as they called themselves, lived in a wild, but still specially regulated way. They predominantly created their own rules and behavioral patterns.

This "brotherly" way of life of the "Flibustiers" on La Tortue inspired a group of ocean-going "blue water" sailors in Chile. On April 4, 1951 they decided to idealistically revitalize the "Brotherhood of the Coast" as an association of sailors. In the following years, this very special men's club, which is not comparable to a "normal" yacht club, spread all over Latin America, Europe and some other coastal countries. (www.secoin.org) It is organized in the form of "tables", headed by a "big brother" and aided by a "scribe" (an honorary secretary). It also reached Germany, where I became a member of Germany's first "table" of the "Brotherhood of the Coast".

I simply liked the somewhat nostalgic and not too serious way of being with people, who shared my summer sailing-passion. One very personal definition of the brotherhood is by a brother with a strong personal connection to Haiti, Bernard Lefèvre: *"The Brotherhood of the Coast is a highly disorganized, loosely organized group of people who are bound by love of the sea and a sense of friendship."*

Having started our serious Montessori work for deprived children in 1986 in Cap Haitien in the north of Haiti, La Tortue soon became fascinating due to the wild legends from the 17th century. Without my "brotherly connections" to La Tortue, I would probably never have ventured there. I might also have missed to be engaged in the nearby northern town of Port de Paix, the departing point of many Haitians trying to reach the shores of the United States.

This "port of peace" became one of the projects for Montessori pre-schools in cooperation with some Canadian Christian school brothers (a more traditional kind of "brothers" than our Brothers of the Coast). Port de Paix, therefore, had to be visited several times. Those visits gave birth to other educational side projects, which simply developed in a natural process of taking action on the basis of obvious needs. This, for example, involved helping to built an extremely simple primary school with the introduction of self-made building blocks (earth with only a little cement) in Haiti.

What did not really work in Ste. Suzanne, here in Port de Paix it worked well – due to the serious commitment of one teacher, Georges Florissant, (here with me on the photograph). He used the claybricks from our imported manual moulding machine to build his school.

A more spectacular project was to help Port de Paix solve their waste problem. This was the city leaders' greatest wish. It resulted in building a connection between this very poor northern town with the town in Germany, where our family-owned company was located. Providing a well-working garbage truck to Port de Paix as a donation from the service provider of our German factory location, Erkrath, created quite some "public movement" in Port de Paix. National TV emitted a story and inhabitants of Port de Paix joined in a new, highly motivated activity to clean their city.

This sponsored garbage truck turned out to be the most modern one of all Haiti and it did useful service for many years. A German volunteer, Bernd Klubach, came along for a few weeks to train some city workers in Port de Paix and later I was asked to send a pair of new giant cartires for that truck to keep it going even longer. It was a nice side project – just by building a suitable bridge from Haiti to Germany.

151

One more "regular" Montessori pre-school project developed right across from La Tortue in cooperation with the same Canadians, our Montessori partners in Port de Paix. They also managed a large school project on the mountaintop of La Tortue. With the help of the responsible Canadian school brother on La Tortue, Père Bruno, this soon became our project pre-school number 18. But – like in Port de Paix – the engagement on La Tortue did not limit itself to providing teacher-training and Montessori material for the school projects of the Canadian brotherhood. Here, the 17th century origin of the new "Brothers of the Coast" provided the starting point of a totally different kind of project. A new vision was born which needed several boat trips over to La Tortue.

Crossing over to the island on one of the small local sailing boats is fun for a sailor. It is not truly dangerous in normal weather, although the rugged small boats are often loaded to their limits.

In Père Bruno's office on top of the turtle mountain, there was always some cool beer in the generator-driven ice box. This was stimulating in Haiti's heat, but on the wall of Père Brunos's office I found something equally stimulating – in a different sense:

Quand Même

Les gens sont deraisonnables, illogiques et égocentriques.
Aimez-les quand même!
Vous faites le bien,
on vous accusera de vouloir en tirer des avantages.
Faites le bien quand même!
Si vous réussissez,
vous vous ferez de faux amis et de vrais ennemis.
Réussissez quand même!
L'honnêteté et la franchise vous rendent vulnérable,
Soyez honnête et franc quand même!
Les gens les plus remarquables, ayant la plus grande
largeur de vue peuvent très bien être vaincus par les gens
les plus médiocres, pourvus de l'esprit le plus étroit.
Voyez large quand même!
Les gens s'intéressent aux opprimés mais, se rangent
du côté des gagnants.
Luttez quand même en faveur des opprimés.
Ce que vous avez pris des années à construire peut être
détruit en un jour.
Construisez quand même!
Les gens ont réellement besoin d'aide; mais peuvent vous
agresser si vous les aidez.
Aidez-les quand même!
Donnez ce que vous avez de mieux et l'on vous remercier
à coup de pieds.
Donnez quand même ce que vous avez de mieux!

This print dealt with the French version of my early guiding slogan from country school-years: "DENNOCH". Somehow, the English translation "even though" or "anyway" do not carry that same power as the German DENNOCH or even the French "quand même". (I will refer to such guiding influences once more in a different context later in the next main chapter of this book and will include an English translation of this French text there.) Finding my personal guiding word, which had supported me frequently in my life, here on top of that very special place in Haiti, La Tortue, was a motivating confirmation that our work in Haiti needed that DENNOCH mentality to avoid giving-up. La Tortue now occupies a special place in my heart – even beyond the "Brothers of the Coast".

The inner connection to the 17th century idea of brotherhood initiated a second activity on La Tortue – beyond the Montessori pre-school on the mountaintop.

Along the coastline of the island, fishermen, all of them descendents of the former imported African slave population, try to make a living from the sea. They are short of everything, which they would need to be successful, like outboard motors, good nets or a cooling system to preserve their catch. The idea (one might call it a "side vision") was born to create a solidarity structure by simply referring to the basic idea of solidarity behind the traditional "Brotherhood of the Coast" – or their modern offspring in the world. Back in Germany, I mobilized our "table" of the brotherhood and found a few followers – at least for an initial phase:

We simply decided to create a "Table de la Tortue" with local fishermen instead of hobby-sailors. New tables of the brotherhood are always initiated by an existing table. Père Bruno was formally agreed to be a special "big brother" (the title of the head of each table of the "Brothers of the Coast", as mentioned above). The leaders of the various groups of poor fishermen on the coast of the island were to become his special fishermen brothers.

In 1988, guided by Père Bruno, I visited the various groups of fishermen. He translated my proposition into Créole: For every dollar, which the respective groups of fishermen were to earn, we, the German "brothers", would add on one of our dollars. This was certainly not a very new creative idea, but it had the advantage to be understood immediately – and was also greatly welcomed by our new local brothers. Since the fishermen basically knew what had happened on their home island some centuries before, the solidarity action was well received.

I had a feeling that some of them thought the German "brothers", who now wanted to help them in a modest way, to be a little crazy. The daily struggle to survive does not leave space for nostalgic reminiscences of past centuries. Since the idea was, however, considered useful, all was agreed on in a harmonious way. It was certainly not an ideal project, since it was not born locally. It still helped to solve real financial problems as long as it could be maintained.

Later on, I simply added the needed money to the initial starting funds from my German sailing brothers and Père Bruno acted as cashier to pay our share for new nets, outboard motor repairs or for whatever the groups decided to need most. A representative of the heads of the fishermen became our contact person and the system continued to function – modestly, but efficiently – for several years. Père Bruno was formally handed the flag number 50 of the table of the Düsseldorf "Brotherhood of the Coast". (All flags are individually numbered, and 50 is considered the size limit of a table of the modern brotherhood.)

A highlight of the small fishermen's project on La Tortue was the celebration of a "boucan" (a feast, traditionally with a roasted pig) on the original ruins of the 17th century brotherhood on the island. All participating fishermen were invited. Our German "table" had donated some t-shirts and caps, since our "big brother", the head of the table of Düsseldorf, was also the head of the yearly Düsseldorf boat show, "boot", a very practical coincidence. A few "brothers" from Europe and from the USA, who happened to sail in this region during that period, joined the festivity. I had the pleasure to pay for the drinks and for a goat, which was roasted instead of the traditional pig. It was a memorable event – and certainly one of the rare fun moments during my later years in Haiti.

Later, when the further deteriorating security situation in Haiti made it unadvisable to travel to faraway places like La Tortue, the small support system unfortunately faded out again. I, however, do not consider this to be one of our failures. It simply became impossible to overcome the growing insecurity with our limited resources. We are, however, informed that the Montessori pre-school project on La Tortue continues to function.

The only practical way to reach La Tortue later on was with small private airplanes. An existing tiny airstrip next to a nice beach section on the island was officially not in use, but easily usable by rolling away a few handy stones. I refuse to speculate for what kind of traffic the landing strip on La Tortue might be used in nowadays sad reality.

Whatever is happening beyond the visible part of poor Haiti on the hidden dark side of this country – like in comparable unjust situations in our unbalanced world – might be an interesting story, but not mine. My contacts with the "elite" in Haiti was and is very limited. What I have witnessed in Haiti, is mainly the daily misery of suffering people, especially of children.

This moves the heart and inspires creativity.
This also gave birth to a vision, which worked.

A vision which worked:
"Facilitators in Partnership" – a micro-grant model

One of my first discoveries in my practical problem-solving work in Haiti was that financially large projects were far less successful than I had previously and innocently expected. This was at least true when large projects were financed by my own country, Germany (perhaps because I looked more closely at those). Especially technical projects like windmills for electricity or mechanical water pumps for irrigation were too big to be handled by the local structures, once the German technicians had left. On the other hand, I saw and met "official" development field workers from my country in Haiti, who did some really impressive micro-level work with their own money. They were not allowed to use the "official" funds of their assigned projects beyond their precisely defined purposes. So they simply collected additional small funds from their church groups or friends at home and used them to open self-discovered bottlenecks in the surrounding of their regular field of work.

The German government was not capable to co-finance smaller projects below German Mark 20,000 (in my early years in Haiti) for understandable reasons: The administrative costs of the bureaucracy at home would simply have exceeded the expected benefits in the field. The German embassies, like those of some other countries, did, however, have the possibility to finance small micro-level projects, originally from the Foreign Minister's own household. These embassy budgets, also "public money" from our taxes, were not limited on their lower end. They could be very small, down to a few hundred German Mark or even less, if considered appropriate. That looked very reasonable – and mostly led to some good bottleneck opening problem solving at the people's level. The small embassy funds were even successfully used, when there was no development specialist in the embassy, who had "deep-down" experience in the field. The vision, which developed in observing this reality, was simple: The system would work even better, if the person in charge for granting the micro-grants would not be a diplomat, who usually has a different kind of job to do, but a development specialist.

This led to the idea to politically fight for the possibility to be able to spend small amounts of public money for micro-level projects without the risk of overspending and thereby killing local initiatives – or with even worse effects. The idea, which simply was born by watching the given reality in the field, led to my first political success in the area of development. It was truly to become a *vision which worked.*

A typical initiative of a man – a baker – in the very informal sector

I have to admit: I originally thought that to build the bridge from a clearly reasonable vision, developed through simple observation in the field, to a political reality working on a larger scale would be easier. It did, indeed, need a lot of detailed work in conceiving, writing – and mainly in convincing politicians and overcoming bureaucratic structures at home in Germany. From the initial idea, even before the formal creation of the Peter-Hesse-Foundation in December 1983, to the inauguration in 1988 and the "final victory" in September 1989, it took almost six years: Two years for the conception and for getting political acceptance, two for finding a suitable administrative structure and two more for a test phase in four countries: the Dominican Republic, Kenya, Zimbabwe and Togo.

In the meantime, another basic micro-financing initiative has won world-wide recognition through the Nobel Peace Prize, awarded to Professor Yunus in 2007 for his micro-credit initiative with the Grameen Bank. Micro-credit has found many followers and is working very well, if properly conceived and managed. I have tried the idea myself in Port Margot in Haiti, as described in the first part of this book. Due to my own experience, I know that it is vital to adjust the idea well to local situations. It also needs time and detailed work to be successful.

Micro-credit – if well introduced – is certainly the most valuable fast working "healing instrument" in development on a micro-level. I consider micro-credit to be generally even more important than my own micro-financing model, giving small grants. Micro-credits have motivating and capacity-building qualities besides directly providing self-help possibilities.

Giving small amounts for bottleneck opening, basic initiatives could, however, be an additional valuable "development instrument" in the world. It is now used as a development tool by Germany in the hands of development workers, which are independent from embassies. There already was one forerunner, who had inspired me (besides the small embassy grants) in the early process of designing my own model: There was a German micro-specialist working for the "United Nations' Volunteers (UNV)" in the late seventies in Africa, who already made use of the same basic idea in his own work. Unfortunately, the UNV system, which is part of the "United Nations' Development Program (UNDP)", did not continue to use this instrument after this specialist had departed. In a visit to the UNV head office in Bonn, Germany, I had tried to convince the very busy leader of this organization to re-activate her good program. This suggestion was verbally well accepted, but without much enthusiasm and with no follow-up action at all (due to a heavy workload, as I was told). It might, however, become a future global vision to add a world-wide scale to our nice German micro-finance model. For the time being, this model serves as an example or even proof that visions can work – and it really serves its purpose: to alleviate poverty in reality.

The following text in italics was part of the "three suggestions" for the World Summit for Social Development in 1995. In this text, I still used the word "help" instead of "heal" which I prefer now. Today, I would also be more careful in speaking or writing about "the poor". I feel today that we need to make a distinction between "poor" and "misfortunate". "Poor" as an attribute is too radical and it is incorrect. Even the most disadvantaged misfortunate people are often rich in other than material views. We in the west or north can learn a lot from many materially poor: in cultural or spiritual domains, for example. My learning process took a while to fully grasp such differences – and will hopefully continue becoming more refined. Anyway, the following English version, written in 1994 for the Copenhagen UN summit, is still valid in content. It was an early attempt to bring the working vision into an international context.

How to reach the materially poor

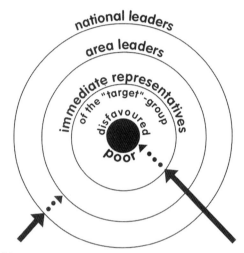

© Peter Hesse

conventional larger projects formulated by "higher" leaders to satisfy their needs

mini-projects for and with the "poor" through experienced **Facilitators in partnership**

The Problem

Funding from outside a developing country to alleviate poverty mostly passes through governments and/or government related central agencies of the developing country, and does very often not – or at least not sufficiently – reach the target groups of the poor. Corruption and/or mismanagement on all levels are frequent reasons for this problem. But even well-intended, honest help projects are often conceived on levels too remote from the truly needy

168

people. The poor are rarely in a position to formulate and articulate their needs in a way that enable public funding from outside their country. Even with best intentions of those "higher levels", who formulate projects for international funding, there is too much diversion and administrative cost involved for effective and direct alleviation of poverty. International funding is rarely direct enough.

An additional problem can be over-funding which kills local self-help initiatives. International funding strategies are usually "demand-driven" – but by whose demand? The only area, where the usual system may work, is for larger infrastructure projects, but not for multiple micro-projects to alleviate poverty through small bottleneck-opening contributions directly for those needy people who try to help themselves. "Trickle-down" rarely works; "trickle-up" is effective. At least for funding, which is intended to alleviate poverty directly by strengthening the productive capacity of the poor, we need a strategy through which the true needs of the poor are established locally in the true partnership with trustworthy facilitators. Only where trustworthy self-help organizations of the poor exist, facilitators do not need to work predominantly and directly with the poor themselves or their immediate self-elected local representatives, but also with the "higher" level of those self-help organizations.

To reach the suffering people directly (or at least their immediate representatives), experienced helpers – facilitators – are needed who are trustworthy, capable and willing to work directly with the poor and their immediate representatives to find out in true partnership where and how self-help initiatives can be supported without damaging local self-help motivation. To bridge cultural and language gaps, partnership facilitators from donating countries or international organizations may have to cooperate with trustworthy local partners, which could be called partnership agents.

169

The purpose of the partnership facilitator model is direct bottle-neck-opening help for self-help initiatives. The final goal of all assistance should be to enable sustainable holistic self-development in peace, freedom and dignity.

"Facilitators in Partnership" – a micro-grant model

Facilitators in partnership should be morally reliable citizens of the donating countries or from member states, if multinational organizations are the donors. They should be mature people who have gained experience with the poor target group, preferably speak their language and respect their culture and value systems. They should be willing and able to locally work as partners with the poor.

They may either be part-time facilitators in partnership, if they mainly work in specific projects with and for a target group or they may be full-time facilitators in partnership if they return to the target groups with no other specific assignment, but after having gained experience there in previous projects.

In the original German model, it was foreseen to install facilitators in partnership through accreditation by the minister responsible for development assistance. This was supposed to be an honor and to be granted in recognition for successful work in former projects with the poor. The state agency or private organizations, who send help workers to developing countries, were supposed to suggest such qualified help workers to the minister. In reality, this accreditation does not (yet?) work, but the responsible minister has delegated the task of selecting and sending out facilitators in partnership to a semi-private organization (German Development Service – ded), who receives funding mainly from the ministry for this task.

The selection process may be structured to be an "honorable distinction" of qualified experienced practitioners or in any other suitable way. It is, however, essential that facilitators in partnership truly accept these guidelines for their work:

170

Guidelines for facilitators in partnership

- *The priority group to receive development assistance should be people who are deprived of their basic needs like clean air and water, food, basic health care and clothing, shelter and learning opportunities for a life in dignity, but who cannot fulfill those basic needs, even though they try.*
- *It is equally important to strengthen the will, the skills and opportunities for self-help as well as for helping others (charity).*
- *Help must be directed to the smallest possible self-help structure.*
- *Working partners of the facilitators in partnership are predominantly the local natural traditional leaders of the poor, as long as they are truly recognized by the poor and do in no way exploit or suppress them.*
- *Groups, including informal groupings and specially neglected segments of the population – often women – should receive priority. It should, however, be possible to help individuals too, provided this is not unjust to the individuals' environment.*
- *All help must be given, consciously observing that it does not create any undesirable side-effects like social injustice towards those, who do not receive help, environmental damage, a passive recipient mentality or new human, technological and financial dependencies.*
- *Help may only be given where those responsible are personally reliable and honestly engaged, live in adequate modesty and possess a minimum of problem-solving capability in the respective value system.*
- *Self-help structures in traditional rural and village environments should receive priority.*
- *Self-help organizations which are not only created to obtain foreign aid are to be supported. Motivation, skills and opportunities to create honest self-help organizations should be furthered.*

171

- *Development goals must not be decided without those who need help. They must participate as partners in all planning and implementation.*

- *Problem-solving paths of those who want to help themselves have priority. To avoid pseudo-modernistic erring, problem-solving paths must, however, be checked through dialogue.*

- *Peoples' dignity, value systems and culture, their spiritual and religious beliefs as well as their human relationships must always be respected.*

- *Logic and rational thinking should only be used predominantly as long as they do not damage local cultural value systems.*

- *Where traditional values block harmonious holistic development because of changes in framework conditions, peoples' attitudes may only be addressed with the utmost care and responsibility.*

- *Those who are being helped must at least contribute their own engagement and must make – whenever possible – some adequate contribution.*

- *All help must lead to lasting improvements and must therefore be reflected beyond its duration.*

- *All help must be limited in time. The recipients' self-help capacity must grow to be self-sufficient.*

- *All technical assistance must be adapted to the future local maintenance capacity and energy resources of the recipients.*

- *Where training is involved, skills and problem-solving capacities have priority over a mere transfer of knowledge.*

- *Problem-solving experience must be shared.*

The key idea of the partnership facilitator model is to enable smallest financial bottleneck-opening contributions directly where they are needed most – along with help to connect people who could better help themselves by cooperating in a given local situation.

172

Facilitators in partnership should also link knowledge on basic needs of the poor with their sending state or multinational organization and be a transmitter for problem-solving know-how.

Financial aspects of the model

Facilitators in partnership shall be given a budget for direct financial bottleneck-opening contributions to the poor. This budget shall allow unbureaucratic fast small-scale help without administrative burdens. The partnership facilitator should have the right to decide himself/herself (or after local consultation with his/her sending organization), who should receive how much help for what purpose. The total amount to be allowed for each needy situation should be limited to 10% of the budget of a part-time facilitator, respectively to 3–5% of a full-time facilitator. There should be no minimum. Full-time facilitators should receive a budget of 2–3 times the amount of the part-time facilitator. Part-time facilitators receive no remuneration for this task outside of their regular pay for their specific main project assignment. Full-time facilitators are paid like development personnel assigned to projects.

Local partnership agents may receive contributions for their relevant expenses, but no salary. Full-time partnership facilitators may also receive some contributions for their relevant expenses, but part-time facilitators only as much as they are active outside of their project areas.

The size of the budgets for the part-time and full-time facilitators in partnership depend on the spending capacity of those help workers. Guided by field experience, it was originally suggested in 1988 that German part-time facilitators shall receive DM 50,000 and full-time facilitators DM 150,000 (plus expenses). Since bottleneck-opening mostly needs very small amounts and since overspending is dangerous, even full-time facilitators mostly need less than DM 100,000

173

per year to be effective. Their own "cost" is, of course, relatively high compared to their budget, but it is more important to spend small amounts well to truly alleviate poverty than to save on the cost of facilitating and waste large amounts of project money as in many conventional big projects.

Facilitators in partnership have given proof of very careful small-scale spending, effectively supporting development self-help initiatives. Of course, it is most important to select the right people for this facilitating task.

The model implies a strong component of voluntary engagement by the facilitators. "Partnership facilitator" should never be considered a financially interesting "job". More important is the privilege to spend public money in a limited way and according to the above "guidelines" with a minimum of bureaucratic procedure and being "officially" trusted to do so.

Of course, there will be more or less administrative necessities remaining according to the sending states or multinational organizations' laws and regulations. But in this framework, there should be as much freedom and trust and the least possible bureaucracy.

Limits of the model

The partnership facilitator model is limited in quantity to the number of suitable and willing applicants. It also needs to be accepted by the respective developing country and it cannot replace larger integrated state projects. But it can be a tool for effective alleviation of poverty with public money from outside through a decentralized, flexible decision structure. It does not pretend to be totally new or sensationally different. But it was certainly new in Germany, when it was inaugurated in 1988 (first as a test in four countries) after four years of conceptual and political preparation. And, most important: It works.

174

Trusting experienced people to spend public money for effective help to fight poverty without damaging self-help initiatives by over-funding and without loss of funds through corruption, is worth trying.

During the initial two-year testing phase in the Dominican Republic and in Africa, I had visited those four countries for one weak each to further "refine" the concept and see for myself, how it worked. The implementing agency, *"Deutscher Entwicklungsdienst – ded"* (German Development Service) did not really like my idea to check and evaluate on my own, how the system worked in practice in those four testing countries. However, since I was ready to pay all expenses myself and since – after all – the concept was written and got to be accepted in politics through my "pushing", they had no real choice, but to agree. I was given all relevant information and was introduced to the four selected personalities. They were consciously mixed from very diverse professional backgrounds to make the test even more significant. They all proved to be most cooperative and gentle to this strange private person, who visited them for one week each. We toured many projects and I noticed that the system basically worked very well – as expected. As also expected, the field experience allowed the integration of some additional recommendations in the final model.

In September 1989, almost six years after the initial formulation of the vision, the model was formally integrated into the "regular instruments" of the German Ministry for Development, as proclaimed by the ministry's State Secretary during a small internal celebration. The extended use – beyond the four initial testing countries – started in the beginning of 1990.

Later, the *"Partnerschafts-Helfer-Modell"* was gradually adjusted during the years and extensively put to use in the development reality, which – after all – was the purpose of the vision. Maybe because the acronym "P.H. Model" sounded too much like "Peter-Hesse-Model" (what I certainly liked, although it was not intended), the name was changed to a more formal and more complicated compound name: *"Programm zur Förderung einheimischer Organisationen und Selbsthilfeinitiativen"* (Program for the support of local organizations and self-help initiatives). As the German Development Service reported in 2007, a total of 70 development workers were then being active in 43 countries in using this micro-grant model.

To sum it up once again: The initial problem, which had to be solved in this case, was clearly learned in Haiti. It only needed open-minded observation of the reality. The resulting vision serves as an example in proving the basic statement in the title of this book: VISION WORKS – even though it sometimes may need some more effort and persistence than originally expected.

10-year celebration of Montessori in Haiti

After 10 years of yearly Montessori training, a total of 412 Haitians had received one of the three types of Montessori pre-school teacher diplomas: Directresses (and Directors), Teachers or Assistants. 42 former Montessori students worked in 26 project pre-schools, created with our assistance. It now started to become difficult to keep track of the didactical quality of the schools. They were spread all over Haiti. It was, therefore, a good rational decision to stop training new teachers for one year and to use the free training capacity instead to systematically follow-up, what happened in the existing projects. In this framework, Carol suggested to organize a one-week training camp in one of the existing project pre-schools in September of 1996. This *"Retraite Nationale"* (national retreat) took place in Haiti's costal town of Les Cayes.

80 of Carols former students participated – including some private ones. The Foundation paid for the food. To join the event, participants needed to get there without our financial support. Sleeping was improvised in a simple camp-like manner. All of this needed some strong motivation. Therefore, 80 participants were not a bad result. On the last day of the successful group training, we celebrated the 10-year event with speeches and some singing and dancing. This was, of course, useful for bonding between the Montessori teachers, who normally lived and worked in different corners of Haiti. So far – so good. What did not work out successfully, was Carol's and my idea to create a sustainable teacher association: an *"Association Montessori d'Haiti"*.

This was an attempt to initiate a democratic structure into a culture, which is not used to a self-regulating form of organization.

177

We underestimated the difficulties to maintain the suggested formal structure. The initiative had already been started by Carol and me in May 1996. The association was therefore not created by the teachers themselves, but by us. The team, which was first installed to organize the new association, was initially named by me – and supposed to be replaced by a democratic structure during the *"Retraite Nationale"*. This plan was well-accepted when we spoke about it with our teachers.

During the retreat, the election itself had a festive, joyful touch. It was almost like in real political life: Those of the participants with good showmanship won the others to vote for them. Lively presentations led to being elected to leading positions in the association. Qualifications were not questioned. Could that be a basic problem of all democracies? Here, in Haiti, it was extreme. Carol and I did in no way interfere in the process and refused to be members of the association ourselves. We thought that it would help to build a more sustainable structure if the teachers were totally free in their decisions and actions.

The 10-year festivities ended joyfully and everybody went home to their work with recharged "motivation batteries". Carol and I were under the impression that we had done a good job. Carol had indeed done a good job. She had been in charge of the framework and the content of the festivities. I felt like i had spent my money well – even including the nice start-off budget for the *"Association Montessori d'Haiti"*! This, however, proved to be a mistake, because I did not observe what I had learned before: Self-help structures must start from the bottom – or at least be seriously wanted there and then organized in true partnership. They cannot be imposed. Especially the job of a cashier was too much of a temptation for the elected person, a seductive pretty teacher.

I had been happy, when this young teacher had been elected to be the association's cashier – simply because she had impressed me. Discretely mentioning this to Carol, she equally discretely condemned me for having such "macho feelings". Although I do not believe that what happened shortly after was in any way connected to the good looks of the cashier, I felt especially sorry because of my positive prejudice.

Not very long after the successful 10-year celebration and the democratic installation of the "Association Montessori d'Haiti", the cashier disappeared with the association's total funds. We did not find out whereto she disappeared, but she was gone and the nice new association was dead. This certainly was a less dramatic failure than in some former situations, but it certainly was not what Carol and I had hoped for. It could have become such a good aspect of our Montessori project in Haiti, if a teachers' self-organized structure would have survived.

Haiti is not only sad.

Chapter III:
Journey inward
and the search for "truth"

To write this chapter of VISION WORKS was the emotionally most difficult decision. What happened during the five to six years after 1989 described in this chapter is relevant for the whole story. What happened, provided the needed inner support to continue making an effort in the world. Therefore that chapter is needed to tell the full true story. One truth on the way to finding "the truth" also helps to make the affirmative decision to write this chapter. Much of what happened "inside" cannot be described in words anyway. So, why worry too much about writing what cannot be explained?

My own realization about the difficulty to write about inner movements is widely shared in the writing of people who otherwise have no problem to publish their own personal views. One example of such a deep writer is Ken Wilber, whose "integral map" is very useful to bring some order into thinking. In my view, Ken Wilber is certainly not shy in his many writings. I, however, feel that we share the view that inner experience can only be experienced. I discovered Ken Wilber's writings – like other deep books – only after having had my own "special experiences".

Somewhere I had read a description of such experience which resonated with me and remained in my mind: What I eventually can describe, is the shadow of a deep experience, not the experience itself. Therefore, I can limit myself here to some essential reporting of what became truly relevant for the messages of this book.

From questioning reality to questioning myself

The process of healing work is in itself a learning process. From irrational emotional reaction while being confronted with situations, which are hard to bear (like people suffering) to trying "to do it right" is also a self-discovery path. When being first confronted with misery (like in 1980 in the Mission Globale in Haiti), I did not question my own motivation. I did not use my rational mind at all. At first, well-meaning, though very imperfect action was at least partly a way to appease my own feelings. The personal process to realize that – if I really wanted to help (not yet to "heal-solve") – I might as well first learn to do it right in practice, was only a first step. Humbly stepping back from "knowing best, what to do" was the next necessary initial learning step on a long path to finding "the truth".

Wise people tend to give advice to someone (like me), who got caught into emotional reactive helping action that one has to develop one's own mind and soul first, before venturing into imposing any actions on others. If this advice is not only a verbal defense mechanism to avoid the emotional need to become active, it is certainly valuable. I, however, tend to believe that learning "to do it right" in concrete outward action is a parallel process to finding the "truth".

This "truth", I believe, cannot be found rationally. This "truth" is embedded in mystery. In my opinion, "truth" can only be experienced. Insights, better: "in-sights", are for me gifts from a dimension which has no name – or many names. In our western culture, we call it GOD. In my inner experience, this view of the divine is too separate from me, from us. My personal experience indicates that the "truth" (you may also call it "light" or "divine energy") comes, is there, when I open up to receive it, when I pray for it, when my soul longs for it.

For me, "truth" also provides answers for the meaning of life, for the "why?" of all existence. There may be good reasons to first dig into one's own soul – in the desert or in some cave. That would mean to follow Christ's or Buddha's initial search through self-isolation or self-starvation. Isolation and starvation were, however, not tempting to me. I always liked – and still like a good life with wine, music, female company and active recreation. I was, however, touched on my own search for "truth" by being active in the world with slowly opening eyes. One such "touching" event was a meeting with a Catholic monk, who spiritually bridges East and West, the Austrian, David Steindl-Rast.

I first met Brother David when I was trying out Zen meditation in Tassajara, a Buddhist center in Big Sur, California, USA. He impressed me in his gentle cross-cultural attempt to find a solution for global unity in diversity, as I saw it. Zen sitting was not my way to meditate, it was simply too painful for my back, but brother David was a role model for me in his serious bridge-building attempt. Shortly after getting to know him in Tassajara, I met him again in the Esalen Institute in Big Sur on the famous highway no. 1 along the Pacific coast of the United States.

Esalen (the name of the former Indian tribe in this area) is a magnificent place, high above the Pacific ocean, with hot springs and an ongoing program of holistic spiritual body and mind workshops – a good place for inner learning and deep relaxation. Here I asked Brother David about his bridge-building way to bring together the spiritual views of the East and the West. I specifically asked him about the difference of prayers in those two cultures. His answer was an unexpected confirmation of what I had been feeling without reflecting about it. He said: "The West, predominantly Christianity, prays with words, the East in silence." But there is a third way, he added. It is "praying by way of doing".

Praying had become a subject of concern shortly after my fiftieth birthday, after 30 years of total abstinence from any religion. During my 10 years in Salem castle, a traditional German country school, interrupted by one year in Phillips Academy Andover, Massachusetts, USA, religion was still "alive" and nicely undogmatic. In Salem, we all prayed together every morning. I participated without being deeply touched. It was peaceful though.

As maturing male adults in a strict boarding school, we were slowly waking up to our time's realities. Those were political realities and more profound realizations of our horrid German past, but there were also personal emotional problems of becoming young adults. Salem was a mixed school. Girls were "untouchable". Sex was no subject. Most of us were very innocent. Even dancing, my early hobby, was rarely allowed in Salem school. Holding hands with my dream girl was my fantasy.

In short, I had other preoccupations than religion. I am not even sure, whether I was ever baptized after being born in New York, USA. In boarding school nobody bothered, whether I was baptized. Only now, at the age of 71, I am asking myself this question. I was, however, formally "received in the arms of the protestant church", as they say in Germany, at some confirmation celebration during that earlier period in school. Those religious formalities never touched my heart – but Pastor Otto did.

It was in the Junior house of Salem castle, in the summer residence of the former abbeys of Salem, *"Schloss Kirchberg"*, where our most gentle Lutheran Pastor Otto was not only our pastor, but simply someone to love and trust. His slogan in life: "DENNOCH" became my life's motto, too – reinforcing itself in later years and receiving additional "sense" on the Island of La Tortue in Haiti: It was the French version of DENNOCH: "Quandmême", which I found there. The original French version, with-

out any indication of who originally was the author, is reproduced in the last part of the previous main chapter of this book.
Here, I am trying an English translation in using "even though"
and "anyway", whatever feels better:

EVEN THOUGH / ANYWAY

People are unreasonable, illogical and egocentric.
Love them, even though!

You are doing it right (good),
you will be accused to extract advantages from this.
Do it right (good) even though!

If you are successful,
you will attract wrong friends and real enemies.
Be successful anyway!

Honesty and openness make you vulnerable.
Be open and honest anyway!

The most remarkable people with the largest viewpoints
may well be subdued by the most mediocre narrow-minded people.
Have an open-minded view anyway!

People are interested in the suppressed,
but they arrange themselves on the side of the winners.
Fight for the oppressed anyway!

What took you years to construct, can be destroyed in a day.
Build even though!

People may really need help, but they can assault you,
when you help them.
Help them even though!

Give your best and people will thank you by kicking you.
Give your best anyway!

Having a problem with this translation, to remain true to the feeling in the words, I still prefer my DENNOCH. It carries emotional power – and constructive anger, which (I feel) gets somewhat lost in the English terms "even though" and "anyway".

One other, deeper influence in my belief system during my school time was a visit in my last year before *"Abitur"* (high school diploma plus two years) in Salem by the retired founder of Salem school (and also of Gordonstoun in Scotland), Kurt Hahn. He was the former assistant of the last German Chancellor under the German Emperor. As a Jew he had to flee Germany during the Nazi time. His lesson was unusual – compared to what we were normally supposed to learn. It concerned life itself.

Kurt Hahn, in my view a truly wise man, referred to the values and pathways to walk in life: *"Always remain open for all learning – but once you have discovered something or a path to be 'right', do pursue the right way even alone and against the prevailing currents."* This did fit my DENNOCH and remained firmly anchored in my belief system.

Apart from those few deeper imprints and a few other good memories during the later years in Salem and during my one year as a guest student in the US partner school of Salem, Phillips Academy, I was relieved to finally leave school and start to discover "real life". This discovery turned around a lot of subjects that were very different from religion. It was a truly lustful discovery time, which I certainly do not regret. It is possibly no coincidence that one passion, which developed during those years, dancing, finally even made sense in helping to "heal" my later life.

Back to prayer:
During my schooldays in Salem, it may not have been very deep

when I prayed, but at least I did participate along with my various schoolmates from different denominations (not only Christians). After school and a wild intermediate year as a (very uncommitted) volunteer in a bank in Geneva, I went to university in Munich, Germany. There, I once went to church on a Sunday to remember some peaceful feelings from my schooldays. But I found this very disappointing. Dogmatic preaching and collecting money for various purposes, which meant nothing to me, made me totally turn away from church – for over 30 years. I never went back to churches – except out of cultural interest when traveling in the world.

There was, however, something I never could explain: When passing a strong Christian symbol, a cross on a road side for example, I regularly had a mild mystic experience. It was and still is happening sometimes that something gently shakes my body when I notice that symbol. I still wonder what could create such bodily feeling, which is very certainly not provoked or created consciously. It became, however, consciously noticed by time, which does not help to explain it.

It was in October of 1988 that all of a sudden something broke open. I suddenly felt a need to pray. It was during a very deep meditation exercise, where I was taken by two lady friends who were more woken-up than me in that kind of exercise. It was new and very moving.

For the first time in my life I had a deep experience of unconditional LOVE – a divine LOVE – impossible to describe. I asked for help and someone did help me to pray, what Christians learn as the "Lord's Prayer". I had even forgotten the words. This need to connect with the divine continued during two more comparable deep meditation sessions. Here the subjects were *"Demut"* (humbleness) and a profound, unspecific gratitude to creation.

This phase resulted in a mental search and in praying questions about our reason of being here on earth, about my sense of being here. I suppose that this is a very normal human question to ask, but it took me over 50 years to get there. There were no immediate answers. But then something significant happened in a totally unexpected moment.

For many years, I could not speak about what had happened and I did not dare writing about it either. This changed only after another "incident" several years later. But this is a different story. I will later grapple with the other, the "unblocking" incident in this book. So, what happened initially?

The key message

It happened on 28 March 1989 in an insignificant hotel halfway from the south of France to my German home in Düsseldorf. In the very early morning (roughly after 3 a.m.) I woke up, realizing still half asleep, but very clearly that I had just started to have a dream, which was not like a normal dream. It was the answer to my basic inner question from some time before during last year: WHY are we, why am I here in this world?

It may sound strange and it certainly felt strange then – but I know in all certainty that this was more than a dream. Maybe I should be more humble and consider this only to be a firm belief. My feeling, however, refuses to accept that reduction to a mere belief. For me, what happened is simply a piece of the "truth", which I was longing for. For the first time in now almost exactly 52 years after my birth in this unexpected moment in an insignificant hotel, I was receiving an answer to my basic question, why am I living here now, what is my purpose, what is our purpose as human beings. In my quest, the personal and general aspects were inseparable.

188

I was not used to write down dreams, although I did have occasionally rather creative dreams which could be turned into fascinating film stories. Here and now in March 1989, I somehow realized that this was not a normal dream, it had a different quality. I knew that I had to write it down, in order not to lose it again. Luckily (still half asleep) I found a piece of paper and a pen and copied down, what I had been told. It was clearly a guiding message. Not the last one, but the very first one and in amazing clarity. It was in my mother tongue, but there was a specific meaning to the words beyond the German words themselves:

Das Ganze muss durch Lernen wachsen. – "The whole (all) must grow through learning". *"Das Ganze"* was truly ALL, the whole, from the smallest to the universal whole. *"Wachsen"*, "growing" had a more qualitative than quantitative character. – It continued:

Dabei hilft Liebe. – "Thereby Love helps". – And the message went on with a sentence which clearly influenced my life:

Ich muss dazu tun, was ich kann. – "I must contribute, what I can".
"Muss" – "must" sounds hard in a loving message. It was, however, clearly meant in a gentle way. It was not like an order, but like a reflection of my own inner disposition towards action. In the sense of active engagement, I (only) must do as much as I can. In further deep reflection about that little word "must" I realized that this divine source was not separate from me. It was also in me, it must be ONE with all. Some later messages and one very special moment of "in-sight" also could only be understood in this way. One later very touching moment even created a direct confirmation of the ONE-ness of ALL.

The first message further continued in providing answers which cannot be considered guiding like the first lines, but which helped me to get a glimpse of what might be called "the cosmic structure". The whole message and especially the added answers were very new to my rational conception. That helped me to accept that the whole message was not originating in my own brain. My skepticism towards phenomena, which I could not "understand", helped me to listen carefully to "messages" from there on and to only trust them, when they were really loving. Less loving thoughts also crossed my mind in this spiritually turbulent time – but they were easy to recognize as such.

In the following years it happened several times that I was given short "in-sights" in my relation to the divine. They were strong helping messages to let me form a belief system which gave me a "direct access" to that source of ALL, which allowed me to include existing religions and at the same time led me to refuse to accept their dogmatic aspects. I am deeply grateful for this period, which also reinforced my holistic conception of that ALL, which has no limits. In that process of finding my inner way, I also felt strongly motivated to continue my "normal" life in the framework of "what I can". After the rediscovery of prayer in the year before, silent praying concentrated more and more on occasionally thanking that unlimited loving power for answering my questions, but also simply saying "thank you" in an unspecific way.

One short message was a particularly unexpected and relevant one about a subject which troubled my mind in the years before and even more so after the initial guiding incident, the prevailing evil in the world.
In a hotel in Paris, while visiting our artists' color customers, deep in the night of 18 November 1990, this same inner voice unexpectedly and directly contradicted a view which I had developed in my work especially in Haiti. Becoming more and more

conscious about misery and evil in the world, I was getting angry. Although I had very limited power to act out this angry attitude, it had become anchored in my mind: Evil must be fought!

To my surprise, the short message was clearly different: *"Das Böse ist nicht zu bekämpfen. Das Böse ist zu heilen".* "Evil is not to be fought. Evil is to be healed". This may not be new to some gentle wise people. It, however, directly contradicted my own grown view. This new in-sight needed first to be digested. I still find it very difficult to act accordingly. But I am grateful for the message.

As shortly indicated above, it needed some years and "another incident" until I dared to speak or write about all this. Speaking is still difficult. Only the first line of the very first message ("The whole – all – must grow through learning") has in the meantime become a publicly declared guiding sentence, which I use without any hesitation (even on top of one of my circular models of reality) after what happened about 5 years later on 9 March 1994.

The liberating message

Exploring various pathways to find more answers in my search for the "truth" and after several other significant answers in equally unexpected situations, I participated in a holotropic breathing seminar with about 300 (!) other searchers, led by Stan Grof, in Switzerland. We "worked" in pairs. Since I went to the seminar alone, I was lucky to find a gentle person to be my breathing partner. One of the pair is stretching out on a mattress and is heavily breathing in following guiding instructions by Stan Grof. The other person of the pair is only paying attention that the one doing the breathing does not hurt himself. There is no other intervention by the watching partner.

It was a deep experience. I, however, did not expect any direct answer to my questions in an "induced" situation, since all "messages" which I had received since the first one in March 1989 were coming without any kind of supporting activity. Real messages were always true gifts from this unspeakable other dimension, which is connected to the "truth". I realize it as LOVE – or "divine energy". It seems to be connected to light (– and to some form of consciousness?). Being basically awake, but somehow shifting to an inward-looking form of consciousness, I did not expect too much to happen.

Then, all of a sudden, I visualized a bright light triangle, pointing upwards. Shortly later, a second bright triangle overlaid the first one – but pointing downwards. Formally it was the shape of the Jewish Star of David where two triangles are forming one harmonious form. This, of course, I knew – but that was not what appeared in front of my inner eye. "My" symbol was clearly composed out of two independent triangles of light. They even differed in brightness. The upward pointing symbol was stronger than the one pointing down.

Even though I was partly in a different state of consciousness, my mind was clear enough not to know or being able to understand, what "my" symbol was meaning, what it was possibly telling me. Then it dawned in my mind that this double light symbol was "something" which I was not expected to know. I took it as a sign that it did not originate in my own mind. Deep in my other consciousness I then saw a few (I do not recall how many) figures appearing. They had no shape, they were just light, moving very gently and in a loving way. Without using any words (unlike in my special dream messages), one of these beings of light created an unspoken, but doubtless message in my mind: Time is now "ripe" (as I understood it) to not keep my guiding messages anymore only to myself. Time – or I (which was not clear) – would now be ready to open up and share my guiding messages. It was not specific, what that being of light asked me to do, it was like a permission, a setting me free in this respect.

My reaction – as I clearly remember – was not at all clear. I still had to digest this totally different message. The question, whether I would have the courage to follow this permission (or was it even an advice?), remains. I will probably never be emotionally capable of sharing all the various answers, which I had received in those five years. Luckily, I do not even feel that I need to share all my personal answers. Words would not be able to describe "it" anyway. For this book I had, however, decided to do my best to at least write about those essential guiding messages.

The other short "in-sights", which clarify my relationship with this unspeakable divine ALL, are mostly very personal. I do believe, however, that the gifts, the moments of "in-sight", which have been given to me, are given to all who pray in whatever way, who seriously ask for such answers. I feel that I have received the gift of some "truth" – "my truth"? – "absolute truth"? This thought continues to be troubling.

Feeling that I have received gifts of "my truth" makes me wonder:
Why should I have received a different "truth"? One, which is different from anybody else's "truth"? On the other hand, the thought to maybe having received some "absolute truth" conflicts with the felt need to remain humble. Therefore, this question remains an open question – maybe until further "in-sights"?

I want to encourage all serious "seekers of the truth" to walk that path themselves. As much as I am convinced that visions have a chance to work, if seriously pursued, comparable guiding answers will be given to those, who are serious in their search. We always have the freedom to act according to what we are being told. That special guidance never gives orders (although I had a problem with the "must" in my first guiding message). We are, however, shown ways to decide – in combination with that other divine gift, which we humans have received: our rational mind.

What I also feel deeply is that the right guiding messages are loving. If they are not, they do not come from the same source. The danger of being mislead can be avoided in my experience, if we only accept loving messages. This in itself was the content of an answer to one of my questions. This LOVE can be trusted.

Besides continuing my "regular" diverse activities in business and in the field of human development in Haiti, the roughly five to six years following the initial incident, which produced the first guiding message, were filled with "deep digging" into soul matters. All I had been reading and writing before, dealt mostly with marketing and management matters, later with politics and human development. I am even grateful to not have been exposed to spiritual subjects, before being "touched" in my soul. In the early years, I used to consider myself to be almost a profession-al skeptic and I did not want to be influenced in my inner views by other people's discoveries. The search for "truth" to me was more authentic, if it was not disturbed by too many preconcep-tions through reading relevant books.

It was only after receiving moments of "in-sights" that my habit-ual skepticism motivated me to verify, what other searchers had discovered. It became a new discovery trip through spiritual lit-erature of all kinds. It finally reinforced my view that my "duty" lay in the field of doing and not so much in the field of pure reflection.

Since the beginning of this new life, I wished to be involved somewhat more in communities, where I was not isolated in my inner search and findings. Somehow "community" seems to be part of an inner path. A conventional church did not satisfy this need. Churches, like any other sacred temple of other religions, were most suited for my inner feelings, when they were empty. They have a strange inner vibration and transmit this vibration to me, if I allow myself to be exposed to it quietly. I became more and more suspicious of anything written by human beings, even the bible.

To try to overcome this inner "reserve" at least partially, I discov-ered one ecumenical Christian institution, which helped to bridge my inner "reserve" towards institutionalized religion. It was TAIZÉ, the foundation of the Swiss Frère Roger near Cluny in France. The vicinity of this medieval high center of powerful dogmatic Christianity with all its former splendor made the con-trast to the positive simplicity of TAIZÉ even more obvious. Since those early "discovery years" of the soul after my fifty-sec-ond birthday, one week in TAIZÉ had become a yearly retreat.

In the huge simple church hall of TAIZÉ, meditative periods frequently led to strong inner movements and to some of the very personal "in-sights". Towards the end of those special five to six years in my life, I also received one message repeatedly, which is even funny and i therefore want to mention it here:

Receiving gifts of "in-sights" became so heartwarming and uplifting that I developed a desire to receive more. It almost developed to be an addiction. However, my inner voice then told me repeatedly: *"Stop asking. You know your way now. You know what to do. Just do it."* – I consider this now to be a great and motivating response, for which I am grateful. It also allows me to smile about and self excuse my waves of greed.

Bridging East and West

On a more consciously reflective level, I am trying to find bridges between our world religions. In my view, one of the worst and most evil developments in our world are all forms of fundamentalisms which overshadow the loving aspects of the great religions. This makes it so difficult to find that "peace between religions", which is also part of our vast vision of "A world in balance", which I share with many active friends. To heal this problem might be one of the most challenging tasks humanity has to face for a peaceful future.

When there were pauses in my active life, my thoughts turned around this question a lot. Such pauses are for example the times during long flights. During one flight over the Atlantic in 1990, when so much happened inside me, I suddenly felt the wish to at least symbolically bridge the two spiritual polarizations of East and West with some form of model. Here below is the result of the transatlantic modeling attempt – including the "ONE LOVE" which later grew around this East-West symbol. When using this double symbol, I put a text around as pictured here:

Vision and hope for ONE world.

**We shall understand and accept to be
ONE in respected diversity
with individual and collective responsibility
for growth towards unity of all in ONE LOVE**

**finally spiritually transcending duality
with the help of ONE LOVE = GOD**

**Western/Christian symbol
for transcending
unconditional LOVE**

**Eastern/Asian symbol
for interconnected
duality – the reality –
here and now**

The Christian symbol of the cross was always problematic for me – even though I did have those strange deep inner reactions, when I saw a cross next to a road. Without digging too deeply into that problem of a cross as the symbol of Christianity, I can at least use this dualistic symbol here above as a symbol of light, transcending the duality of the ying-yang.

The "color sermon"

Since the spiritually "heavy" period of the five to six years after the reception of the first guiding message were also physically heavy, my double occupation of managing our family business and of further developing the projects in Haiti led to physical heart trouble. On 13 February 1996, I needed to be operated on my heart and received five bypasses. All went well and I, of course, was most grateful not to be one of those few patients, who do not wake up again after such a long heart operation. I felt a need to express my gratitude.

Five days later it was Sunday and I was for the first time allowed to carefully get up and walk around a little in the hospital. Like in most hospitals, there was a prayer room downstairs. Since it was Sunday morning, a young pastor was doing a Christian ceremony. I came in a little late and sat down in the last row, when something significant happened:

The young pastor was preaching about colors!
Why should this be significant?

Well, having just been operated successfully was also a good moment to plan to change my somewhat hectic life with its double working agenda. Both occupations, managing our color manufacturing family business and working for the Haiti projects could not be done blindfold. Both occupations were full-time jobs if I wanted to do them right. And I did want to do them right. Therefore, I had to make a decision: Color manufacturing or working to give children a chance.

I liked both jobs. Although the color manufacturing business was not started by me, but my ancestors, it still had been a challenge after almost total wartime destruction to rebuild and strengthen the Schmincke factory internationally. The Haiti projects had also become successful and equally challenging. So, what to do?

Leaving Haiti would not yet have been really possible without endangering, what Carol Barratt and I had started together over 10 years before. Haiti – unlike color manufacturing – was our own creation. Schmincke was "only" (partly) inherited. But what would happen to our family company, what would happen to all the good and trusting people, who worked for us there? Simply leaving would have been most difficult without prior settling the situation and finding a suitable successor. The color sermon was like a wake-up call to practice responsibility.

I was deeply touched. So was the pastor, when after the service I told him about my dilemma. Not being very knowledgeable about the writings in the bible, due to my skepticism about writings by human beings, which are supposed to be some last truth (at least by some people), I had no idea, how much color there was in the bible. Unconsciously, the young pastor had done a good deed in sharpening my consciousness to be responsible in my inherited profession. Leaving Schmincke right after the operation might have been possible to explain and for others to accept. However, after that sermon, leaving the color plant was no immediate option anymore. My plans for life had to be readjusted.

In my mind it was clear that hard choices are necessary at a given time. Leaving my business, even though I was deeply connected to that business by family tradition and my own successful work, might be necessary in order to follow an inner call. But at this time, the inner call was clearly asking not to leave (yet).

And so I remained president of our family company for almost three more years. That allowed enough time to carefully search and find a qualified young successor. Haiti trips were reduced to once a year after the operation. Life calmed down a little, but plenty of challenges remained and new, bigger ones appeared with the beginning of the new millennium.

After "traveling inside" I questioned myself on the geographical scope of needed engagement. Haiti was and remained in the foreground. But why not extending the scope of activity beyond Haiti? After all "the whole, the all" of my initial guiding message was at least as large as our world, our globe. An initial hesitation of "going too far" was slowly fading in the light of global challenges and my further extending consciousness. Being more free to act according to my inner voice since 1999 is like a new gift of life. One more reason to be grateful.

The Learning Spirals

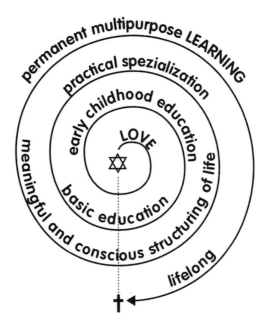

The combination of inner and outer learning, which happened during those years in Haiti, also asked for some visualization of the learning process. I always liked round models for visualization since they avoid linear models, which are rarely "real". Truly dynamic are spirals. Therefore, I originally used this spiral to visualize the learning process in life:

Since I considered this version of a "Learning spiral" as not yet dynamic enough, I drew a three-dimensional version in the nineties, first published in my German book: ***Von der Vision zur Wirklichkeit,*** *von Lernwegen zum Erfolg; von der Möglichkeit, SINN-voll zu leben"* (From Vision to Reality, on a learning path to success and the possibility to live with sense) *Cogito-Verlag, Kaarst-Büttgen, Germany, 1999, ISBN 3-00-4473-6.* The book dealt with various fields of personal learning from the beginning of my active life in business, politics and inner life.

My text to interpret the meaning of the spiral (on the next page) developed with time. It illustrates a vision, of how a fulfilled life could develop. I did not try to picture my own learning, but "only" the way I would like it to be.

Dominique Veyre, a French artist of calligraphy and illumination and teacher of my wife, Isa, did the following full page artwork (measuring 60 by 80 cm) to illustrate my learning path – as she saw it.

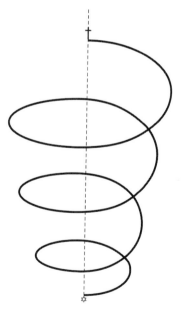

der Lebenskräfte

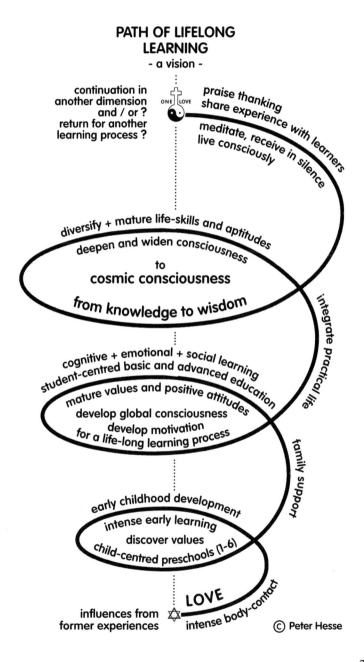

PATH OF LIFELONG LEARNING
- a vision -

continuation in another dimension and / or ? return for another learning process ?

ONE LOVE

praise thanking share experience with learners

meditate, receive in silence live consciously

diversify + mature life-skills and aptitudes

deepen and widen consciousness

to
cosmic consciousness

from knowledge to wisdom

integrate practical life

cognitive + emotional + social learning
student-centred basic and advanced education
mature values and positive attitudes
develop global consciousness
develop motivation
for a life-long learning process

family support

early childhood development
intense early learning
discover values
child-centred preschools (1-6)

LOVE

influences from former experiences

intense body-contact

© Peter Hesse

203

Chapter IV:
Reaching for global change
as the path widens

In the beginning of my engagement in Haiti, I frequently stumbled over my own basic question concerning my "interventions" in this country:
What gives me the right for any kind of intervention at all?

Shouldn't it be "none of my business", what the Haitians do or don't do in their own country?

This was a serious question after the first negative experiences while working in Haiti. My own inner development, however, allowed me to become more conscious. This resulted in a firm view on the question of the right (or even the moral obligation) to intervene – and also on a clarification of:

My motivational background

After my inward journey I now firmly believe that ALL is interconnected through the inner nucleus of all that exists through an all encompassing divine SPIRIT. This, of course, includes all human beings in ONE world in diversity. This asks for responsibility and solidarity. There are certainly additional rational reasons for healing and problem solving action in our world. World peace, physical as well as economical and social security and prosperity for all beings need active individual and global solidarity. But beyond all additional rational reasoning, we human beings have the freedom and face a challenge, mainly due to our interconnectedness and rooted in a cosmic consciousness, to co-create a balance in solidarity which

1) protects and preserves the grown and further developing base of all that exists, i.e. nature;

2) enables peaceful loving togetherness of people, capable to lead a life in dignity in social structures, which are defined by the "golden rule";

3) allows all people to benefit from the fruits of research and creative productivity – according to their engagement and efforts – in an open, fair and efficient way. This requires a global market economy which, however, must be effectively limited by the correcting factors 1) and 2), therefore a global "Œco-social market system".

ONE world in balance is a vision.
ONE world in diversity is a reality (at least in my consciousness).

"The whole, ALL, must grow through learning", is the first guiding message which anchored itself in my inner system. Desired and accepted spiritual guidance in combination with rational reflection gives birth to visions. From vision to action is a path to walk on. I see it as my path. Besides actively taking part in life with my own limited possibilities, for me this means trying to build bridges from visions to reality – and to connect people.
All adds sense to (also my) life.

This summarizes my inner motivation and basic view for action in our world. The intention in writing this forth chapter of the book was not to try to formulate one more development theory, but to concentrate on some basic guidelines of work born out of my own practical experience during the first years of activity in Haiti. This practical experience in problem-solving was originally influenced by my former life as a management trainer and manufacturer. As such, I was predominantly interested in people: those who came to my trainings, those who worked with me in business and, last not least, my customers – therefore my learning happened mostly on the micro-level. There, "solidarity in humility" seems to be the appropriate guiding expression.

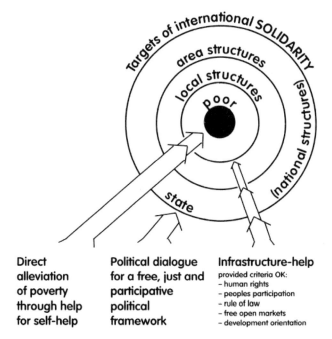

| Direct
alleviation
of poverty
through help
for self-help | Political dialogue
for a free, just and
participative
political
framework | Infrastructure-help
provided criteria OK:
– human rights
– peoples participation
– rule of law
– free open markets
– development orientation |

The same question, concerning justification for interventions from the outside, must also be asked on a global level. My view of all encompassing interconnectedness through ONE divine SPIRIT cannot be limited to individual human beings. The world community is interconnected as ONE in diversity. All are responsible to practice solidarity and intervene with compassion, when and where this is truly needed and possible. Between individuals, the golden rule ("do not do to others, what you do not want them to do to you") clearly sets limits to interventions. Globally, this is much more complicated. But the dilemma still needs to be addressed – and solved, if possible. Since the question, when and where interventions are permitted in a development process, is delicate, the whole issue must first be responsibly and deeply reflected in a holistic (or integral) way, before it can be formulated in a political vision.

In 1993, I had already felt the need to ask myself this question. In the brochure for the 10th anniversary of the Foundation, I wrote an article in German on the dilemma of development assistance versus intervention. As mentioned before, those years were for me heavily loaded with inner movement. This made it even more difficult to find the right answer in my own mind and soul. In practice, this question greatly depends on grown cultural value systems in the world, which cannot be overlooked. Firstly, however, I had to get a clear picture in my own mind.

To again summarize my basic learnings in the first ten years in Haiti, I realized that *nobody, nothing can* **be** *developed,* but that solidarity was and is still needed. Solidarity is, however, one form of intervention. It is easier to first look, which kind of interventions in solidarity are effective. To practice solidarity, I found two major development "instruments" to be effective on micro-levels and got involved in their use:

Micro-financing through micro-credits and micro-grants for immediate healing of problems and – for long-term healing – early and continuing learning for life.

The functioning of those "instruments" cannot be seen independently from a suitable framework – political, social, environmental, economical, cultural and technological. Those framework conditions were, of course, out of my reach, when I tried to find "my" solution to the problem of interventions in the world. Later, now, I do believe that as a thinking, feeling and learning being and as part of civil society, I even have a moral duty to also "get involved" in our world's framework conditions.

In the first roughly ten years of my involvement in development, my consciousness had not yet accepted such necessity. I also did not even believe in the vague possibility to get involved in global framework conditions in some effective way. But reflecting about it was still needed. Here is the essence of those reflections fifteen years ago:

The dilemma boiled down to the controversy between intervention and freedom. As a European (a "member of old Europe", as we liked to see each other in our circle of friends), I firmly believe in the unconditional priority of all human rights, as they are publicly acclaimed and respected in most parts of our (at least western/northern) cultures. Spiritually I see freedom as the greatest divine gift to humanity – next to LOVE. Legally and spiritually this individual freedom is clearly limited by the golden rule (at least in principle).

The sad fact that the golden rule is not at all respected by all humans and by humanity as a whole, is in my view the origin of evil. I see evil as the price of freedom. But not all erring, not all mistakes can be considered to be evil. Freedom clearly incorporates choice. Whether such choice is made in a "good" way, is not up to me or up to us to decide. Freedom without choice would not be freedom, and I feel that we have to defend the right to make mistakes – our own right to mistakes, but also the right of others, of individuals and of all groups, nations and states. This makes interventions so difficult.

As a human family we must (and always did) organize us in some way and give us a legal framework. Today, democracy is the key to find the best possible middle course for this legal structure. At least, I cannot think of a better alternative. Since without any doubt we are only ONE world in diversity, we need a legally binding global law and, therefore, also global democracy – including (finally) a world parliament.

Since installing a functioning democracy is also part of the freedom of groups of humans, we must accept or at least tolerate other organizational solutions – as long as the freedom of human beings in such "other" legal frameworks is not totally disregarded. Since only a relatively "fair" and transparent global democratic system can decide, when human freedom is disregarded in an intolerable way, we will not reach any definite solution for our problem until we have organized ourselves democratically in the global village.

In my German article of December 1993, I came to the following conclusion (to appease my own mind): *"Since freedom to develop individually includes diversity and erring, we must differentiate between seemingly erring ways, which happen in freedom and framework conditions where freedom to develop does not exist. Only to enable development in freedom, interventions should be permitted – and even asked for."*

I am sure that many other people have dealt with these problems and probably even published their findings. Unfortunately, I did not know where to look for such solutions, except in my own mind and soul. My article for the 10th anniversary of the Foundation ended with this attempt:
"It may be a utopia to want to co-create a world, in which every human being joins in with his contribution in free, conscious, self-chosen diversity, treating himself and his social and natural environment in a loving way, in respecting the differences of all others, contributing to the creation of ONE world in peace and liberty. This, however, must not remain a utopia, but must transform itself into a vision to go for. Every step in this direction is progress."

Now, 15 years after this had been written, the world has become even more complex. This is not only due to globally shifting human power structures visible behind our time horizon, but to the growing need to extend global consciousness to cosmic consciousness. Science is getting more knowledgeable about the structure of our universe. We, for example, are learning to better understand where we, humanity and our world, are positioned in the middle of an incredible cosmic size scale from the smallest to the largest. We know that we certainly are not eternally existing as a livable planet. On the other hand, the potentially "usable" time on earth is marvelously huge (in terms of human life) – if we do not destroy the basis of our existence, nature. This implies great challenges for development, but equally great responsibility for future generations. Cosmic consciousness allows us to realize those dimensions.

Asking for *cosmic* consciousness may be asking too much in a time, where the majority of people are still struggling with their daily survival problems and cannot even permit themselves to think globally, to open up to a global consciousness. Other people have found their inner peace by living their lives in a more or less happy way without bothering what might follow after they have died.

For those, who care about what will happen on earth after they are gone, at least a global consciousness, with subsequent global responsibility and solidarity is an imperative mental requirement. Besides caring for themselves and their immediate surroundings, our most urgent common problems in the world (like affordable food and drinking water for everybody) can only be "heal-solved" on a world-wide scale. That requires at least a global, if not cosmic consciousness as a precondition for successful global healing action. In that light, our momentary differences in daily national and regional politics look ridiculous.

Such reflections will unfortunately not change much in practice. They may, however, encourage the birth of visions for the needed feasible changes on all levels.

In practice, Haiti continued (and continues) to need much of our efforts as well as our funds. But Haiti also continued to be the essential learning field for needed change, including in politics – here in German development politics. Now the scope of consciousness had widened and the motivation to tackle the "new dimensions" had further grown, opportunities for change on a scale reaching beyond Haiti became visible.

Another vision, which worked – at least partly:
A new priority in German development politics

When money is concerned, change seems to need considerable effort. This was certainly true in the case of the micro-grant model, which was described earlier in this book. It is fascinating to listen to Professor Yunus telling his story of the beginning of his fight to introduce his most successful micro-credit model in Bangladesh. New ideas and visions seem to hurt old habits and beliefs even more, when money is involved. Bank officials and administrative bureaucrats do not differ too much when it comes to accepting change, which touches their own established systems. It is comparatively easier to get political consensus for change, which makes sense, when there is no *direct* financial consequence following a political decision. At least in my own experience it is relatively *easier to make a vision work in politics than in administrations.*

I would like to encourage the readers of this book to engage themselves in political subjects, whenever they discover weak points in the existing political situation in their country.

212

Therefore, here is an example as to how relatively easy and simple it can be to make a vision work in politics:

Again it was simply due to observation of the reality in Haiti that I realized that something was wrong in the political decisions of my own country, Germany. In this case, educational policies were badly adjusted to the basic needs in the world.

Germany is rightfully proud of a rather successful traditional educational concept, named *Duale Bildung* (dual education). This means that in order to become fit for life, a combination of practical and theoretical education is useful. The learner works as an apprentice in a real business during limited hours and goes to a vocational school for the theoretical part. In our German culture, this works very well.

At first sight it might look logical to export to the field of development, what has proven to work at home. Unfortunately, positive experience at home does not necessarily fit into other cultures, as I had to learn in making my own mistakes on my micro-level. Educational concepts also need preconditions in the system itself, which may differ in developing countries. When I asked myself, which kind of educational development Germany preferred to co-finance, it quickly became obvious:

Requests for installing *Duale Bildung*, as we handle this in Germany, were readily accepted by our development bureaucracy. Other forms of "higher" education have also frequently been asked to be supported by developing countries. In those cases, it is tempting to please the demanding countries by fulfilling their wishes for other political reasons beyond poverty reduction.

Financing vocational or other "higher" education is certainly also a necessity, but in allowing this to be a priority, basic education for the less fortunate population is being neglected. This is precisely what happened in Germany's development policy. The small portion of the budget of the German Ministry for Development, which was to support developing partners' education, was predominantly going into these "higher" sectors.

One argument often used in politics explains, why this is supposed to be the right way: Basic education, especially primary school, should be one of the most basic duties of any state. Therefore, it is not necessary to co-finance such development from the outside. The developing states will deal with this basic need themselves.

"In principle", this is a good argument. When, however, a state is not even capable of providing such basic service to its population, the most disadvantaged part of the population has even less chance to develop. The gap between rich and poor is widening further. A principle – even a good one – must also pass the practice test.

In Haiti, this was obvious:
Primary school, though on paper compulsory for everyone, was simply not available enough in quantity and even less in quality. In the countryside of Haiti, less than one percent of "teachers" do have a teaching diploma. Only the small middle class and the tiny "elite" can send their children to those few private schools, which are sometimes of better quality.

Becoming conscious about this prevailing situation created my "educational vision" for Germany's development politics:
Basic education, especially primary school, but also including pre-school from the age of 3 years, wherever possible, must become **Germany's new priority** for co-financing education.
There was nothing spectacular in this vision. It was born out of observing the reality and simply using one's responsible

"thinking-machine", the human mind, to find a healing-solution for the children's missing starting chance in life – not only in Haiti.

I was not the only person who observed the prevailing reality in the field. Kurt Gerhardt, a well-known German radio journalist, also shared my opinion that basic education is of the utmost importance. He had gained this insight in two years of practical work for the German Development Service in Africa. It was easy to meet him on that basis. We decided to act together. The vision became our vision. The goal following the initial vision was soon clear and became an objective: *a parliamentary vote for a new priority in Germany's development politics.*

We decided on a simple plan of action and a strategy to make our political vision work:
First, we decided to ask one personality, who was already working for basic education in the German institutional framework, Dr. Udo Bude, to join our core group.
Second, some additional academic weight was to be added to the group. Our vision had now become our "vision in progress".
Third and major step: We had to find out, who was most important to get our ruling parties to introduce a bill to parliament, win their support and get a positive parliamentary vote.
And, last not least, we must win the Development Ministry's acceptance, so that they did not feel left out in this process.

The very first step was immediately settled through a simple telephone call. Dr. Bude immediately accepted to become part of the team. After all, he could only benefit for his work. To gain added academic support, our second step, we researched who might be asked from the academic educational field to give our vision some additional backing. This resulted in a list of 20 people,

17 educational scientists and our core group of three. We invited this group to one single meeting, which worked out well. These specialists did not need to be convinced. We only needed to find a time slot for one meeting. After a short discussion, we formulated an appeal to the German Parliament. Up to this point, all went smoothly and fast as anticipated. The next step asked for only a little more effort.

In many countries, development policies are not a purely administrative question, but are to be decided by parliament – if there is one. Luckily, Germany has a functioning parliament with working groups for most relevant questions, which are to be decided by parliament. There are, of course, also public parliamentary debates, which look good on television (and sometimes good for those who take the floor), but the real work is done in an *"Ausschuss"*, in a parliamentary committee.

My political learning process had shown me that it is most important, who is heading the *"Ausschuss"*, which is responsible for a given question. The leader decides the working agenda. He or she can decide, what shall be debated by those parliamentarians belonging to the relevant *"Ausschuss"*. Once the subject of a vision is on the agenda, the problem is well on its way to being solved – provided, of course, the subject, the vision, makes sense.

There was no question in the case of our vision of a new German political development priority that basic education was most important for poverty reduction. Since poverty reduction is officially an overarching top priority for all development efforts that link was made in a credible way. The backing of our "group of 20" would simply add additional credibility to the case.

The first part of our third step: finding out, who leads the responsible *"Ausschuss für wirtschaftliche Zusammenarbeit (AWZ)"* (parliamentarian working group for economic cooperation), was easy – even before internet transparency. It just needed asking. In our German parliamentary system, it is good practice that the important parliamentarian working unit is not only headed by the leading political party, but that there usually is a vice-head – or even a parallel leader – from the second most important party. To obtain their names is easy. To win their hearts may sometimes be the more difficult part – but it was not so in our case. The *"Ausschuss"* leader from the Christian Democratic Party (CDU), my own party, already shared many of my basic micro-level views with me. The leading member from the Social Democratic Party (SPD) would be more skeptical, if directly approached by someone, who was involved "on the other side" like me. Therefore, Kurt Gerhardt was asked to win him over to also agree to a hearing in the responsible parliamentarian committee.

Luckily, in Germany there are only few differences between our major parties in development questions. Human development unites people, who normally are supposed to fight each other to be elected. However, when it comes to political decisions, there are still games being played to win over one's party opponent. Our vision was, however, so well grounded in reality and so well supported by the appeal of our "group of 20" that we quickly reached our intermediate goal: to get a hearing. Since Kurt Gerhardt was a well-known professional radio journalist, we quickly agreed that he should present our vision in the committee hearing.

All went amazingly well: One of the two parties in the *"Ausschuss"* reacted first and formulated a proposal for a bill, the other one (my own party, CDU) was a little less quick. In order to save their face, the CDU had to add some small amendments to agree to a committee proposal from the Social Democrats (SPD).

Only one year after the initial meeting with my journalist vision partner, on 30 October 1990, an almost unanimous vote in the Federal Parliament gave Germany a new direction for the educational development policy.

Priority for basic education.

Only the few new parliamentary members from Germany's unified East abstained in the voting. Global matters were not what those new members of a democratic parliament were used to deal with in former East Germany. The whole German public was too busy with the re-unification of Germany during this period to even notice such relatively small policy change. But we felt good – at least for the moment. Our primary objective was reached, the vision worked.

It may not always be that easy to get a voting by the legislating body or to convince the relevant power structure in different governmental structures, but it certainly is worth trying. Political power structures are usually much too busy to solve daily problems and to react to "hot" events rather than work on long-term healing and problem-solving. Civil society has many more possibilities to be actively engaged in visionary conceptual work than it is usually believed. This is no plead for sheer activism, but for motivated engagement in relevant matters which need political change. *Visions do work.* Just go for them!

In our above-mentioned case, we were successful on a political level, but not yet on the often more problematic administrative level. Here it was our strategic step number four, which proved to be less successful. It still made it worth-while to pursue the initial political path. The rest is a long-term ongoing struggle which, however, can finally be successful too, once the political preconditions are being settled.

In our case, we did continue as planned: Our core group of three plus one of the specially engaged scientific supporters together visited our Ministry for Development to appease their feeling of getting new orders which did not originate in their walls. Yet this did not work in a fully satisfying way. Though nobody dared to openly contradict the new formal development priority, until now reality has not yet been changed as much as we, the civil society "visionaries", had hoped. This struggle still goes on.

In the meantime, I wanted to "cement" our political achievement as much as possible and make sure that *Early Childhood Education* was to be included in "basic education".

In our political vision, basic education *("Grundbildung")* included the age group from 3 to 6, my own major concern. To ask for this in absolutely clear terms would, however, not have been wise, since in the late nineties the utmost importance of learning in the early years of life had not yet arrived in peoples' consciousness. It already was a main step to change the political educational priority from "higher" to basic education. To be sure that the early years were at least formally included in the new official priority, I asked German Development Ministers twice to publicly reconfirm in discussions after public events, that Early Childhood Education was still part of Germany's priority for "basic education". I always got confirming responses – in public. In reality, however, other development priorities frequently took over again. Politically, the "basic education vision" clearly worked. In reality, the struggle is a continuous one.

Only recently Germany has caught on in recognizing in mainstream politics that Early Childhood is a most important period for human development. As a founding member of the umbrella organization of Germany's roughly one hundred major NGOs in development, "VENRO" *("Verband Entwicklungspolitik deutscher Nichtregierungsorganisationen")*, I joined a working group on education *("Arbeitsgruppe Bildung")* in the ministry. Since that time I try to add my voice to reinforce the basic aspect of Germany's official development practice. This helps to keep the flame burning.

In the first years of this struggle, there were only very few colleagues even in the working group on education, who shared my view on the importance of early education. But since the shock of Germany not reaching one of the first places in the OECD Pisa studies (evaluation of European achievements in school), public opinion and mainstream politics started to change positively. Our country or to be precise, mainly one female Family Minister, is now asking for much more and better "Early Childhood Care and Development". In the Dakar "Education for All (EfA)" goals, this was clearly asked for as the first of six educational goals *("Expand Early Childhood Care and Education")*.

This may finally also have a positive effect on the Development Ministry's attitude to act more in accordance with the real needs for the less favorite majority population in our global village and at the same time follow, what our parliament has asked our administration to observe. Sometimes change simply needs more time, but without actively working for that change, it might just not happen at all.

The United Nations open up for civil society

In Haiti, the work was certainly still to be continued for some time in solidarity with the Haitians themselves, when I became interested in the work of the United Nations. In the beginning, I was sure that this one-world organization would be the key to solving our world's social problems – including those of the most needy countries, like Haiti. It took many more years to adapt this idealistic expectation to our reality. However, the United Nations could and should be more powerful and more effective in global social questions. How this vague vision might one day become reality, was still to be learned.

Information on a forthcoming specific UN conference on social matters sounded promising to me in the early nineties. Announcements and a call for participation in the "WORLD SUMMIT FOR SOCIAL DEVELOPMENT" in March 1995 in Copenhagen, Denmark, provided the needed optimism. It was to be the first UN conference which opened up a little to civil society movements. This happened mainly due to the open-minded leader of that Conference, Ambassador Juan Somavia (from Chile – later to become head of the ILO). Just in time before that conference, even smaller NGOs (like mine) were given a chance to at least meet in the vicinity of the official country delegations. It was not much of an opening, but better than nothing and I registered to participate.

Since I did not only want to come to Copenhagen to learn, but also to share my own learning in the field of development with like-minded people, I prepared a document containing three "SUGGESTIONs for ONE WORLD DEVELOPMENT".

The first suggestion was, of course, based on our Haiti experience, but also included a more general political project, a German "INITIATIVE PRE-SCHOOL EDUCATION for children in ONE world".

The second suggestion on "project management" was mainly based on my former life as a business person, a management trainer. It did concern the Haiti engagement during the very first years. Seminars on project management are described earlier in this book in connection with Miot's northern village Ste. Suzanne .

The third suggestion ("Facilitators in partnership") was dealing with a "vision which worked". It was born from simple observation in the first years of my Haiti engagement. This vision was simply born out of a visible need in the reasonable administration of reality. The vision developed well before my own "inner awakening" and therefore has already been treated at the end of the second chapter of this book.

All three suggestions can been downloaded as pdf documents under www.solidarity.org/en/one.html.

In a cover letter *"To government and UN officials, NGOs and individuals who are engaged in ONE world development at (or around)* the WORLD SUMMIT FOR SOCIAL DEVELOPMENT" I wrote in October 1994 – filled with new spiritually enriched motivation and hope:

The Social Summit hopefully will produce consciousness, visions and goals to be pursued. It will hopefully further intensify the motivation for ONE world development among all those whose task is policy- and decision-making on all levels. But declarations of intention will have to be filled with concrete and detailed action by governments, the UN, NGOs and individuals. This works best if all conscious people who are involved in this process cooperate through

222

information, constructive criticism and open-minded partnership to pursue the best ways to action.
The three papers in this folder, the result of the practical work of a small German NGO, are supposed to be an input for such exchange. Please make use of these suggestions wherever they may help.
We gladly await your response for further conceptual and detailed improvement – for ONE world.
Yours sincerely – Peter Hesse

Here is the title page of the first suggestion, using as a title the key message, described in Chapter III, "Journey inward and the search of truth":

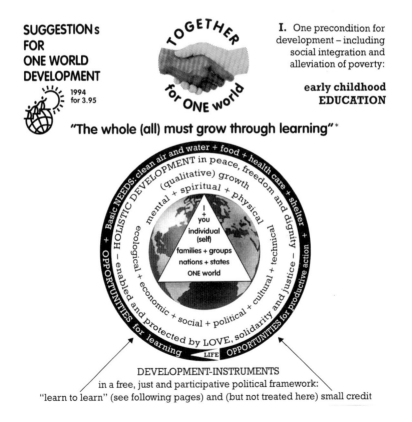

SUGGESTIONs
FOR
ONE WORLD
DEVELOPMENT
1994
for 3.95

I. One precondition for development – including social integration and alleviation of poverty:

early childhood
EDUCATION

"The whole (all) must grow through learning"*

DEVELOPMENT-INSTRUMENTS
in a free, just and participative political framework:
"learn to learn" (see following pages) and (but not treated here) small credit

223

Many hundreds of these fold-ers, held together by a nice little heart-shaped clip, where distributed, most of them from hand to hand. The response was most disappointing. I can count the positive responses on the fingers of my two hands. But I learned something from this idealistic attempt:

Most people are understandably most interested in their own sub-jects. Writing papers and even making concrete suggestions, which are based on concrete experience, are only reaching the consciousness of other – often equally engaged – people, if they truly manage to pass through the other person's heart. A plastic red heart is not enough to enter a living heart. But I tried it any-way. Without being "touched", our system seems to filter out even very useful information. Tons of paper are being printed and distributed with best intentions – and with very little effect. I can only hope that the readers of this book let themselves be "touched" by some living reality.

Only then, dear reader, I can really hope to reach your hearts and your motivation to actively participate in healing the evils of our world.

This may sound a bit pessimistic, but it is what I experienced in reality – and not only in my own reality. Otherwise, many more thinking and feeling human beings would join in civil society healing work. But I have not yet given up hope and this book is another attempt to encourage readers to let themselves be touched by the world's realities and join in the global action.

The World Bank story

In 1997, on the new ONE-world path, I had accepted an invitation to an international conference in Florence, Italy. There I met Dr. Mary Young. She is a pediatrician, deeply devoted to globally promoting Early Childhood Development in the World Bank. Our Haiti project found her interest. She commissioned a first evaluation of our project through the Word Bank and than invited me to join a World Bank conference on "Investing in our children's future" in April 2000. As one of four case studies, I was invited to report on our Haiti project. The other cases were from much bigger groups: the Aga Khan Foundation, the Bernard van Leer Foundation and "Step by Step" (funded by George Soros). It was a strange feeling to be compared to such wealthy groups, but I learned a lot in this fascinating conference. Mainly thanks to Dr. Mary Young, it was the first time that the World Bank had seriously treated Early Childhood Development.

Two years later, the World Bank did a second evaluation. A specialist from Dr. Mary Young's department, Simone Kirpal, came to Haiti and evaluated several early childhood projects. Both evaluations of our project are quoted in our homepage: www.solidarity.org/en/eval.pdf.

The second one was publicized by the World Bank in a large report in 2002 *"From Early Child Development to Human Development – Investing in Our Children's Future"*, The World Bank, 2002, pages 309 to 316*. The evaluation was very positive for our project. A reproduction of those seven pages is contained in the annex of this book. But more important: That same World Bank conference in the year 2000 produced valuable facts and impulses to "give children a chance". These facts and impulses should at least become "mainstream" knowledge in the World Bank itself.   *(Here in this book on pages 361-369)

I only hope that at least those engaged individuals, who work for "our children's future" in the world, do take the time to take notice of the diverse experiences and scientific findings in favor of consciousness Early Childhood Development. There is so much knowledge existing in our world on the value and importance of the early years that it would be a shame for humanity, if this knowledge is not sufficiently transferred into political mainstream activity.

All deceptions on the path of learning to "do it right" must be set aside in our efforts to reach the hearts of many people. The World EXPO2000 in Hanover, Germany provided such an opportunity:

World EXPO2000 HANOVER

Preparations for the World "EXPO2000 HANOVER" in Germany started in a chaotic way – at least as seen from an engaged civil society viewpoint. As part of the German Non-Governmental-Organization (NGO) community, I was invited for basic consultations. This, of course, was better than being confronted with a finished concept. The openness of the preparation process was, however, rather limited. This resulted in protests and controversies by the engaged NGO community. After realizing the potential possibilities of an active participation in the world exposition, I decided not to be held back by fighting for ideal NGO principles of cooperation.

My vision was to use the EXPO2000 to promote the possibility of high quality Early Childhood Development (ECD) even for deprived people in whatever way. Our Haiti project was to demonstrate that possibility. I, therefore, adjusted (opened up) my general vision of an active participation to the given framework – and first of all researched that framework more deeply. On that base, I simply contacted those who were in charge of designing the overall structure of the EXPO presentations. This direct approach proved to be working well.

My vision was further developed and transformed to a goal, to demonstrate the proven possibility of establishing high quality Montessori pre-schools in poor situations, like in Haiti, with the help of local Montessori teacher-training. – I wanted the "Haiti Model" to be shown in the given EXPO2000 framework.

From there on, preparations were still a little frustrating in some details, but while larger NGOs continued to argue about principle questions, I was able to start planning in a concrete way. It was a typical case of project management. I only had to remember what I had been teaching in my earlier management seminars – and act accordingly. The result of this preliminary process was promising:

The first successful step was that our Montessori pre-school program in Haiti was accepted officially by the central organization of the EXPO2000 to be a *"Registered Project of the World Exposition Germany EXPO2000 HANOVER"*.

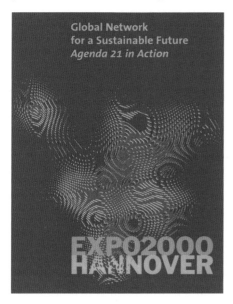

Global Network
for a Sustainable Future
Agenda 21 in Action

EXPO2000
HANNOVER

The title of the project was *Early Childhood Education* in the category *"Projects all over the world (international)"*. – So far, so good. That was exactly what I had wanted. It was the necessary first and very important step, but the real work had to start from here.

Since I had been going ahead on my own to find acceptance in the EXPO2000 concept, the group presentation of Germany's "One-world NGOs" was losing importance for me. Too many voices and too many diverse interests were hampering a noticeable group presentation. The prolonged discussions about principles of the role, NGO presentations were to have in the EXPO2000, did not make it easier to come to conclusions. Having chosen my own way to proceed and having been basically accepted, did, however, not yet mean that our Haiti project was being physically presented in the EXPO2000 itself. There was to be one international house for all world-wide NGO projects. A small organization like mine would have been lost in the multitude of small presentations. Therefore, I looked for a more promising alternative in the projected concept of the exhibition.

My "working argument" towards the EXPO organizers was that Early Childhood Education or to be more precise, pre-school from age three to six, is a "basic right". It, therefore, should somehow belong to the projected EXPO section on "basic needs". In the preliminary research it had become clear that there most likely would be a separate big hall dedicated to all "basic needs". It was to become hall number 6, a huge place indeed.

The first step in this second venture to find a suitable framework to present our Haiti project was not yet to get a physical space in the "basic needs" hall. It was to be included in a preliminary presentation, a large book on the *"Global Network for a Sustainable Future"*, published by the EXPO2000 already in October of 1998. In this preliminary book presentation, there was room for only four "basic needs" projects. Each project was to be presented on two double-size DIN A4 pages in German and English with color photographs. We were lucky to be included under the heading *"Early Childhood Education – Away from the Streets"*. Having been accepted in this publication was an indirect

228

assurance to also be visibly presented in the "basic needs" hall no. 6. – Now the detailed negotiations and the planning procedure could start.

Co-financing of NGO contributions in the EXPO2000 was normally handled by the staff of the *"Gesellschaft für Technische Zusammenarbeit – GTZ"*, Germany's main semi-private project-executing agency in One-world development matters, who was also involved in the selection of worthwhile projects. Since I had chosen a more direct approach for our EXPO participation, I only had to inform the GTZ office to avoid bad feelings among those in charge there. I could not expect any major contributions from their budget, since we had not been chosen by them. Since the GTZ funds, however, all derived from the responsible Ministry for Economic Cooperation *(Ministerium für Wirtschaftliche Zusammenarbeit – BMZ)*, I approached the ministry directly and was lucky to be granted a nice standardized amount independent from the GTZ budget. This was given to a few "cases" like mine, when a project was accepted by the Ministry itself. Of course, we never saw that money (which was no problem). It was fully used by the EXPO organizers of the "basic needs" section to finance what we finally agreed about:

Carol, my Montessori partner in Haiti, agreed to design a display in making use of a nice Haitian tradition: painted cut metal structures. After clearing the concept with the Indian chief designer of hall 6, we conceived a big, cave-like structure. Visitors were supposed to enter in this room-size structure and see the difference of a traditional teacher-centered "Kindergarten" and a child-centered Montessori pre-school. Carol sketched those two different didactical approaches on paper and her brother, Michel Guy-James, a young professional designer, transferred his sister's drawings on metal. Haitian craftsmen cut the metal sections and painted them in bright colors.

The making of the display in Haiti by Carol and Michael Guy-James

230

The whole structure was carefully packed in big cradles and shipped to Hanover. What sounds so simple here, needed a lot of detailed work – and, of course, Carol's and her brother's full engagement. I worked on the written explanations of the project, which were posted at the entry of the structure and used in the exhibition's documents. The explanations had to be short, fitting to those of the other exhibits – yet clear and convincing. Arriving at some accepted conclusions needed some fierce, but friendly battle of words with the EXPO team.

Foto: Werner Maschmann, Kassel, Germany

Another, slightly less friendly battle was fought with the chief designer of hall 6, when it came to details like painting the floor in using our two-dimensional first "learning spiral".

I had privately commissioned a Haitian artist living in Germany, "Zaneda", to paint the floor in using our original spiral. As an artists' color manufacturer, it was of course not difficult to provide an acrylic quality paint, on which visitors could walk without having to fear to destroy the painting. This became a nice practice test of durable art work, which could be walked on!

Preparing the presentation of our educational Haiti model was altogether a challenging task for our small Foundation team. It was well received by visitors – even though the whole EXPO2000 was overwhelmingly huge and complex. The EXPO2000 was practically impossible to see in only one day. It was very complex due to the multitude and variety of impressions, which visitors had to digest. Even the very motivated young EXPO guides, often students who took the half year off for this challenging job, were lost when being asked specific questions.

When I realized this problem during my own initial guided tours for "very important persons" in the "basic needs" hall, I offered some additional training for EXPO guides. This was welcomed by the EXPO training team, since the guides had only been given a general instruction on the multitude of exhibits in the EXPO. Many guides gladly excepted my private information sessions. That proved to be useful – and fun. After all, the purpose of the whole work was to raise consciousness for the need – and the possibility – of good Early Childhood Education as a "basic need". Many young EXPO guides were very engaged to participate in this consciousness-widening process.

All in all, the EXPO2000 HANNOVER was a strenuous, but worth-while advertisement for the possibility of Early Childhood Development through Montessori pre-schools even in difficult situations. It could have been even better, if an additional idea would have been realized as conceived, planned – and basically agreed by the responsible organizers:

When reflecting about what could best convince visitors about the importance and the beauty of Early Childhood Education, I just had to remember my own moments of joy, when I saw children in Haiti working with the Montessori material with bright eyes. Observing Montessori pre-school children at work with the special didactical material is simply touching. That had to become a "sub-vision" of the whole EXPO project. Therefore: Why not show real playfully and seriously learning children to the visitors of the EXPO?!

It was to be expected that many of the young mothers working in the huge world exhibition in various functions from June to November 2000 would have children in the right pre-school age of three to six. Why not offer them to professionally take care of their children at least during part of the working day in the EXPO itself? It was easy to conceive a suitable framework to allow children to work like in a regular Montessori pre-school without being in any way disturbed by visitors, but still clearly be seen and observed. Mirror glass walls, for example, which can be looked through only from one side, are widely known from many crime movies.

My EXPO partners were immediately enthusiastic. We planned all the needed details like space, location and informing the mothers who were going to work in the EXPO staff of the possibility to integrate their pre-school age children in that special

Montessori pre-school during their working time in the EXPO. Carol was willing to come and bring two or three of our Montessori teachers from Haiti to stay in Hanover for the whole duration of the EXPO. We even discussed the legal visa requirements and special work permits. The top EXPO organizers basically followed our suggestions and all was set to go and become a beautiful reality.

Finally there remained only one bureaucratic battle, which still had to be won: Legally the children were considered to be "working" in the EXPO2000 – and, of course, children at that tender age are not supposed to work! In Hanover, it was the *"Ordnungsamt"* (municipal department for public order!), which created that problem. We were, however, hopefully believing that this last problem could also be solved when – at the very end – the financial EXPO budget was overstressed. That finally "killed" the idea.

And what happened to the nice and partly self-explaining Haitian metal art display, which Carol and her brother had designed and which had been a convincing part of the "basic needs" hall?
The German state of North Rhine-Westphalia (NRW) bought most of the displays in the "basic needs" hall for very little money after the termination of the EXPO. We were hopeful that our Haiti display would be reconstructed in some other place as we were told. But for many years nothing happened – until now, only one year ago, when I received an invitation: Essential parts of our colorful metallic Montessori demonstration from Haiti are now being shown in a very decorative way in a children's museum in the German Rhineland. – A nice ending for that story.

In the new Millennium global challenges beyond our important, but narrow field of early education became gradually stronger and consumed growing parts of the available energy. Haiti, however, continued calling. The organic growth of our basically successful educational project had to be further supported. Haiti even continued creating the needed impulse to extend our work beyond Haiti itself. My first, somewhat sad deceptions in being admitted to participate in the United Nations' Social Summit as an NGO without being able to tintroduce in a more effective way, what I considered to be valuable experience into the UN system, made me look closer at the United Nations. It soon became obvious that the existing UN structure needed to be revitalized. This later gave birth to a new vision, although I should have been warned by a former experience in trying to change some traditional rigid structure:

The failing vision to reform university

My deception with the possibilities to influence change through civil society engagement in the framework of a UN conference like the United Nations' World Summit for Social Development in Copenhagen in March 1995 created the desire for some change in that UN system. That desire was unspecific in the beginning, but it brought back memories of former efforts in comparable fields, of producing change in existing rigid institutions. From the beginning of my active life, I refused to simply accept, if a system was in bad shape. While people in the late sixties took to the streets to loudly protest and "fight the system", some other people, like myself, tried a more peaceful and conceptional approach to produce change. In the sixties it was the educational system in Europe, which – in our view – needed to change.

Together with a Belgian friend, Willy Verbruggen, we had an idealistic vision to reform academic economic studies in Europe to teach more practical subjects like basic management. As described in the very first pages of this book, I had been part of a group of former students of *"Betriebswirtschaftslehre – BWL"* (business economics) in Germany, who were frustrated about the predominantly theoretical subjects in our studies. Instead of joining protests in the streets, we wanted to try a more gentle approach for change. In 1969, Geneva looked like the best place in Europe to start such a venture. We managed to obtain permission to use the building of the former League of Nations to assemble an engaged international group of people for a first discussion. This first meeting paved the way to a valuable conceptional achievement, but it did not really make our vision work as we idealistically thought.

In the same year, also in Geneva, another German, Professor Schwab, had conceived a vision, which later became the big World Economic Forum (WEF). There were early contacts with this organizer of the WEF in 1969, which I remember well (but Professor Schwab did not, when I talked to him about this much later). He had once contacted me in the very beginning, but I did not believe in his vision (what later proved to be my mistake). Being preoccupied with our own educational vision, we did not pay attention to this other visionary, whose persistence led to a remarkable success.

Our educational vision only partly worked in producing a realistic concept. But even a good concept does not change anything, if it implies change in rigid structures like the European academic systems. Our initiative started as the *"**Committee for Management Education in Europe**",* but reduced itself gradually to a German initiative and in 1973 became the nucleus of the *"Deutsche Management Gesellschaft"* (German Management Society). Until 1975, we had organized 17 mostly two-day meetings with (in total) 163 participants in different cities in Germany. Only the very first meeting in 1969 had been in Geneva. Everybody paid his/her own expenses. My secretary informed the other group members on the outcome of each meeting. The early vision became more realistic and quite feasible in being slowly "boiled down" to the German situation. We now "only" wanted to have practical management training included in the educational system in Germany. It turned out to be a real nice, useful vision – on paper.

Our instrument for the realization of that vision was a *"Management Bildungskonzept"* (management training concept) in four steps: Basic step for secondary school, second step for University level, third step for post-graduate levels and forth step for life-long continued education. As an intellectual and at the same time practical concept, it is still valid today.

After the 17th group meeting in September 1975, we printed a small brochure with the details of our four-step management training concept in German (which is still available in limited quantities on request from the Peter-Hesse-Foundation). The essentials of this concept can be found under "publications" in the German section of our homepage: www.solidarity.org. We formed different "lobby groups" with a concentration of members from one of the major German political parties in each group. The goal was to "intrude" into the existing academic structures with this concept through the existing party structures. It was not envisaged to fully replace the traditional theoretical studies, but to simply add a more practical component to the study program for future economists and also for other academic fields, where some management skills would be needed later. But sadly enough – we even failed with that moderate practical vision!

We had planned in a very concrete way that our lobby groups would try to get into the academic system of the German *"Bundesländer"* (federal states), where our respective political party was in government at that time. (In Germany, education is under the jurisdiction of the federal states.) The "entry strategy" basically worked well, but not our full vision. Together with one colleague from our group, I managed to get invited into the conceptional group for secondary school of the Education Ministry in our federal state North-Rhine-Westphalia. After a few very tiring and formally structured meetings, we gave up. Our vision was confronted with the traditional theoretical academic system, which resisted change and which is still partly alive in Germany today.

Later some new private management schools were created in Germany and our nice management training concept is being partly used by those former group members, who professionally remained in the educational field. I consider this initial venture to be my most fascinating flop and a good example of a good vision, which did not work – even though it was and still is a good concept. Fact: The (academic) wall we wanted to pierce gently for a more useful bit of learning was simply too firmly built – somehow comparable to the United Nations.

One aspect of that failing vision was positive: During that time, I was learning a lot about modern management and in this framework developed my management circle models. This added professional quality to the start of my initial career as a management, marketing and creativity trainer.

Much later, after opening my eyes to the world and after becoming more and more critical in view of sad realities in global structures, I was informed about the very first World Social Forum

(WSF) in Porto Alegre, Brazil, in 2001. Remembering with some regret not to have believed in the challenges of the earliest stages of the (later) World Economic Forum (WEF) in 1969, I still hesitated again 32 years later to immediately join the first WSF in Brazil.

As a relatively conservative German businessman, the WEF could have been an appropriate framework for action and appealing to me in the framework of my new global interests. The WEF had, however, become too expensive for the co-owner of a medium-size family business and in the beginning was anyway limited to very big companies (as I had been told). Therefore, I dropped the WEF idea.

In the very beginning, the World Social Forum in Porto Alegre seemed too "radical" to me – although I was fascinated about that new visionary movement, which wanted to counteract the more conventional WEF with the needed social content. In the beginning there was a lot of red-flag waving and wild protest against all traditions. It was like in the late sixties, when young people protested in the streets of western capitals (not only in San Francisco). Again, like in 1969, I wanted our protest to be more constructive. It was obvious to me that constructive renewal was needed and that the economic mainstream politics were in the grips of a market fundamentalist dogma. So I finally decided to join the second WSF in Porto Alegre in 2002 at least as an observer.

In the German delegation of about 300 people I was the only active member of the CDU party. As far as I could see, I was also the only German businessman. There was, however, a small, but qualified minority among the over 100.000 participants from a constructive global business community in that second WSF in

Porto Alegre. I, therefore, decided to come back next year with my own "constructive program". This became the birth of my first vision of a renewed United Nations. The lesson learned 30 years earlier in the case of our academic European reform vision, namely that changing rigid structures is most difficult, was brushed aside with new global motivation.

The World Social Forum
is more than „only" protest.
It is living proof of
ONE world in DIVERSITY.

Motivated groups and individuals **can** help to further constructive global **change.**

This is why we want to share what works –
to make our ONE world more peaceful and just. We, the German Peter-Hesse-Foundation „SOLIDARITY IN PARTNERSHIP for ONE world in diversity" herewith cordially invite you to those **3 workshops – in English:**

1. One most important challenge is the future of our children. Therefore: How to **Give deprived children a chance through quality ECD** (Early Childhood Development) **with limited funds.** 20 years of experience in Haiti – presented by Peter Hesse – (with requested participation of UNICEF).
Time and place:

2. Successful political interventions in the case of German development politics: **From Vision to Reality ! How to succeed in democracies.** Peter Hesse presents reasons for his own failures and successes as an NGO. Time and place:

3. Organized by **CONGO** (CONFERENCE OF NGOs IN CONSULTATIVE RELATIONSHIP WITH THE UNITED NATIONS), www.ngocongo.org facilitated by CONGO in cooperation with Peter Hesse:
United Nations Reform – transparent + democratic + participatory. NGO-expectations /-visions /-hopes towards a renewed United Nations. Introduced and moderated by Renate Bloem, CONGO-President, presented by Peter Hesse and other CONGO-members from around the world.
(Please see Peter Hesses personal vision/hope for a UN-reform on the back of this leaflet.)
Time and place:

The vision of a renewed United Nations

During the second WSF in 2002, I felt that a growing number of constructive, active people from around the world could be reached. Therefore, I started formulating my vision of a **"United Nations' Reform** – transparent + democratic + participatory" as one of three subjects for the WSF in 2003, again in Porto Alegre. During the year 2002, I discussed my vision with other interested visionaries. One of them was specially helpful: the director of UNOPS, the UN Management Organization, "Assistant Secretary General of the United Nations", Dr. Reinhart Helmke. He agreed with me on the need of a UN reform and gave me some valuable hints for the condensed one-page version of my reform vision, fully reproduced here as follows – unchanged as written in 2002 for the WSF 2003:

We need a strong, renewed United Nations!

*This is a **vision** which could and should be transformed into realistic political goals and objectives.*

To all members of civil society, who are somehow engaged for ONE world in diversity.

*United Nations were and are a vision. World war II had provided the global shock and motivation to initiate our UNO as an instrument for peace. By now in 2002, it became visible what worked and what did not. The new global shock created by September 11, 2001 could have provided renewed impetus for a needed UN-reform. This impetus is almost lost again and starts dissolving in frustration about the predominant escalating "war on terrorism" – instead of also healing the underlying causes of the unjust and predominantly materialistic development-reality in our world. **The UN could and should be a*** *main actor in healing our world chronic illnesses like poverty, the majority-people's missing chances to satisfy their basic needs, like the lack of good learning possibilities. But **the UN suffers from its own bureaucratic power-structures.***

*"**A better world is possible**" is more than a Porto Alegre activist's slogan. It is a true statement and could be effectively carried forward by a renewed United Nations, whose leaders and staff-members would then, hopefully, be measured by their managerial success instead of by well-sounding strategy-papers.*

***We need a UN which practices "good global governance" in participation with civil society** (NGOs/PVOs, science, business and the world religions).*

*Overlapping UN-sub-organizations and territorial egocentrism are consuming too much energy. A lack of transparency adds to the dilemma. We do **not** need a top-down central world **government**, but **a truly democratic, transparent and unbureaucratic strong, firm, but gentle, coordinating agency, facilitating dialogue**, based on **all** human rights and on shared values. We need a UN capable of helping to solve global problems – but also respecting regional and local structures – down to communities and families – for **ONE world in diversity**.*

*Such a reformed/renewed United Nations must be based on **values** and **principles**:*

A renewed United Nations respects, follows and protects global **values**:

– *The **golden rule**: Do not do to others, what you do not want them to do to you.*

– *Growth in holistic **quality** – instead of mere quantitative material growth.*

242

– *Favoring what furthers* **community** – *but respecting individuality in its diversity.*

– *As a central value: Undogmatic true* **spirituality**, *enabling Love and compassion.*

A renewed United Nations must also follow/include such **principles**:

– **Subsidiarity**: *Regulating and doing only what can not be better regulated and done in smaller structures (regional – like European Union – national, local or individual)*

– **Democracy** *through direct election of global delegates (min. 1 per country; in larger countries 1 per 10 Mio inhabitants) – a 2ⁿᵈ "chamber" next to the existing structure.*

– *Active* **participation** *of all sectors of civil society – respecting the elected structures.*

– *Enforceable* **global law** – *including international court of justice – protecting* **all** *human rights and nature + securing fair starting chances for the weak.*

– **Transparency** *in all UN-procedures, goals, -objectives, -plans and -structures.*

– **Peacekeeping** *and (if needed) Peacemaking through a* **strong** *global police-force.*

– *Reformed Security-Council and strengthened ECOSOC, truly* **capable to decide**.

– *Own* **financial sources** *(like tax on speculative global money transfers).*

– **Integrated** *democratic global finance- + trade-institutions (IMF, World Bank, WTO).*

– **Separate policy advisory and operational functions** in efficient UN sub-structures.

The guiding principle for all of us should be: MITEINANDER / TOGETHER / ENSEMBLE.

*Only the last but one line in the envisioned "principles" for a renewed UN was soon changed in the ongoing learning process: The line "**Integrated** democratic global finance and trade institutions..." was changed to a more realistic (but unfortunately still rather utopian) version: "Global finance and trade institutions, which **serve** humanity...".*

In a longer version, not fitting on one single page, I added an additional sentence in the desired principle on democracy and a second UN parliament chamber: *Such a second chamber must also include representatives of the world's indigenous people, who live partly separated by political borders in diverse unnatural situations. Those representatives should be chosen by the indigenous peoples themselves.*

After arguing for my (further improved) vision in various publications, speeches and activities, like in the following World Social Fora (WSF) in 2004, 2005 and 2006, I finally realized in 2006 that I was again defending utopia. Therefore, in the WSF in 2007, I did not present my UN vision anymore. It had to be reconsidered in a more realistic political way, but was not given up. In the meantime, I concentrated on the Early Childhood subject and on our new vision of a world in balance through an Œcosocial market system. So in my Nairobi seminar, I presented the Global Marshall Plan, calling it "Global Solidarity Plan".

Since my first skeptical participation in the WSF in Porto Alegre, this social movement has gradually, but steadily become more constructive. This may have helped to also provoke the World Economic Forum (WEF) to include some social and environmental touches in their program. In addition, a World Spirit Forum, just one week before the WEF in the neighboring valley in Switzerland, Arosa, has well developed. I twice participated also in this open-minded, undogmatic spiritual event. It helped to recharge the motivational batteries. For me, the World Spirit Forum became particularly rewarding, because there I met Susan Baller-Shepard. She contributed most valuable suggestions for this book and also helped me to refine some of my German/English terms.

The World Spirit Forum also raised important questions:
Why isolate the different global aspects of a fulfilled life, the economical, social and spiritual aspects? Is it not a shame that we cannot yet have one single global platform, uniting spiritual, environmental, social and economic aspects for a more balanced better world? All is interconnected anyway. We should develop a "United Vision" for our ONE world in diversity!

Back to the United Nations' problem:
Concerning an urgently needed global structure, which could "handle" effectively our integral world problems, which cannot be handled on "lower" levels, following the subsidiarity principle, just a humble vision will not be sufficient. Kofi Anan, the former Secretary General of the United Nations, had truly made an effort to adjust his huge organization to the needs of our time. He got entangled in the hardened postwar structures, which were created mainly to avoid a third world war. He also did hurt himself in potentially touching the interests of imperialistic thinking state structures and the comfortable life of those, who now benefit from the UN system as it is. Renewal from the inside of the UNO must still be tried to at least heal, what is possible. But real renewal will need basic rethinking from qualified outside sources.

After I realized the utopian character of my treasured vision of a renewed United Nations, I had to find a solution, which would at least contain the seeds of a possibility to become reality. That brought me back to looking at the original conceptional work, which was preceding our existing United Nations. That gave birth to a new further "improved vision":

Just as there was a devoted think tank officially charged by the USA, Great Britain, the Soviet Union and China in 1944 to develop the security structure of the United Nations in Dumbarton Oaks near Washington, D.C., USA, we today need a renewal of such a think tank in some neutral place in the world. This think tank should be composed of a mix of engaged people from various relevant sectors of life (like science, religions, business and social as well as environmental movements) from all areas of the world. Democratic political structures should not be excluded. But they should in no way dominate the initial conceptual work. Globally conscious politicians from a few respectable countries could initiate such a conference. As a starting point, the original concepts of what is today the relatively powerless "Economic and Social Council of the United Nations – ECOSOC" could be used for practical reasons to avoid to "rediscover the wheel". But to wait for renewal only or predominantly from inside the United Nations will most likely not make much sense.

We need a new integral vision of a peaceful, fair and just balanced world organization as a result of a new think tank. The conceptual result of a new think tank must then be widely made known and could be discussed in a fair and totally transparent open global consultation process.)This process could be comparable to the new consultation process, which derived from the Global Marshall Plan Initiative. Please see pages 266-274.)

246

Elder statesmen and recognized ethical personalities could form a filtering body to eliminate utopian extremes and power games. Existing world rulers from democratic countries could chaperon the process to make it stronger and more visible without interfering in the design of the content.

The final outcome of such a search for a global solution would probably not need a totally new organizational framework. If it is conceived independently from the existing power structures, it could be based on the existing representation of all the states in the United Nations and on an additional world parliament (a second chamber). If accepted by enough countries, such a renewed concept could slowly and gently be merged with those United Nations' outer structures, which do exist already.

If the suggested values and principles in the utopian ex-vision above would at least be considered by a visionary think tank, the attempt of the humble vision for a renewed United Nations may not have been totally in vain. It is mainly up to new generations to participate in building our new sustainable world. We older ones should, however, assist in the healing process, when being asked to do so. We could then rest with a better feeling that we have contributed "what we can".

Chapter V
Researching guidelines
for our world to heal

28 years of learning and doing in Haiti was useful, fulfilling and frustrating. The world now adds a new challenge. The "global vision" of more and better early education for all is not new. It is shared by many people and institutions. Helping to provide a starting chance in life for all children in our world remains the key purpose of our engagement with our limited possibilities. Education, however, is "only" one important factor in conscious global development. Qualitative growth to truly become ONE peaceful striving world in diversity involves all aspects of people living in community with each other and with nature.

Widening and deepening the scope of consciousness implies also rational clarity and understanding of the managerial tool box to solve our problems and to (re)search guidelines which can help to heal the miseries in our world.

Terms and definitions

Not to fall into the trap of dream walking, I feel that I need to clarify, to define my "working tools" – at least as much as this is possible. For me, definitions are such working tools. I feel that it would be helpful to use clear terms from the field of management when we make suggestions for "ONE world heal-solving".
Graphic models, by preference round ones, are additional instruments which I like for transparency and clarification. They help me to bring order into my subjects – and into some humble conclusions from the work in Haiti and in the world. My definitions and models are not pretending to be unique or scientifically elaborated, they are merely the results of my own reflections.

They may, however, serve other bridge-builders as starting points for their own views.

When working in the field of "development", the term itself must be clearly understood:

"Development" permanently happens in all structures from the micro-cosmos to macro-cosmos, in all aspects of existence. Consciousness, values, attitudes, skills and knowledge; body, mind and spiritual insight of human individuals; all groups, nations, states and ONE world develop permanently more or less fast and consciously. Or in other words: "Development" simply happens in all aspects of existence. In order to promote and to co-initiate a desired integral development, all aspects of human development are of special concern, from the individual to humanity as a whole. The respect for and the protection of the biological base of all being, i.e. nature, is – must be – a limiting factor for all material and technological development.

Visions, goals and objectives

"Visions", as used here, are mental images of potential future existences or happenings, which can be possible in principle. Such visions may develop in many ways, in various mixtures of emotional needs, rational analysis and inner guidance. Here, visions are used only in a positive, constructive sense. Horror visions are another aspect of our reality. They may also have a wake-up quality in our reality. I do not deny the reality of horror visions; they touch me, too. Since our existing reality is full of such negative visions and even their reality, I do not need (or want) to add more to them. I, therefore, will not even try to contribute to the multiple descriptions of our existing global horrors and human misery. Everybody, who cares for our planet and for life on earth, knows enough about the dark sides of our existence.

My constructive visions aim at consciously desired change. I consider them to be first steps in working for a peaceful, just and fair world.

Many visions can be transformed into reality through a spirited management process. Visions can truly work. They have a real driving and motivating force. Visions may be daring. They **should** even be daring and challenging to make the expected change worth the effort. Visions should not be mixed up with utopia. Utopian images may be creative and fun – and it does not hurt to imagine utopia. Utopia and fantasies may even stimulate creativity, but the difference is: A "real" vision carries at least the seed of possible reality. I feel that visions are even useful, if their realization does not succeed. If I would not truly believe this, I would be permanently frustrated due to my visions, which did not work, although they were potentially possible – and therefore no utopia.

Visions imply *change*. Change happens slowly and seemingly without conscious effort – but visionaries want more and faster change in the desired direction. Desired change rarely happens without effort. The path from vision to reality needs bridge-building and mostly a lot of effort. These efforts are, however, rewarding. The mere wish for a vision to become reality rarely works. Visions become reality through a conscious goal-setting and planning process, permanently accompanied by analyzing, deciding and communicating processes. Such a procedure is called management. This rational process becomes truly valuable if it incorporates spiritual values – ideally, if love is involved. Change in a loving direction is the spice of life. Visions should be inspired. They should be spirited to become inspiring.

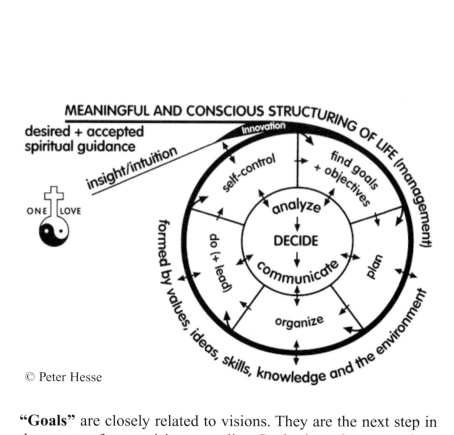

MEANINGFUL AND CONSCIOUS STRUCTURING OF LIFE (management)

desired + accepted
spiritual guidance

insight/intuition

ONE LOVE

innovation

self-control

find goals + objectives

analyze

DECIDE

communicate

do (+ lead)

plan

organize

formed by values, ideas, skills, knowledge and the environment

© Peter Hesse

"Goals" are closely related to visions. They are the next step in the process from a vision to reality. Goals show the way as how to proceed in pursuing a vision. They indicate the direction. Goals must be transformed into concrete objectives through analyzing all possibilities on the path to realization. Such analyzing process may be more or less formal and complicated. Often it is sufficient to simply use the divine gift of a logical mind to define objectives on the basis of given goals. Modern management has developed instruments like "force field analysis" to structure and clarify this analyzing process.

Here is an illustration, which I used in my own German management seminars to illustrate hindering *("be-hindernde")* and supporting *("fördernde")* forces, which influence the analyzing process in a management setting.

252

(be) hindernde
Kräfte

besondere Schwächen
besondere Stärken

fördernde
Kräfte

"Objectives" should always be combined with dates, when the objectives should be reached. Well-formulated objectives should also include some measurable quantitative data to control the results, whenever this is logically possible.

The real challenge in a management process from a vision through a goal to an objective – and onward through planning to realization – is often the "human factor" on the way. This is a predominantly irrational factor, which can hardly be anticipated rationally. It must be "felt" intuitively and gently integrated on the way from a vision to the desired reality. Good management needs more than rationality.

253

Due to the "human factor", but also due to changing "hard" facts in the analyzing process, visions are not necessarily remaining fixed. Visions may change. In that sense, too, they may "work" in a reality which demands flexibility. "Working" can also be understood as "changing" in the sense of a vision that changes. The meaning of "VISION WORKS" as used here is, however, not this flexible aspect of a vision. Our visions here in this book are considered to be more or less firm and strong motivating images of the desired change.

From a management perspective in the business world, the path from clearly defined objectives to reality passes through planning, organizing and leading for controlled realization. This second phase tends to be less problematic in reality than the first creative phase from a vision to objectives. To obtain precise objectives in business, one must pass through a detailed analyzing process and observe many legal and policy restrictions. This is the phase for the most important management decisions. Once precise and clear objectives are defined and accepted, the process still requires effort, but often will be less dramatic. In other words: The last phase of a management process from clearly defined objectives through planning and realization in transparent organizational structures and procedures (simply) involves more or less rational work and efforts (at least in well-managed businesses). The path from clear objectives to the desired results is the implementation part of management. This is mostly the easier part of the process.

In political life the opposite is often true.
In states or in other single political units it seems relatively easy to agree on goals – and sometimes even on objectives. Planning (in the sense this term is used in management) and putting plans into actions is, however, frequently more painful in the political

reality. In politics, the term "plan" is often misused. What in politics is called a plan or even an "action plan", in reality is more like a goal, a list of good intentions or, at the most, a list of objectives.

A political objective is like a promise. In political life, however, it seems to be difficult to keep promises. Only when goals and objectives are shared, co-signed by a number of states, objectives are more difficult to forget. Such enlarged transparency can create political pressure. But even internationally agreed objectives are no guarantee for realization. This can be seen when we look at what happened to the *"Millennium Development Goals (MDGs)"*, which were formally signed in 2000 by 189 states:

The **Millennium Development Goals (MDGs)**

By 2015, all signing United Nations Member States have pledged to:

1. **Eradicate extreme poverty and hunger**
   - Reduce by half the proportion of people living on less than a dollar a day
   - Reduce by half the proportion of people who suffer from hunger

2. **Achieve universal primary education**
   - Ensure that all boys and girls complete a full course of primary schooling

3. **Promote gender equality and empower women**
   - Eliminate gender disparity in primary and secondary education preferably by 2005, and at all levels by 2015

4. **Reduce child mortality**
   - Reduce by two thirds the mortality rate among children under five

5. Improve maternal health
- Reduce by three quarters the maternal mortality ratio

6. Combat HIV/AIDS, malaria and other diseases
- Halt and begin to reverse the spread of HIV/AIDS
- Halt and begin to reverse the incidence of malaria and other major diseases

7. Ensure environmental sustainability
- Integrate the principles of sustainable development into country policies and programs; reverse loss of environmental resources
- Reduce by half the proportion of people without sustainable access to safe drinking water

8. Develop a global partnership for development
- Develop further an open trading and financial system that is rule-based, predictable and non-discriminatory. Includes a commitment to good governance, development and poverty reduction – nationally and internationally.
- Address the least developed countries' special needs…..
- Address the special needs of landlocked and small island developing States
- Deal comprehensively with developing countries' debt problems…..
- + 4 more sub-goals.

The MDGs still remain a compromise in view of the real misery in a world out of balance. They could even have been called "Minimum" Development Goals. In that limited degree, they are, however, a valuable first step which could create hope for the world, if seriously pursued. For individually engaged people and for Civil Society Organizations ("CSOs"), the MDGs are an excellent instrument to remind their respective states to keep the promises to help healing at least some of the worst problems in our world.

From a formal management perspective, the eight main goals and the sub-goals under goal number 8 are well-formulated, "correct" goals. Most of the sub-goals under the goals from number 1 to 7 are formulated as "real" objectives (they contain measurable data). Whether the precise objectives are sufficient in content to "heal" the relevant global problems, is a different question.

Like many other engaged people, I do not consider the MDGs daring and complete enough. Not daring enough, where they contain precise quantities, and incomplete concerning the development problems which they treat. It must, however, not have been easy to get 189 states to agree at least on what they did. In the case of the MDGs, the result is remarkable since it is rare in politics that states agree on any concrete numbers at all. Mostly agreed goals remain rather vague and, therefore, are even less binding than objectives with at least modest numbers and dates, which are shared by many states. Unlike "objectives" formulated by only one state, here is a possibility of signing states mutually reminding each other of what they signed. Failing to pursue objectives in states does feed opposition speeches and is extensively used in election campaigns. This, however, is no guaranty that such objectives are truly pursued in political reality.

The first sub-goal under the 8th MDG *(Develop further an open trading and financial system that is rule-based, predictable and non-discriminatory)* has special relevance in the framework of a later subject in this chapter of VISION WORKS. This goal addresses the key problem of our reigning global economic order – a disorder, which is one main reason for a world out of balance, as I see it. This disorder must be "heal-solved".

"Heal-solving"

Why do I suggest to use this strange word "heal-solving" here?

I prefer the word "healing" to "helping" or "aiding". Both terms, "helping" as well as "aiding", sound patronizing. These words may create the impression of an intervention from the outside or from a superior situation. "Helping" makes sense, when the word is used referring to one's own activities, like in "self-help" or in emergency situations. In the early years, I innocently used the word "helping" extensively in my original guidelines. It may not be important, how the healing or problem-solving process is called, but it forced me to reflect on the inner meanings of the various words which are being used in this process. This reinforced my skepticism about the interventionist word "helping", which I now try to avoid.

The word "healing" refers mainly to beings which heal themselves. Some animals can even re-grow parts of their body, which were cut off. With human beings, a wound heals. Healing is like developing. Nobody, nothing can **be** developed – or healed. No healer can really heal. He can only stimulate or advance the healing process, a natural or learned capacity which, of course, is to be highly valued and praised. The main work is, however, done by the one to be healed. Development and healing happen from inside.

This may be an extreme position – especially in the eyes of the healing profession. The only human healing, which truly comes from "outside", in my view comes from some unknown and unspeakable other dimension. But here the question is, whether there is a difference at all between "inside" and that very special "outside". This touches a different subject, a spiritual belief system, which reaches beyond our subject here.

In the witnessed reality of trying to heal development problems, my view grew steadily and firmly that (at least on a micro-level) healing must happen from inside the healing system. In any case, it helps to be careful and conscious about the hidden meaning of words like "helping", when referring to actions from outside. "Heal-solving", in my view, is an expression, which fits reality. "Solving", the second part of this expression indicates a "softening" of "hard" facts. It is connected to "melting". Angaangaq ("The man who looks like his uncle"), a gentle Inuit shaman, uses the image of "melting the ice in the heart of people" as a pre-condition for problem solving in the world.

"Solving a problem" is work done by individuals or groups. In my experience, "solving a problem" often involves team work. It always demands community between the healed and the healing and it often also involves an enlarged community of those concerned in the process. Heal-solving is a mutual process in which the people, who want or need to be healed, take the initiative and – whenever possible – lead in the problem-solving process.

The verbal creation "heal-solving" by a German, whose mother tongue is not the English language, is a result of reflections about the one principle, which proved to be of utmost importance in the 28-year learning process in trying to "heal-solve" problems, mainly in Haiti. It became a leading principle for successful interventions that *desired development – or healing – must start from the inside of those, who want to develop or heal themselves.*

At this point I would like to add that a seemingly opposite truth is not contradicting the strict application of the above subsidiarity principle: When looking at any kind of organization or structure which wants to develop its value system, to improve in a moral sense, to give guidance for those who work on all levels, it is important to realize that such change must start at the top. A staircase must always be cleaned from top to bottom. Those seemingly opposite views are no contradiction. They fit together.

Reflections on the meaning and content of words which are used in acting in the world became a need in the process of developing my own consciousness. When dealing with visions, it is also useful to reflect about various levels, where visions are "at home".

Levels for visions

Visions and goals differ greatly when we look at the various levels, where development takes place. There are three levels to distinguish: basically the macro- and the micro-level – and a relative vaguely defined mezzo-level between the two extremes.

On the macro-level in states and in ONE-world, visions are relatively rare – at least in the political world. There are powerful visions on state macro-levels like those proclaimed by Martin Luther King jr. or Mahatma Gandhi, but they are rarely proclaimed by ruling politicians. Professional full-circle management procedures, which start at the level of visions or goals, are also rare in politics. There are too many obvious problems to be solved in our world. This provokes states and international institutions to jump to solutions. To go beyond discussing big problems and their desired solutions, needs some reflective distance and a holistic/integral approach. Besides proclaiming objectives in omitting the needed preliminary analyzing process, politicians tend to directly suggest solutions. Solutions sound strong. They help politicians to get re-elected.

In international institutions, especially in the United Nations' system, agreements must be found between states to get the states' commitments. Here, vague goals are more frequent. Precise objectives carry the burden of commitment, if there are formal signing processes involved. Where there are precise objectives, they usually represent compromises on relatively low levels. The MDGs are a good example.

There is more room for visions on the various mezzo-levels. These mezzo levels are somewhere positioned between states and the micro-level of people and their immediate surroundings. Humanity has, for example, formed cultural identities during centuries, which today often differ from existing political boundaries. This naturally creates human frictions and political problems. The Kurdish people without their own state or African people in unnatural colonial borders are such examples. On such intermediate levels, visions at least help to rally people behind the visionaries for desired change. Such visions, I feel, have more power than politically declared goals or objectives – except when there is a visible possibility of political realization of such goals and objectives as results of a transparent analyzing process.

Visions, even when they only carry a small seed of potential reality, can be the start of potentially powerful people movements. One such example is the slogan of the World Social Forum: "A better world is possible". This is a very vague and imprecise vision – but it wakes up people and creates engagement. In this case, the vision was born in civil society initiatives, therefore on a mezzo-level. "A better world is possible" is certainly very vague, but it touches many hearts and draws up to 100,000 people (including myself) to join the yearly gatherings since 2002. This vision is so powerful, that it created a global movement and does even have a (mild) wake-up effect on politics.

Visions are "at home" on the micro-level. They are great instruments to start working "on the ground" for desired change. On the level of people, visions can be as varied as there are individual people. Such diverse visions are born out of multiple types of rational and inspired dreams and hopes. They can be condensed into "visions, which work" – if the visionary dares to pursue his or her vision. In this realm, I have gained my own experience. Some visions did not work – but others did. The wish to share such experience and to encourage other visionaries was one motivation to write this book. Most of my engagement in practical development matters (as well as in political work) started on the micro-level and derived from learning in the field.

When change is desired on or from the micro-level, a simple proclamation of an intention or a vague goal are too weak to stay alive. Reality runs over mere wishes, hopes and good intentions. There is a difference between visions on the one side and vague goals on the other side, which cannot really be precisely described. The difference can, however, be felt. Vague goals are often mere proclamations. Visions carry motivating power in themselves – and: Visionaries do not give up easily.

Creating a vision may be simple. One only must look closely at reality, follow one's inner divine guidance and/or ones rational logic and visualize what that reality could and should look like. Maintaining such a vision is much more strenuous – but needed. Here the real work starts. This is not only true for individual visionary work, but also for those large "group visions" which the collective reality in our world is creating.

One outstanding very macro-level vision is only hidden behind the above-mentioned Millennium Development Goals (MDGs). It is a fair and just new and sustainable world order. The signed and declared MDGs are valuable, helpful and luckily they are concrete, but the MDGs themselves are far below the level of encompassing visions. They represent a minimal agreement to solve some of the worst problems in our world of today. It is an outstanding achievement that these MDGs found at least verbal support by all those 189 states in the United Nations, who signed them in 2000 in New York. Most conscious people, who woke up to notice the present state of our world, did and still do agree that much more should be achieved much faster to save humanity from destroying itself. However, those MDGs can be a beginning for needed sustainable change – if at least they are reached by 2015.

The vision of a world in balance

Together with a growing number of people from all areas of life, I share a "real" vision for a "better world", which truly can benefit all humanity – including even those few, who now gain huge additional fortunes yearly at the expense of the vast majority of people. For me, this vision was reinforced in Haiti. Dealing with problems in Haiti on a micro-level, further clarified that not all problems can be solved locally. Some issues have to be addressed on a global level. This boils down to the need of a more just and fair world order. This vision sounds simple, it is in fact simple and clear, yet still amazingly difficult to be transformed to a widely accepted political goal. It is: *a world in balance.*

An "equity factor" is used by the German Professor Dr. Dr. Franz Josef Radermacher in many of his books to define an economic balance in mathematical terms. Such scientific definitions may help to clarify needed directions for change. They also assist the development of global visions. To create and pursue such visions should be the tasks of our governments. As long as our elected (or otherwise accepted) leaders do not effectively manage to heal global illnesses, we, the thinking and feeling conscious citizens must not hesitate to take action. Here is the "equity factor":

Slowly those citizens waking up in the world are forming a new kind of global structure: the civil society. This mostly still virtual gathering of people is now becoming real. It started to self-structure itself beyond a mere feeling of being united by dissatisfaction and anger. One such concrete civil society structure, created only 15 years ago in South Africa, is CIVICUS. This umbrella organization of globally concerned groups and individuals is growing rapidly today. I joined CIVICUS as a member in 2008 after convincing myself of the usefulness of this constructive structure. I like what CIVICUS does and where they want to go. It can be summed up, that we in the woken-up civil society must not only help in the concrete healing of misery in the framework of our limited possibilities. We must also raise our voices against oppressive, destructive and unfair government policies, where we encounter them. We must also be politically engaged in the framework of our accessible legitimate governance structures.

In the eye of formal national and multinational structures, new global movements – like CIVICUS – lack formal legitimacy. In most cases, we are neither elected nor chosen by formal structures. Our legitimacy is evolving as a new dimension of the way humanity organizes itself in today's transparent global village. We are original structures, newly formalizing ourselves on the basis of multiple constructive initiatives. Our roots are in a global consciousness and responsibility for the ALL. This new self-made legitimacy, of course, can only be accepted by society, if we, the active members of civil society, truly act responsibly and observe the golden rule.

Responsible engagement and practiced subsidiarity, giving priority to the smallest possible unit, more and more also demand a common concern for our "global commons". Examples are our concern for clean air and drinking water for everyone. Those essentials cannot only be treated on regional or local levels, they concern top global levels, too. Beside their doubtless regional and local aspects, those essentials – as many others – need global solutions on the basis of global visions. As long as there is no widely accepted and enforceable legal structure functioning effectively for all human rights and global commons in our "ONE world in diversity", civil society must pursue our visions and fill the gap for a world in balance. We must unite in open and transparent structures of engaged individuals and groups.

The Global Marshall Plan Initiative

In 2003, a group of scientists, ex-politicians, business people and constructive civil society "activists", mainly from Austria and Germany, created the "Global Marshall Plan Initiative" to counteract the economic dogma of market fundamentalism. I was actively involved in that conceptual work from the very first year. It had become evident that the dogma of totally unlimited markets, which Europe and parts of the globalised world had imported from economic views in the United States (and to some extent from the United Kingdom), was not able to fulfill its promise for a better balanced world. The global gap between those few, who continue gaining huge fortunes and the vast majority of the rest of the world – including the "middle classes" – is growing constantly. This development is not sustainable – not even for those few, who are benefiting from it at the moment. Either the whole global system will end in turmoil or the lucky minorities have to build even more guarded fences around them. Both alternatives are not desirable.

As a young economist, I had already been engaged in the expansion of our postwar socially balanced market economy ("*Soziale Marktwirtschaft*") into other fields in Germany's society since the beginning of my adult life. Especially in the early group of young business owners and leaders ("*Junge Unternehmer*") well over forty years ago, we were working on political concepts to introduce our successful, socially balanced market system into health care and into a more pragmatic business education. During my internal candidacy in the Christian Democratic Union (CDU) for the German Parliament in 1975/76, I had also been engaged in conducting seminars on our successful socially balanced market economy for members of the CDU. The formation of a "think and action tank" for a better balanced world order in 2003 was, therefore, immediately fascinating me.

266

The initial vision of the Global Marshall Plan Initiative, already in transition to the form of a goal, was and still is to conceive a concept of an ecologically and socially balanced market system for our globalised world. Together with the general vision of a "world in balance", such a global design of balanced markets could already be called a goal, since it does not only indicate a final situation, but already shows a direction for further analysis to formulate precise objectives. The whole concept coincided with my thinking and feeling. I, therefore, joined this engaged group from the beginning in 2003.

After some initial exchanges in the rapidly growing group, the first culmination was the formulation and a public proclamation of a programmatic text in November 2003 in the castle of Stuttgart , the *"Stuttgart-Declaration"*. After further growth of the core group, the Global Marshall Plan Initiative met in Vienna, Austria, in October 2004. There, we agreed on our vision in a more detailed way:

"A world in balance
 – in harmony with nature
 – in peace with cultures (especially between religions)
 – in peace with societies
 – in worldwide prosperity
in which every human being can reach his/her desired potential."

Beyond this basic vision, which – due to its general character – is easily accepted by most thinking and feeling people, our more controversial visionary goal of a new world order had to be refined. This vision is not that easy to digest by traditional politics, as ie interferes with their hierarchical power. The new envisioned world order will have to contain a set of international rules and regulations, which will limit the abuse of economic power. The envisioned new world order should be able to safeguard our biosphere, i.e. nature. Such a new global order must also provide the political and legal framework to prioritize the fulfillment of the basic needs of all people.

In this controversial vision, markets with transparent competition would still have an important function to direct the flow of goods and services – but not in an unlimited way. This implies the enforceable respect for all human rights in all international agreements, especially in what is already agreed today in the World Trade Organization (WTO). This would also need the harmonization of contradicting world-wide agreements and declarations. It would also have to include the right of nations to develop themselves in individual ways in the interest of their people – at least during a transitional period. Such individual ways would, for example, have to include the right to protect their markets as long as needed until they were strong enough to face international competition.

Totally open markets in our view lead to exploitation of the vast majority of people by only a very few globally powerful business structures. A new and more just world order would, of course, also have to find fair alternatives to "nation-centric" agricultural subsidies as they are practiced by Europe and the United States. They make it difficult for developing countries to compete with their own agricultural production in the markets. A new and better world order would need to be rooted in a global – if not even cosmic – consciousness.

Our ecologically and socially balanced economic vision is in no way supposed to be a return to state-administered central markets, since that would mean a return from one extreme, our momentary market fundamentalist dogma, to the other extreme of socialism. We argue for a "middle way", a true balance, for the needed new global root design. We call such a desired ecologically sound and socially acceptable system an **"Œco-social market system"**. This system, in German: the *"Öko-soziale Marktwirtschaft"*, is being propagated since 1992 by the former Vice-Chancellor of Austria, Dr. Josef Riegler, in his *"Œco-social Forum Austria"*. In 2001, it became the *"Œco-social Forum Europe"*. Dr. Riegler is also one of the founders of the Global Marshall Plan Initiative.

If the content of the initiative looks too much like a European concept for people around the world, we can refer to a goal, which is – after all – signed by 189 states in the framework of the MDGs: Under the important, though vague MDG number 8, *"Develop a global partnership for development"*, there is a rarely quoted, more precise first sub-goal: *"Develop further an open trading and financial system that is rule-based, predictable and non-discriminatory."* I feel that this fits very well to our intentions in the Global Marshall Plan Initiative, especially the demand that a trading and financial system must be "rule-based". We also ask for firm binding, "rule-based" global regulations. As mentioned before, "non-discriminatory" implies fair differentiated treatment of nations, which are still not equally "strong" to allow those states to protect themselves until they are truly equal in strength. It is in this first sub-goal under the eights MDG that I see the hidden vision of the MDGs.

The name "Marshall Plan" was borrowed from the most valuable concept, which a former United States' Foreign Minister, George C. Marshall, had initiated in the U.S.A. after World War II, in order to support the reconstruction of Europe after the war. This was no pure altruism, since a strong Europe was considered useful as a shield against the communist block, but the Marshallplan was still a most valuable concept to redevelop economically. Our choice of name "Global Marshall Plan" was also supported by the vague hope and wish to integrate the United States' administration into this initiative. When speaking about the initiative outside of Europe, for example in workshops at the World Social Forum, I call our concept a *"Global Solidarity Plan"*. I feel that this fits the content and is more easily understood and accepted. The name "Marshall" sometimes made people believe that the concept has some military connection. In the meantime, the Global Marshall Plan Initiative has, however, found broad acceptance far beyond Europe. It is now probably too late to change its name.

World Social Forum 2007 Kenya, Africa.

For ONE just and peaceful world in diversity – for a world in balance

you are invited to join working for a better world in two workshops offered by the German Peter-Hesse-Foundation.*

1. – High quality Early Childhood Development for all
through child-centred Montessori quality-preschools (age 3-6) also in Africa – as successfully proven to be possible in Haiti by the Peter-Hesse-Foundation since over 20 years.

*For **time and place** please refer to German and official WSF- programs.*

2. – Œco-social market system – to replace worldwide market fundamentalism.

A socially just and sustainable concept which functions through fair competition in free markets – but under agreed values and globally accepted and enforced rules – promoted through a global Solidarity Plan ("Global Marshall Plan") to replace the market fundamentalist dogma which is reigning – and unbalancing the world – today.

On the basis of the general vision *("a world in balance")*, the initiative shares a long-term final goal which can be summarized in a short paragraph:

A new **root-design**, a legal framework for a peaceful and just world order in our global village, a world-wide **Œco-social market system** as a world order framework for global trade and a peaceful society in **ONE world in diversity**. Free markets should have binding, enforceable and democratically agreed limits to freedom. Basic ILO* and environmental standards should be interwoven in a binding way with agreed trading standards, especially with the WTO, the IMF and the World Bank, in a legal framework of international law, respecting all economic, social and cultural as well as general human rights. All should be value-driven by the global **golden rule**.

---

*Basic ILO standards, which are considered to by part of general human rights:

Nr. 29 (1930)	*– Forced Labor convention (still containing exceptions).*
Nr. 87 (1948)	*– Freedom of Association and Protection of the Right to Organize Convention.*
Nr. 98 (1949)	*– Right to Organize and Collective Bargaining Convention.*
Nr. 100 (1951)	*– Equal Remuneration Convention (men and women in comparable work).*
Nr. 105 (1957)	*– Abolition of Forced Labor Convention (all types of forced labor).*
Nr. 111 (1958)	*– Discrimination (Employment and Occupation) Convention.*
Nr. 138 (1973)	*– Minimum Age Convention (connected to school age).*
Nr. 182 (1990)	*– Worst Forms of Child Labor Convention.*

As an intermediate goal, the Global Marshall Plan Initiative wants to help, to politically support, but not to exonerate, the 189 states and international organisations, who formally pledged to reach the Millennium Development Goals by 2015.

Quantitative and strategic goals of the initiative are new, fair international funding sources, which do not harm trade, for co-financing urgent development needs and to allow global standards. In the beginning, the initiative had considered to target 100 billion US-$ yearly as was suggested by some respectable international institutions and researchers. This precise quantitative goal is now being discussed and re-evaluated. The world may even need more, to heal itself. More funds might be needed for a better balanced world, it would be well invested money for a peaceful, striving future in the global village.

Methododical goals are seen in an efficient and transparent, democratically controlled administration to handle additional new international funding as well as to administer carefully directed use of such new funds. Guidelines for such action should be the *ownership, capacity development and empowerment of those without power* – following the guiding principles: *transparency, subsidiarity, participation* and *environmental sustainabililty*.

Strategic international activity of the Global Marshall Plan Initiative in 2008 was the initiation of a global consultation process for a free, just, ecologically and socially balanced world-economic order – to replace the market-fundamentalist dogma.

The process is quite alive and not fixed in all details. Only the vision of a world in balance and in particular a balance between ecological, social and economic components of what we call an *Œco-social market system* remains firm in principle.

The power balance between the three aspects of our vision: ecology, social and economic needs should be based on a broad international consensus. The content of this design must still be elaborated in detail by many more thinking and feeling people to obtain objectives, plans and suggestions of organizational structures. This is an open process. Qualified views from all sections of global society must come together. To reach that stage, we initiated an international consultation process to define what might be called *"a planetary contract"*.

The consultation process was formerly inaugurated on 5 March 2008 in Berlin under the guidance of H.R.H., Prince Hassan of Jordan. Some basic ideas had been prepared by the German entrepreneur Frithjof Finkbeiner in cooperation with a group in the United States, initiated by James B. Quilligan along with 40 other contributors from our Initiative, including myself, to start the consultation process. Under the slogan **Save the World Now**, a **Coalition for the Global Commons** was formed. The initial paper (for details, please see www.global-commons.org) proposes seven essential courses of action:

1. Living the Principles of Global Spirituality, Ethics and Values

2. Achieving the Millennium Development Goals

3. Protecting the Common Global Resources

4. Restructuring Economic Rules and Institutions

5. Establishing New Forms of Governance

6. Generating Multilateral Financing to co-finance the Implementation of International Standards

7. Realizing Human and Social Potentials.

Hopefully, many thinking and feeling individuals in our global village will participate in the consultation process to share their views on an integral concept for a world in balance, which will benefit all humanity and the ecology, which is the material base of all life. Precondition for fruitful participation in this process is a global or even cosmic consciousness. We seek an agreement on the content of global needs, of *"global commons"*. The goal is to agree on a concrete vision of a world in balance, which shall be suggested to politics after a serious of conferences from the year 2012. The process hopefully will also help to heal religious extremes, further inner and outer peace between the worlds' religions and pave the path to a global undogmatic true spirituality, enabling love and compassion.

My own participation in this process up to now dealt mainly with point seven: *"**Realizing Human and Social Potentials**"* on the basis of my own practical experience. I will continue to suggest my own views on best possible individual human and social development to be included into a global concept of effective development in and for ONE world in diversity.

Enforceable rules for global business

What is firmly intended, is the replacement of the ideology of market fundamentalism by a more balanced concept. Some people also call market fundamentalism *"neo-liberal"*. In my opinion, the word "neo-liberal" is misleading. It sounds much too positive if you look at the words as such: "Neo" means "new", which is basically positive. "Liberal" has its linguistic roots in "freedom", which is also very positive. "Liberal" has, however, a totally different political meaning in different cultures. In the United States of America, "liberal" tends to be what Europeans call "left". "Liberal" in Europe varies regionally and also with time, but it certainly does not mean "left" today.

All functioning states have enforceable legal rules for their national industry and commerce. The globalised world does not have such rules. There are, however, some voluntary rules for "good behavior" of globalised business. For example, one such set is stipulated in the ten behavioral rules of the *"Global Compact"*. Nine of those rules were suggested by the former Secretary General of the United Nations, Kofi Annan, in 1998 and initiated in 2000. The tenth rule, "transparency", was added a few years later. This is certainly a good start, but those rules are not yet very precise and they are not enforceable. Multinational companies can always claim that they are forced to disregard some rule because their global competitor does so, too.

Appealing to large business units in our globalised world through the Global Compact and/or other comparable voluntary sets of rules is not enough to assure good behavior – although such attempts are important initiatives. Even though sustainable development must start and be rooted in the smallest possible units, positive change in the world also needs the engagement of the top leaders of big business.

Here I have to repeat a German saying: where values and good behavior are concerned, a staircase must be cleaned from the top. The top leaders are vital to create the right attitude for change. There is no contradiction in arguing that in the spirit of the subsidiarity principle "trickle-up" works better in development than "trickle-down". Top leaders can lead the way through value-based initiatives for change. Good leaders will recognize and support the importance of the smallest units for desired change.

The 10 Global Compact Principles:

*Businesses **should** –*

based on the Universal Declaration of Human Rights:
1. *support and respect the protection of internationally proclaimed human rights.*
2. *make sure that they are not complicit in human rights' abuses.*

based on the ILO's Declaration on Fundamental Principles and Rights at Work
3. *uphold the freedom of association and the effective recognition of the right to collective bargaining.*
4. *... the elimination of all forms of forced and compulsory labor.*
5. *... the effective abolition of child labor.*
6. *... the elimination of discrimination in respect of employment and occupation.*

based on the Rio Declaration on Environment and Development
7. *support a precautionary approach to environment challenges.*
8. *undertake initiatives to promote greater environmental responsibility.*
9. *encourage the development and diffusion of environmentally friendly technologies.*

based on the United Nations' Convention Against Corruption (later completed through the intervention of the NGO "Transparency International"):
10. *work against corruption in all its forms, including extortion and bribery.*

"Businesses should..." is very nice – and should not even have to be explicitly declared, since all those good principles are already internationally agreed and signed by most states in various forms and at various times. The principles are in no way binding. They are voluntary commitments, which are monitored – but not enforceable. The Global Compact simply asks companies to "embrace, support and enact" those principles "within their sphere of influence"… This is good – but weak.

When the Global Compact was launched in New York in 2000, it still included a vision, which has seemingly fallen asleep in the meantime: Good, pro-active behavior of global business was originally supposed to reinforce the minimal (originally nine) principles of the Global Compact. One of the early active personalities in the United Nations' System, who helped to launch the initiative of the UN Secretary General Kofi Annan was the Assistant UN Secretary General and Director of UNOPS, Reinhart Helmke (mentioned before in connection with the United Nations reform vision). I had met Mr. Helmke when he was still the Resident Representative of the UN Development Program (UNDP) in Haiti. We had become friends and Mr. Helmke invited me to his New York Global Compact launching activity in the framework of his UNOPS-work. I presented a concept, a suggestion for pro-active engagement of multinational companies in developing countries on the basis of our Haiti experience. The idea was simple, it was not even a vision:

Multinational businesses, which maintain production units in developing countries, mostly employ also young women who are mothers of small pre-school age children (from about 2 to 6). Why not invite those employed mothers to bring their children to a Montessori pre-school which the company is setting up next to the production unit? In a few companies around the world, the basic concept is already being used in the form of a "normal" Kindergarten. If the company hires a qualified Montessori pre-school teacher instead of some "normal" child care, it would not cost the company much more, but it would tremendously benefit the children – and raise the morale of the employed women. If a qualified Montessorian could be found, which would be possible in many potential cases, he or she could offer Montessori teacher training (like we do in Haiti) to the surrounding community. As far as I know, this would be new. The children of the area, the social structure and the company would all benefit from such an initiative, reaching far beyond the company's production unit.

My presentation was gently appreciated by the international business representatives, but nothing concrete ever came out of this suggestion. When I later questioned Global Compact personnel informally when we stayed in the same hotel during an international conference, I got the impression that indeed the original desire to add a pro-active component to the Global Compact was silently abandoned again. Only more recently the additional idea of pro-active company engagement in social fields seems to be picking up again.

Again, a good idea is not enough. To become a vision which works, it must be pursued by the visionary. In this case, other priorities at that time were not allowing me to invest more energy into my own suggestion. If I live long enough to keep this simple idea of spreading Montessori pre-schools through company initiatives alive, a time will come to transform it to a vision – and go for it to make it work.

I am convinced that multinational companies will have to wake-up to much more pro-active engagement in the globalised world in their own interest and in partnership with the surrounding populations. Hopefully, there will then be a better chance to convert such a simple idea into a vision, which works. Other visions should be created and pursued by visionaries with a global or cosmic consciousness and with relevant practical experience. The whole – all – must continue to grow through learning.

Guidelines for "heal-solving" solidarity work

My 28-year-long learning process with people in need has produced some suggestions for successful action, which can be summarized in a number of principles, in guidelines for action. They were also integrated in my contributions to the above-mentioned Global Marshall Plan Initiative. Those most basic guiding principles are equally valid on the micro-level, when working with people and their direct representatives, on mezzo-levels and on a country's macro-level as well as on a global level. Here they are again:

– TRANSPARENCY of all development goals, objectives, plans and activities,
– SUBSIDIARITY – giving preference to the smallest possible unit,
– PARTICIPATION of all, who are concerned for true holistic (integral) development – and:
– SUSTAINABILITY of the natural environment, the base of all existence and of our cultural heritage.

Those basic principles are widely accepted and may even sound a bit simplistic. I am, however, sure that if they were truly and fully observed in reality, development efforts in our world would by now have been much more successful than reality shows. Sustainability is at the same time an important guideline and a very basic vision when applied to nature and to our global cultural heritage. Social and economic structures are the results of people's efforts to serve their needs and desires. They should be sustained, as long as they function well in the interest of humanity.

There are additional guiding words, which can also be applied like principles, but which should better be considered as methodical development goals. Those guiding words indicate desired working directions. They are not yet precise objectives with quantitative and time specifications, but most important general action goals. They do not describe any kind of development like the "Millennium Development Goals (MDGs)" or the "Education for All (EfA) Goals", which are content goals. Those methodical development goals are relevant for all trustworthy levels in formal structures like states, regions or global institutions:

– EMPOWERMENT of those without power,

– CAPACITY DEVELOPMENT to initiate self-help structures – and particularly delicate:

– OWNERSHIP of those, who want to develop themselves.

These first two methodical goals are equally vital for the micro, mezzo- and macro-levels. On the micro-level, on the direct level of the concerned individuals, all three goals are even of the utmost relevance and importance. The ownership goal, however, stops to be a valid goal upwards on the ladder of formal governance structures, were trustworthiness must be questioned. When corruption exceeds an acceptable basic level, it is counterproductive to pursue this valuable goal. Here, such ownership may simply lead to even more corruption.

Increasing the power and developing the capacity of corrupt structures may still be defended in some situations as measures to fight corruption. However, fully applying the valuable ownership principle to corrupt states is a grave mistake made by well-meaning donors. Here it is often said that corrupt states will change for the better when given a financial chance to develop their governance structures. That is wishful thinking as long as those in corrupt governments do not overcome their egoistic attitudes (or as long as their populations cannot chase them out of government).

280

For a donor state or an international structure it is, of course, much easier to transfer large amounts of money from one banking structure to another. Even when seemingly strict control mechanisms are being agreed by donors' and recipients' structures, there is still too much room for misusing funds. Even in situations, where states truly make an effort to use budget money in a good way, the temptation of large amounts being transferred to the recipients' budgets can be simply too much.

The ownership goal should always be applied together with these three principles: *transparency, subsidiarity* and *participation*. In this context, it is in my view a most valuable goal and working-tool to almost guaranty success in development efforts. Especially on the micro-level, on the level of the people themselves, ownership is a key to success.

Transparency is vital for success on all levels, but much easier to realize on the micro-level than on "higher" levels. On the people's level there is more possibility of a social control. Where everybody knows each other, it is much more difficult to act in a secretive, corrupt way.

Subsidiarity as a most valuable principle which, I feel, is not getting enough public support. People "on top" unfortunately often do not like the principle. There is a fear that sharing power with "lower" levels, as the principle asks for, may have negative effects on the "top". In reality, at least in good management, the success of an organization can greatly increase if the subsidiarity principle is fully applied. The same could be true in formal structures, in states – and certainly on a global level.

The principle *participation* is a tricky one. It is easily claimed and often proclaimed (I include myself and my Foundation). There are, however, psychological stumbling blocks involved, which are difficult to overcome. Participation is directly connected to partnership. They may almost be considered to be a pair of guiding words, since they are so closely linked to each other. Partnership mostly leads to participation, but not necessarily the other way around. Participation is even possible – and valuable – without true partnership.

Partnership is truly a valuable word, which carries an important emotional value in itself. It is a programmatic expression, which I consciously used in my Peter-Hesse-Foundation's working name: *SOLIDARITY IN PARTNERSHIP* – later, after the Foundation's creation, enlarged to *for ONE world* and later again to *for ONE world in diversity*. This reflects my own waking-up processes and is meant in a programmatic way – beyond just being a working name. All the more, the word *partnership* must be critically reflected. It carries the danger of being misused.

The difficulty of true partnership

I would like to shortly quote here, what I wrote in December 1993 for the 10th anniversary of my Foundation. My German article was titled *"Partnership in the field of development cooperation – problematic, but needed to heal misery"*. Here is the essence of those reflections:

Partnership is used a lot as an expression, but also often misused. It, therefore, needs clarification. I define partnership as a participation on the same level of rights, on "something" people share in common. This could be a shared goal, a shared task, a shared path. This does not necessarily need to be all-embracing, but honest in relation to the limited "case". Such partnership does not necessarily require participants, which are totally equal in type and strength, but participants, who are at least truly willing to achieve "something", which is clearly defined in common. This is the rational level. There is, however, an equally – if not more – important level, a mutual "wavelength", an emotional aspect. Partnership needs basic harmony, this does not exclude content-differences. Harmony is difficult to limit to the "something" which shall be achieved together.

In the field of development cooperation, such true partnership is rarely to be detected. Here one side usually wants to "help" the other side – often at least partly ideally motivated (even if an official participant is involved). Rarely both sides are comparable in type – and in strength. Equally rarely the development goals are truly and deeply shared by everybody on both sides. After realizing those differences, strength of character is needed on both sides. The helping participants must be willing and capable to "feel" like the participants on the other side and their environment. The helping side must be willing and capable to learn. The recipient side must be able to resist dependency of the giving side, and resist the reduction

283

of their own desire and motivation for self-initiative. Most impor-
tant: The recipients must be able to maintain their dignity. One other
requirement in such partnership is directness. Since it is frequently
difficult to truly work with the people themselves, but with their rep-
resentatives, the integrity of those representatives is important.

To summarize the problems of true partnership in short: The biggest
problems are hidden in the "soft" qualifications of partners and fre-
quently also in their "egos".

In my own experience, a second level of problems became evident: It was not only difficult to establish true partnership
between the materially giving and the receiving side, there were
– and are – equally problematic relations inside the donor groups.
Here there are frequently power conflicts, which might be compared to the macho struggles in the animal world, where mainly
males fight for dominance. I have seen some amazing situations
even – and quite frequently – between fractions of the basically
same religion, in their diversity. That realization was not anticipated by me before venturing into the fascinating field of human
development.

Chapter VI:
From Haiti to Africa – and onward

In the years 2006 and 2007, visiting Haiti was not advised. Just sitting in a hotel (which always would have been possible) does not help us in our work with local partners. Therefore, Carol and I had to cancel projected visits twice. Written exams for our Montessori teacher-students were given with Carol's distant guidance only. She submitted her exam questions to our two local trainers, Naomie and Heliana, by e-mail and both supervised the written exams together. Naomie tested Heliana's students orally, Heliana those of Naomie. No new schools were opened during those two years, but existing project pre-schools grew further. Even without us being involved personally, the "system" slowly continued to grow.

43rd Haiti visit in February/March 2008

From 26 February to 5 March 2008, I planned my 43rd visit to Haiti together with Carol, since there had "only" been 23 kidnappings for ransom in Haiti in the first three weeks of February 2008 – a big improvement in security matters!

Specially to prepare detailed facts for the annex of this book, Carol had given me an overview about the status of our project pre-schools in February of 2008. Not all of the 53 school-projects who received some help to get started since 1987 are still in existence. Some returned to a "traditional" style, with some others we have lost contact and therefore have to consider them as being lost. It has become impossible for us to visit the growing numbers of project-schools systematically in the last 10 years as we did in the first 10 years. Insecurity has added to this dilemma. We now have to rely more on reports given by "our" teachers.

The extension of the internet and recently of mobile phones in Haiti have made this partly possible.

The listing of all pre-school projects in the annex of this book, together with some short explanations, is only as complete as possible. During the turbulent 21 years since the opening of our first Montessori project pre-school (not counting the first "traditional" Kindergarten in Ste. Suzanne) with 12 very different governments, change is one of the few things one can always count on. Unfortunately, this permanent change does not bring much improvement to the disadvantaged parts of the population in Haiti. Looking back, Carol and I therefore were surprised ourselves, how many projects are still functioning well – and growing steadily. To shortly summarize this here:

– 53 school-projects received help from the Foundation

– 36 are known to still function in 2008

– 18 function well as Montessori pre-schools

– 17 function – but more or less slipped back to traditional pre-schools

– 2 of those schools have again changed administration and are coming back to the Montessori method

– 1 more school is functioning – but we do not know how

– 3 schools are located far away and we do not have enough contact to know, how they work

– 11 schools are closed – for known and understandable reasons

– 3 relatively new schools are also potentially good projects – but they are waiting to receive their didactical material during 2008 from this year's material shipment.

In view of the political and economic turbulences of the past 20 years, it is surprising that not more projects are lost by now.

Those few pre-school ventures, which had been started in Haiti by large organizations with other didactical systems (and much more money) even had to suffer more. At least those of our pre-schools which function well are steadily increasing in size.

In most of the cases, where Montessori project pre-schools turned back to "traditional" forms, the reason was a change in ownership or leadership. Especially where some religious groups were our initial partners, a change of the responsible priest or nun usually made them accept many more children than a well-functioning Montessori class can take. There, quantity was or is considered more important than quality. At this point, I just want to mention the most recent "failing case", which is particularly interesting – and sad:

One of my very first project-partners in 1981 and 1982, who maintains an orphanage and receives support from some religious groups in the USA (and also some from me), Pastor Cassey, had later opened two project pre-schools: "Coeurs Joyeux" (our no. 26 and no. 27). We trained the needed teachers for him and all started nicely. One pre-school is in Carrefour, near his orphanage, the other one in the "Cité Soleil", Haiti's most (in)famous slum. As we learned now, in February 2008, Pastor Cassey had recently opened a third, but now "private" Montessori pre-school: "École Cassey-Maria". This pre-school is supposed to function well, as we were informed – with children of better paying parents. Pastor Cassey's former Montessori project pre-schools now had to be counted as two of those, who returned to more "traditional" forms – simply due to neglect and greed.

I admit that such incidents make us sad – and angry. Since we, however, have to live with these sad stories if we want to work in

Haiti, it does not help to be angry. We, therefore, might as well turn back to the more positive aspects and outlooks of the work. We must not lose hope, but trust in the future. Future intensified cooperation with the University QUISQUEYA is such a positive outlook on a better educational future for Haiti and its children.

As planned in 2005, one of our best former students, Willande Antoine, was inscribed at QUISQUEYA in 2006 for a four-year study program to obtain a formal teaching license. She is supposed to start teaching Montessori pre-school didactics to other teacher-students in the University QUISQUEYA after obtaining her teaching license – hopefully in 2010. This is part of a long-term concept to integrate our private Montessori teacher-training into the university program in a sustainable way. Plans for this future structure of our teaching program in Haiti were already initiated in 2004, discussed and basically envisaged in 2005. This agreement now needed to be formalized to endure. To accomplish this next step, or at least to carry it one step further, was one of the objectives of the 43rd Haiti visit. It was to be my last visit before the accomplishment of this book. Carol has returned in the summer 2008 for the yearly exams. She plans to submit a curriculum proposal to the university as requested during our meeting with the university on 3 March 2008. Carol will also help starting a new school project – possibly in Jacmel, where an active local NGO (St. Joseph's home) showed interest.

Six complete assortments of Montessori didactical material from the quality producers "Nienhuis-Montessori" in Holland and 480 of the new manuals "MONTESSORI Atelier" had just arrived in Haiti before our visit in February 2008. Unfortunately some of the material was stolen on its way from the ship to its destination in Haiti. (One more sad experience.) The remaining new material will, however, still help to add classes to existing project pre-

288

schools and to start new school projects. The University QUISQUEYA will also need one set of didactical material.

We have been helped by the "Agro Action Allemande", the Haitian branch of the "Deutsche Welthunger-hilfe" to liberate the new didactical material from the bureaucratic Haitian customs service. Otherwise even more of the valuable Montessori material might have been lost somewhere on the way. This large and very effective German NGO is our most valuable partner since the beginning of my engagement in Haiti – even before the creation of the Peter-Hesse-Foundation. Since several years, we are even allowed to maintain a desk and filing cabinets in the office of "Agro Action Allemande". When, due to insecurity and part-time absence from Haiti, we could not maintain our small own training center anymore, our German NGO-friends opened their office space for us. This practical support is, of course, most valuable, especially since we are not present in Haiti anymore on a permanent basis.

Political obstacles from the macro-level

Germans, who are engaged in Haiti either in the name of Germany's big development implementation structures or in private Non-Governmental Organizations (NGOs) and even the German Ambassador in Haiti are worried and sad about a political development in Germany: Haiti and some other needy countries have been barred recently from the list of those countries, who are to receive official development assistance. Donating countries are in the process of concentrating their work on a lesser number of countries and on specific subjects. This could theoretically be reasonable if there would be firm commitments in the framework of the donors' harmonization efforts, resulting from the "Paris Declaration" (for details please see www1.worldbank.org/harmonization/Paris/finalparisdeclaration.pdf).

Crossing off a country like Haiti from an official list of an active donor country, however, carries the risk that good existing aid-structures are also being neglected along the way.

Concentrating and harmonizing world-wide development efforts may sound good in distant planning bureaucracies away from the field – on a macro-level. Whether this desired harmonization between donating states and international institutions really works in practice, however, remains to be seen. In any case, development strategists must watch out not to interfere with successful micro-level initiatives. Small initiatives may not count in development statistics, but in reality they are often more effective than large expensive concepts.

During my visit to Haiti in February/March 2008 all engaged people from Germany, whom I met, were worried. Those people make sincere efforts to solve existing problems of the poor population and try to help healing them ("heal-solving", as I call it) together with their local partners. Of course, there might also be fear involved that their jobs could be in danger. Reducing the worries of truly engaged people to this personal aspect of fear, would, however, be wrong in most cases. Sustainable development needs durable structures – and more time than some theoretical central planners are ready to concede to the practitioners in the field.

Montessori teacher-training manuals

During 2006 and 2007, while working in Haiti was too dangerous, Carol had continued to work on her two training manuals in French and in English in her African "exile". Both manuals were published by the Peter-Hesse-Foundation in Germany in 2007. Here is the cover in a reduced size (with integrated explanations from the back-covers) of "MONTESSORI Workshop" in English.

MONTESSORI
Workshop

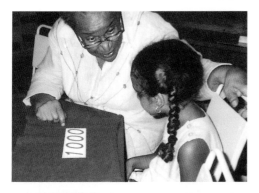

This book contains concise information that explains Montessori education, and describes in detail the proper use and handling of the Montessori didactical materials important to the practical implementation of the Montessori philosophy.

The concrete activities described will help teachers to maintain a learning environment that assists children to acquire knowledge through their own activity.

Over 250 photographs and illustrations of Montessori materials, and children working with these materials, will help parents understand the daily activities of their children at school.

This book is also excellent for home-schooling since it prescribes the progression of activities for all subjects in the pre-school curriculum for children in the 3 $\frac{1}{2}$ years before primary school.

Carol Guy-James Barratt

291

The original books are finished in a durable way – for intensive long-term use – in the large European A4-format.

Here are a few sentences from the foreword to the English version of the teacher-training-manual:

"MONTESSORI Workshop" *is a procedural manual for working with children of 2 1/2 to 6 years of age. It gives detailed descriptions on how to use Montessori didactical material for children in the three and a half years before primary school. "MONTESSORI Workshop" describes the basic philosophy behind the method and explains how the classroom functions on a daily basis. The manual also facilitates parents' comprehension of their children's activities.*

Content of the 283 pages of the "MONTESSORI Workshop", a teacher's manual with over 250 illustrations – for work with children from 2$^1/_2$ to 6 :

The importance of Quality Early Childhood Education (page 7 – and here below).
Montessori education (main subjects):
What after Montessori? The philosophy. The teacher's role (pages 8-14).
Technical use of the Montessori material (pages 16-18).
Practical life exercises (pages 19-42). + **The sensorial materials** (pages 43-83).
Language (extract):
Learning a second language, literacy, materials, the verb game (pages 85-121)
Mathematics (extract):
Numbers, quantities, addition, subtraction, multiplication, division (pages 122-199)
Cultural Subjects (subject-categories):
Geography, history, science, living organisms, craft, art, music (pages 201-254)
Starting your Montessori class (pages 257-272)
Discipline and evaluation (pages 273-278)
Bibliography (pages 279-282) + **On the author Carol Guy-James Barratt** (page 283)

We warmly thank Carol Guy-James Barratt for not only having sustained our Montessori pre-school project in Haiti during those 20 years since the beginning of the first one-year training cycle in Cap Haitien in 1986 – but also for her valuable contribution to give children in many parts of our world a starting chance in life through the writing of these books.
P. Hesse.

In the meantime, Carol has continued to work on the further improvement of her training courses for future Montessori pre-school teachers. Two workbooks in French are in preparation and shall be printed in Haiti in 2009:

A work-book to be used in conjunction with "Atelier Montessori". It contains 12 reading assignments which require written responses for greater comprehension of the Montessori method and its application.

The second work-book, "Je sais écrire" (I know to write), also to be published by the Peter-Hesse-Foundation in Haiti in 2009, is an exercise-book, which follows the Montessori material for training the fingers and the hands to control a pencil. It also promotes letter-sound and letter-pattern recognition, writing individual letters, words and sentences. An advanced exercise furthers understanding of the significance of the written word by allowing students to write down own ideas.

Since it was not possible to "liberate" our big shipment (the above mentioned Montessori materials and the 480 books) from Haitian customs before Carol and I arrived in Haiti in February 2008, I brought as many of the heavy books in my suitcase as possible. One of them was reserved for a ceremonial hand over by Carol to the responsible Assistant Dean of the QUISQUEYA University, Dr. Gilles, at a mini-seminar for students and some interested visitors on 3 March 2008. It was a very special meeting, since the day before, on 2 March 2008, we had received the visit of a very special guest.

The visit of the AMI president in Haiti

André Roberfroid, the president of the *"Association Montessori Internationale – AMI"*, did come to see for himself, how our Montessori pre-school system functioned in the most simple framework of our projects in Haiti. I had met Mr. Roberfroid on recommendation of some Swiss AMI members to present the newly printed first version of the "Atelier Montessori" to him. Frankly speaking, I did not think that AMI would be interested in what we were trying to accomplish in Haiti. Before André Roberfroid, a former high ranking UNICEF diplomat in the United Nations' system, was elected for the AMI-presidency, AMI did not bother much with Montessori efforts in poor countries. AMI was created by Maria Montessori and André Roberfroid is the first AMI president who does not directly descend from Maria Montessori herself. He is opening this renowned didactical elite-organization for the world. This was a radical change in the true spirit of Maria Montessori. He checked Carol's book and also asked some of his AMI members to do the same. They found "nothing to disagree" in "Atelier Montessori".

Spontaneously, Mr. Roberfroid had accepted my invitation to have a look at our Haiti work himself. He made it possible and arrived early in the morning on Sunday, 2 March 2008, tired from a long voyage, but with an open mind. On Monday, after being briefed on our work by Carol and me, we visited two of our typical Montessori pre-schools early in the morning in Liancourt behind the coastal town of St. Marc. When I realized that even the professionally demanding president of the most noble Montessori association appreciated our work in Haiti, I invited him to contribute a foreword to this book. I am happy that he agreed.

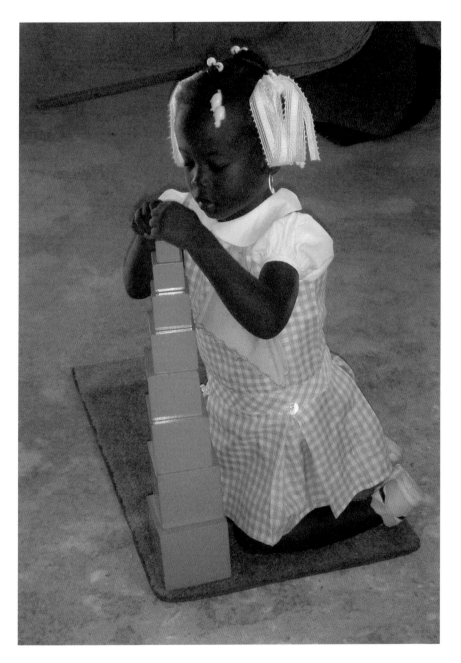

298

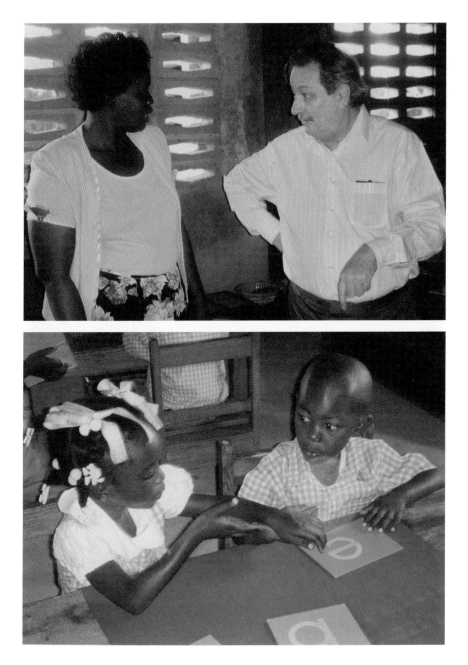

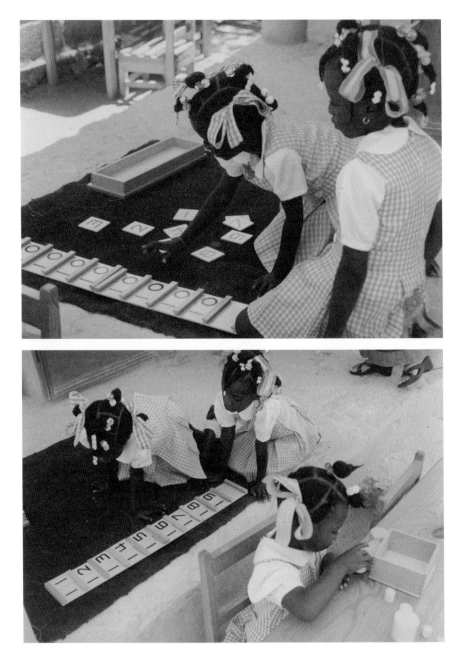

Time for lunch

Returning from the Liancourt-field trip, we went straight to QUISQUEYA for the programmed Montessori mini-seminar and for Carol's formal hand over of a copy of "Atelier Montessori". André Roberfroid spoke to the audience about the global scope of Montessori and about his positive reaction after having visited our pre-schools. This created some fruitful discussion and certainly helped to back up the work of our Foundation in Haiti in this academic setting.

Early on Tuesday, 4 March 2008, Carol, Mr. Roberfroid and I traveled on a small "Tortugair" day flight to Jérémie to visit two Montessori pre-schools in the far south of Haiti. These schools for predominantly deprived children in Haiti, whose foundations were not originally initiated through us, are situated in Mackandal and Caracoli, two sections of Jérémie. Those were the locations of this year's "mobile training center of the Peter-Hesse-Foundation".

The Caracoli school project had been originally created as a private initiative by a French Montessori specialist, Mrs. Jeannine Arnaud. It was later taken over and enlarged by the *"Kindernothilfe"* (a larger German Child-aid-NGO). A German religious NGO and a support group in Cologne (our neighboring city in Germany) started the Mackandal project. This support group and the responsible catholic priest in Caracoli were not satisfied with the quality standard of their 21 teachers, even though in the beginning of those projects there had been some teacher-training involved. We were asked to help – and agreed to offer two years of teacher-training through our "mobile training center". This mobile unit consists simply of some Montessori didactical material and our trainer, Heliana. Training is always done in the afternoons in connection with a Montessori pre-school for the needed practice with the children in the mornings.

When we arrived in Jérémie, Heliana was right in the middle of her second training year with her Montessori material – and with some problems to be solved. The locality, directly next to a *quartier populaire* (a slum-like quarter) could not be locked, and Montessori material is getting stolen – even by people, who do not know how to use it, a sad frustrating side effect of poverty in Haiti.

During the first year (2006/07), Heliana had taught the new one-year preliminary course, which Carol had developed and initiated in 2004: The more our Haitian Montessori system reaches deeply into the countryside, such preliminary work becomes a necessity and is a significant advance to safeguard the quality of Early Childhood work in Haiti – for the benefit of the children.

The importance of the first years of life

It may remain difficult in Haiti – even with two full years of training – to reach a perfect professional standard for early childhood education. Not even in so-called "developed" countries like my own country, Germany, professional training for work with young children is given the needed political (and financial) attention. Teacher-training for secondary and advanced education is still considered more "valuable" than for basic education (including pre- and primary-school). The older the student, the better the salary of the teacher and the higher his/her social prestige in society. Until not very long ago, caring for children under the pre-school age of three was considered even less valuable.

In Germany, the relatively bad results in the OECD's (Organization for Economic Co-operation and Development) educational comparisons (the so-called "Pisa"-studies) had created a shock and a potentially healing wake-up call in public opinion. Now Germany even plans to improve child-care facilities *(Kinderkrippen)* before the pre-school age of three years. Adequate teacher-training is now at least a political subject. Very slowly some politicians, hopefully including finance ministers, begin to recognize the immense importance of the full six to seven first years of children's lives.

In some parts of our world, there are still rather unfortunate attitudes and traditions concerning the preconditions for a "fulfilled life" (theoretically a human right, as proclaimed by the United Nations). In parts of Asia, early cognitive "drill" starting latest at the age of three, is considered a precondition for success in life. Parents, who can afford to do so, submit their children to such early "drill" to get them admitted to the "very best" (most demanding) schools right from the beginning. Comparing educa-

306

tional results in various countries has been most useful for the needed wake-up calls – at least in Europe. In Finland, in the far north of Europe, teachers for early childhood and for primary school are equally well-trained, well-paid and socially respected, which simply goes together. Since Finland came out first in the OECD-comparisons, this not only provoked some reflections, but it also started to create positive re-actions in some other parts of Europe. Maybe, hopefully, this new opening will become also a financial reality – for all children in our world.

In Africa, like in Haiti, Early Childhood Development for the less fortunate majority population is still mostly based on civil society engagement. "Trickle-down" effects from formal educational recognition to real practice on the ground are yet to develop. It is hard to get this heavy train ready to move and to bring it up to speed for a better balanced world. We want to further this development through helping "trickle-up" models in Africa to become visibly successful – like in Haiti.

Voodoo celebration in Saut d'Eau, Haiti

310

Carol with our team of volunteers Bernd Klubach and Wolfgang Buchkremer

Carol and Naomi with students in the Centre Montessori in Port-au-Prince

Iris Großmann and Peter Schneider, German volunteers in the early years

The path leading from Haiti to ONE world in diversity.

After the initial opening of the United Nations to civil society activities and after my own widened consciousness, I did not see the work in Haiti any more as an isolated local initiative. It, however, still had to be developed further to become truly sustainable. The engagement in Haiti was not at all what Carol and I had expected when we started with our main project, the yearly training of Haitian Montessori pre-school teachers. It needed more and longer efforts to make the vision really work. Caught in this activity, too much energy, time and inner engagement had been invested to simply give up. We were caught in our own self-imposed prison – with, however, some bright sunlight shining through small windows of success.

To seriously "give children a starting chance in life", some kind of more individualized early care and development would certainly be needed in many parts of our world – but most certainly in poor regions of Africa. – But, why should Montessori didactics be particularly useful to improve Early Childhood Development in Africa? – After all, Maria Montessori developed her method mainly in Europe. Is this a new camouflaged attempt to "colonize" Africa?

Well, if Africa could maintain some traditional values where children are brought up by the whole village, where they are carried on their mother's body tightly and lovingly, where grandmothers play a loving experienced part in the early education of children, a European methodical import may be questioned. However, Africa is part of our globalised world. Healthy traditions can only survive in isolation. Such romantic isolation does less and less exist in our global reality. Since what matters after all is a decent starting chance in life for all children, we might as well look for what works.

Montessori – the trainable method

Certainly, the Montessori method does not necessarily need to be the one and only method. Any didactical system, which puts children truly in the center of attention and which allows them to learn together in mixed aged groups is basically suitable. All that matters is the best possible development of the child. There are also other child-centered didactical approaches for that delicate and vital age before six.

Rudolf Steiner's Waldorf schools also put the child into the center. Other organizations have adapted Maria Montessori's basic developments and created their own system, like the U.S.-based "High-Scope" company. In Italy, the region Reggio Emilia has created child-centered pre-schools which are praised by demanding educators. The "Step-by-Step" initiative, financed by George Soros, also follows those lines. There are more good approaches to overcome the old teacher-centered methods mainly memorizing some text – with or without cognitive "drill-components".

To teach in a Waldorf school would, however, be rather difficult for someone, who does not share the anthroposophical way of thinking. "High-Scope" is a commercial company. Would they work in most moderate conditions with rather little possibilities to make money? Reggio Emilia needs an expensive child/teacher ratio – mostly unaffordable in less fortunate situations. Montessori is also a demanding method – if fully understood in all its complexity – but Montessori can be adopted in steps, so that children can benefit from the beginning.

What makes Montessori so particularly suited also in deprived situations, has been learned and proven in Haiti. Here, the situation is somehow comparable to where Maria Montessori made her first observations: with children who are less fortunate than average children. The reasons for those less fortunate preconditions are certainly different. But what counts is that even children who are less well nourished or who live in less caring families with less early stimulation have an natural learning capability and mostly like learning – provided the learning environment is suitable. My major argument for Montessori is very simple and practical: ***The Montessori method can be trained*** – even by teacher-students from less favored backgrounds with little scholastic preparation. This is the reality in most parts of Haiti – as in many parts of Africa.

Two opposing prejudices against Montessori are equally wrong:
* The method is only (or at least: especially) for children with learning problems
– and the other extreme:
* The method is expensive; it is for children of rich parents.

The truth is simply:
All children benefit from being able to chose their own learning speed. Learning follows the observing guidance of teachers to lead a child in an orderly environment from more simple to more sophisticated learning steps, from touching to understanding, from concrete to abstract. Even with teachers, who do not (yet) fully integrate Maria Montessori's holistic philosophy in their minds and souls, the children will benefit. Teachers (in the beginning) merely have to know how to handle the didactical material and to observe the child's advancement with the material. They have to maintain order in the classroom in a quiet way – without shouting or beating. There, the children will feel safe to learn by themselves with the didactical material. They also learn to share their acquired new skills with smaller children, acquire an attitude of solidarity towards the weaker, the younger. The children thereby "learn to learn" for life. What could be more important?

Besides the vital aspect of self-learning in the Montessori method with the help of the well conceived Montessori material, there is also room for more conventional learning through "being taught something" like in art and music classes, in nature or in group lessons. Montessori can help to bridge existing social gaps and to help the less fortunate to catch up. This is the Haitian reality: Children coming out of our project pre-schools are mostly "doing better" in primary schools compared to children from an "upper-class" conventional pre-school. The reality in Haiti's most problematic environment is simply convincing.

Reaching for Africa – and beyond

20 years ago, the "Association for the Development of Education in Africa – ADEA" had been formed by African ministers south of the Sahara. The former general-secretary of ADEA, Monsieur Mamadou N'Doye, had already invited me to a consultation-meeting with leading ADEA-Africans near Paris a few years ago. He had heard me pleading for more and better Early Childhood Development in a conference in Germany. This did "fit" to what ADEA wanted to promote and so finally led to an invitation to join the "ADEA-Biennale" in Libreville, Gabon, in March 2006. The subject in this African ministerial meeting was divided in three equally important parts:
Early Childhood Development, Primary School and Adult Literacy.
The official guiding question of this conference with 40 African ministers and over 500 educational specialists was: *"What makes Effective Learning in Schools and in Literacy and Early Childhood Development programs?"*

This (to my knowledge) was the first time that Early Childhood played such an important part in an African conference of this

317

importance. In the six "Education for All EfA goals", Early Childhood was already referred to, but not yet in this prominent form like in the 2006 ADEA-Biennale. There was new hope – especially now in Africa. Unfortunately, there were no Ministers of Finance from those African countries in that big conference in Gabon – but still, it looked like a new beginning.

Therefore, I accepted the invitation to join the ADEA Biennale in Gabon as a civil society member of the German delegation – at my own expense, of course. In the initial plenary session, I used the possible three minutes for an appeal to the delegations and advertised our "Haiti model". The message simply was that good quality pre-school for deprived children between the age of three and six is a proven possibility. After this short plenary intervention, several of the most dynamic African Education Ministers – all strong women – approached me for more information. This resulted in 35 relevant addresses of potentially interested African educational officials.

In 2007, there was another opportunity to advertise for the "Haiti model for Africa": in the World Social Forum (WSF) 2007 in Nairobi, Kenya. I had participated in this event by offering various workshops – like in all former WSF since 2003. In the African WSF in January 2007, one of the workshop subjects was: *"High quality Early Childhood Development for all through child-centered Montessori quality pre-schools (age 3–6) also in Africa – as successfully proven to be possible in Haiti by the Peter-Hesse-Foundation since over 20 years"* (see copy of this WSF-invitation on page 270 of this book). 75 WSF-participants, all of them connected to African civil society initiatives for children in various ways, came to this workshop. About 40 addresses were retained.

Later in 2007, when our new Montessori teacher-training manuals in French and English were printed, I followed up all those leads in a mailing, introducing the manuals "Atelier Montessori" and "Montessori Workshop". Only a few responded from both groups, the educational officials and the African civil society, but the wake-up process is still alive in Africa. Even though the immediate reaction to my initial mailing to Africa was not satisfying, I felt DENNOCH the need to pursue the goal to introduce our Montessori teacher-training manuals in Africa.

The participation in the ADEA-Biennale in 2006 had been encouraging and motivating. Therefore, I tried to get invited again to the next Biennale in May 2008 in Maputo, Mozambique. Initially there was no response from the organizers. The DENNOCH-principle does, however, not allow to give up so quickly. Finally I did get invited. I had asked the German Ministry for Development to put me on the list of the official German delegation as a private "NGO-appendix". That worked well. The DENNOCH-principle had functioned again.

On ADEA's twentieth birthday in 2008, the Biennale in Mozambique even included North-African states and was therefore getting even more relevant for the development of education in Africa. The subject was to be "Beyond Primary Education in Africa". The need to expand education in Africa beyond primary school was reaffirmed widely in Maputo. In many contributions, the focus was, however, still on primary school. Early Childhood Education did not really fit into this working agenda. I had hoped that the training of rural teachers as one desirable aspect of further education after primary school could be acceptable to be discussed. Our Haiti experience had shown that young men and women, who only had finished primary school, could become good Montessori pre-school teachers. They only needed an open heart for children – and an intensive one- to two-year training like Carol had developed in Haiti. This practical experience did, however, not at all fit into the prevailing mind-set of African education officials. It seemingly was too basic. The value of Early Childhood Development was still not rooted enough in the minds of the official educational structures in Africa.

African Education Ministers were rightly concerned about the urgently needed strengthening of some kind of general or vocational further education. Teacher-training was considered to be most important – but as a higher, next step in educational development after secondary school. This view certainly can be justified, but it leaves out the most disadvantaged rural populations who have (as of now) practically no chance to benefit from some structured Early Childhood Development system. In the program of the 5-day event of Maputo, I did not find any "niche" where I could "sneak in" with my basic view.

There was only one new concept, which offered the possibility to bring into discussion the age group of 3 to 6. It was the idea to consider 9 to 10 years of school as "basic education" in the framework of the "Dakar Education for All (EfA) goals" (as mentioned before). Considering a total schooling-time of 9 or 10 years could fit perfectly into the central Montessori concept of child-centered education, starting at the age of 3 and going on to the age of 12 (or 13). In this view, I felt strongly supported in Maputo:

After having met the new dynamic president of the Association Montessori International (AMI), André Roberfroid, and having appreciated his open-minded ways of thinking, I thought that his thinking would fit into the goals of the ADEA-Biennale – and that Africa would benefit from his engagement. So I asked him, whether – if invited – he would accept an invitation to the

320

Biennale. He responded positively to that question. Since I had finally found my way into the Biennale through the German delegation, it was easy enough to convince ADEA of the importance of the new AMI-president for the future development of education in Africa. All it took was one telephone-call – and he got invited. We arranged to be assigned to the same hotel for easier communication.

During the whole conference, I learned to appreciate Mr. Roberfroid's diplomatic sensitivity. We both pleaded for ECD whenever possible during the discussions. André Roberfroid avoided to mention Montessori – except when he had to introduce himself in the discussion. Directly pleading for Montessori as an ideal model for the age of 3 years onwards could have created resistance. It might have provoked negative feelings among some education professionals from the African states and international organizations. As mentioned before, Montessori is frequently considered to be "something for the elite". This holds true for Africa, too. Mr. Roberfroid therefore "only" pleaded for the universal human right to learn and suggested to remain open and to continue discussing separately, at which age the new basic-education concept of 9 or 10 years could or should start. Without respecting and following his careful diplomatic formulations in my own formulations in the discussion, I might have created even more resistance than there already was to accept the usefulness of our Haiti experience.

Early Childhood was clearly one of the three ADEA-topics during the last Biennale in 2006 in Libreville, Gabon. There, I had found a strong positive resonance by ministers and other officials after presenting the Haiti model in a short 3-minute-intervention in a plenary session. In 2006, to my own amazement I had, however, found resistance from a small working group on ECD, who even banned my Montessori leaflets from a corner of the ECD-table by hiding them below the table. Our practical achievements in Haiti seemed to disturb their views of the status quo of ECD. I was sad and angry. Then again, in 2008, they even "forgot" to invite me to a side-meeting on ECD at the Biennale in Maputo. This example of a turf war, of protecting one's "playing-ground", instead of seeing it as common ground, instead of constructively working together, needs a strong DENNOCH-principle to continue "even though" (or "anyway")!

There were, however, some strong positive personalities in Maputo who hopefully will join André Roberfroid and myself in our vision to spread the Montessori method and philosophy in Africa, too and especially for deprived sections of the population. There are already a few countries and projects, where the relevance of the method is being recognized. In Côte d'Ivoire, Democratic Republic of Congo, Kenya, Senegal, South Africa and Tanzania, Montessori is already working successfully. Our Haiti model can now demonstrate the possibility to make use of Maria Montessori's valuable findings for the benefit of children even in unfortunate situations. Here, Carol's teacher-training manuals in French and in English can provide the needed assistance. They can facilitate training for the age group from 3 to 6 in a way, which is well adapted to comparable situations – especially in deprived rural areas of Africa.

A dynamic lady from UNESCO, Ann Therese Ndong-Jatta, a former Education Minister from Africa whom I had met in Gabon in 2006, was newly installed to be the responsible person for education in Africa. Her constructive contributions gave us hope for the future. More valuable contacts were made by the AMI-president and by me, which made our self-financed trips to Mozambique look well worth the effort.

For me, this was also an occasion to continue my own learning process – at least in the subject of international diplomacy – but also concerning the multiple problems in Africa. During the ADEA-week in May of 2008 it became obvious that the educational situation in Africa is extremely diverse – to put it mildly. There are many human, political and financial restrains making it extremely difficult to at least reach the educational compromise goals two and three of the Millennium Development Goals (MDGs) (please see previous main chapter) – and even more so the six Dakar *Education for All (EfA) goals* – excepted by 164 countries in 2000:

1. Expand early childhood care and education
2. Provide free and compulsory primary education for all
3. Promote learning and life skills for young people and adults
4. Increase adult literacy by 50 % by 2015
5. Achieve gender parity by 2005, gender equality by 2015
6. Improve the quality of education

In the ADEA-Biennale in Maputo in 2008, the first EfA goal seemed to be forgotten during plenary sessions. It was simply brushed aside by the actual problems in fulfilling the other goals. Closing or at least narrowing the educational gap between Africa and those parts of the world, which are economically further developed will need much more efforts in Africa itself – and from hopefully growing solidarity-movements for a better balanced world. The growing global acceptance of an Early Childhood Development model, which gives children a chance to develop themselves, their communities and countries, however, remains a vision which can and must work.

Early learning – a basic solution

As a first step, it must be firmly recognized beyond the educational sector that human beings learn best in their first six to seven years of life. As a next step, it must become mainstream knowledge that a method is most effective to allow children to develop to their full potential if those basic criteria are respected and put into practice:

– mixed age groups
– free choice of what a child wants to learn at a given moment – and
– a teacher's attitude to serve the child, to put the individual child in the center.

A precondition for this is the love for children. This love will flow back from them.

Looking beyond my personal and the Foundation's commitments, the need to "grow/develop through learning" must be seen also in a truly all-encompassing world-wide dimension:

Beyond the need to learn for a fulfilled individual life, our global village community must learn to live together as part of our natural environment. There are climatic changes, which cannot be influenced. But beyond those natural changes, our complex biosphere is in danger to be destroyed by humanity. To at least seriously try everything possible to solve that super-macro level problem, all human beings, at least those who are in powerful positions, first need to develop a true global (or even cosmic) consciousness.

On that basis, humanity needs a global vision to at least reduce future global disasters as much as possible. Rising sea-levels will most certainly create misery first in lowlands, especially for less favorite dense populations like in Bangladesh, but also in other costal areas in the world. This will add to social misery due to unjust framework-conditions on our planet and lead to total disaster – if we do not manage to heal our global unsustainable structures. The earth will recover in future planetary time dimensions, but humanity is in serious danger of losing its soul.

This potential danger is known to all thinking and feeling people, who do not close their eyes to the facts. Additional words like these here may not change anything, but they still must be written to avoid the impression that better solutions on micro-levels alone may be sufficient to solve our global problems.

With this in mind – micro-level problem solving must DEN-NOCH be pursued.

On a path to the future

When this book will be printed, it is too early to make a definite statement as to the future of the Peter-Hesse-Foundation. The human path on this Earth is, of course, naturally limited. I, for my part, hope to have at least tried *"to do as much as I can"* as i have been guided. I also hope to be given some more time on earth to contribute to building bridges from visions to reality. Every additional day is a gift and a joyful mixture of conscious living and a "good life" in a very down-to-earth way. Preparing myself to depart into an unknown other dimension is a challenge.

But my own future departure must not mean that the work of the Foundation shall stop. Foundations are created to survive their founders. The Foundation's 25th anniversary on 7 December 2008 is a good opportunity to set the stage for its future beyond my time. Ideas on how the Foundation's work could be carried on do exist. There are even concrete alternative visions, which could work well. Evidently, such a small foundation like my own cannot go on alone in a sustainable way without the engagement of motivated people. The future vision therefore involves partnership. My preferred partners shall be the "Deutsche Welthungerhilfe" ("Agro Action Allemande"), whith whom we worked so well since the beginning of the Haiti-engagement. In any case, the Peter-Hesse-Foundation shall slowly grow during my lifetime – and beyond.

Behind my hopeful visions are hiding some uncertainties – not concerning the basic direction and the possible partners – but concerning the possible final size of the small Peter-Hesse-Foundation. It is envisaged to let the Foundation grow financially after my departure – and it will grow. But how much and when this is fully feasible can only partly be decided by myself. I have to live with that uncertainty at that moment.

One fact, however cannot be denied:
The work done in Haiti, which is now slowly spreading to Africa, could never have been accomplished without one special person: Carol Guy-James Barratt. Her work with teacher-students and with deprived children in Haiti is rooted in success in the still sad daily reality in Haiti. Her personal engagement during all those years have recently (in 2007) been topped by her intellectual achievement in conceiving and writing her Montessori pre-school teacher-training manuals "Atelier Montessori" in French and "Montessori Workshop" in English. The Peter-Hesse-Foundation had the honor and pleasure to publish these very practical and essential works for the growing need of more and better Early Childhood Care and Education. Carol's books will be most helpful at least in all those countries, where French or English are spoken. This work will certainly live longer than our earthly lives. It will benefit many more children in our world. Therefore, I have no reason to be sad about an uncertain future. What could be done, had been done. Certainly as long as we, Carol and I, live – and hopefully much longer – this work will bear fruit.

We should not forget the over 700 – mostly female – Haitians, who have been directly or indirectly trained by Carol to be devoted Montessori pre-school teachers and who have helped children (mostly) in Haiti to get a better start in life. They all have benefited from her work – and their pre-school children have gained all those wonderful human qualities, which Maria Montessori has discovered in the small child, if it is well guided in the crucial early years.

Others are also to be mentioned with gratitude:

First of all my wife, Isa. Although in December 2008 we will only be married since 2 1/2 years, Isa has helped me in my work in many ways, since we met six years ago. Many suggestions were contributed by her for this book – including the title itself (at the breakfast table some time in 2007).

Heaven-sent was Susan Baller-Shepard, the bright and profoundly spiritual pastor from the United States, whom I met in January 2006 in the World Spirit Forum in Arosa, Switzerland. Her professional input of the "right" expressions and conceptual details were essential for the completion of this book.

Looking back I realize that my life's work, or at least the work of the last 28 years, was almost always influenced by women! That includes my former female partners before my first marriage. It includes my first wife, Ting-Wen Fan from Taiwan, and also my half-sister, Dr. Ariane Hesse, who came along to Haiti in the first years to bring dental care to Ste. Suzanne.

I sincerely hope that some readers – women and men – with a global or even cosmic consciousness will feel inspired by this book. May it help, that some of my mistakes on my learning-path can be avoided by future visionaries on their own ONE-world path.

Dear reader: If ever you should feel discouraged, please pursue your visions DENNOCH.

Annex:
Work in Haiti,
facts and figures

Since this book is mainly based on the 25 years of the existence of the Peter-Hesse-Foundation plus the 3 early learning-years, which led to the establishment of the Foundation, some facts and figures on the work in Haiti are compiled here for additional information.

From the beginning of our work in Haiti, we have regularly documented our "ups and downs" in yearly trip reports. In 1990 and then for our 10th, 15th, 18th and 20th "Foundation anniversary", we have published DIN A4-size brochures. They were all donated by our printers, "druckpartner" in Essen, Germany. One of the printers, Gunter Kirsten, became a true friend and valuable supporter – beyond "normal" sponsoring. With the exception of one version in English for our 18th birthday, all these documents are in German. Learning-results for ONE world development were always added to the factual reports. Some of those more general in-sights are integrated in this book. The path walked on in all these years was never a straight one, there were detours and sideways which all served to widen the path, the views and the resulting scope of action. It all led beyond Haiti and also beyond early education into the world and into the inner self. But Haiti and Montessori remained firmly anchored in the heart. To honor the "Montessori soul" of the Foundation, Carol Guy-James Barratt, this annex starts with an article, which Carol had written for the twentieth anniversary brochure of the Foundation – in her mother tongue, English, in the otherwise German brochure of 2003:

On approaching a Haitian school for the first time in 1983, I was reminded of chanting monks. As I came closer, the chanting became more and more jumbled and I realized that there were different groups of children all reciting their "lessons" at the top of their voices. At close range the sound was almost unbearable. Occasionally there would be a loud bang as one of the teachers would hit the desk to bring the children back to attention. The infamous stick, ally of the Haitian teacher, is used to enforce discipline, the proof of which shows on the backs, legs and the palms of pupils.

Physical violence is the tip of the iceberg of problems, the Haitian school system is being confronted with. Shortage of books, the absence of any kind of visual aids and – above all – learning in a foreign language without comprehension seem to make rote learning an attractive solution. Classrooms are usually packed with 60 or more children to one teacher. Past assessments of a number of Haitian schools have indicated low teacher competency in several key subjects, including math, sciences and social sciences. This is not surprising since more than half (59%) of the teachers have less than a high-school-level education and only 0,4% of the teachers have teaching diplomas.

More than half (55%) of Haiti's children still do not attend school. Private schools outnumber public schools by 70% at the elementary level and 90% at high-school level. All pre-schools are private, this means that most poor children are excluded from education at the most crucial stage of their development. Concern for these children influenced the Peter-Hesse-Foundation to introduce Montessori education in 1985.

The Montessori Method proved to be a suitable answer to several problems of helping teachers with a low level of education to be functional in the classroom. Since teachers lacked the ability to effectively use printed materials, the introduction of the Montessori didactical materials helped to bridge the gap between language and

330

the acquisition of skills. Explanation on the use of the materials in the mother tongue fostered comprehension. These materials, when used correctly, are self-explanatory, and children can derive information from them without depending solely on the teacher.

The didactical materials – mostly made of wood and plastic – compensate for the shortage of books that is the norm in most Haitian classrooms, and they are cost effective since they do not need to be replaced frequently. (The training center is still using most of the original materials bought in 1985.)

How well the materials are preserved and the philosophy is followed, depends a great deal on who owns the school. In general, schools that are owned by institutions and exchanged administrators often are the most likely to fail. In some cases, schools were converted back to traditional when the new administrator felt that having 60 children in a classroom meant that more children got a chance to go to school, and that children came to school to learn, not to play and, therefore, did not need toy. The Montessori didactical material was then removed from the class and the traditional black-board and stick returned.

Schools that are owned by teachers do much better. The reason for this is that the teacher has an immediate responsibility and must raise funds to support the school. This is done by charging school fees to children who can afford to pay (the fees are usually set to match the income bracket of that particular area) and still include children who cannot pay by granting scholarships. About 50 % of the children attending these schools are given scholarships. This not only assures the sustainability of the school by making it self-financing, but also assures the quality of the instruction, since the teacher will lose the children who can pay fees if the school gets a bad reputation.

Protecting the quality of education to match international standards is a massive challenge. The problem lies mainly with the attitude of

331

some teachers who instinctively resort to hitting and treating the children as a herd, rather than individuals. Another problem lies with some teacher trainers, who have been taught by rote themselves all through their school lives and tend to slip back into that system.

In one case, a trainer was upset because she was not given the answers to the exam questions so that her student teachers could learn them off by heart (trading in comprehension for rote). In another, several disagreements which involved changing the Montessori philosophy to accommodate traditional repetitive learning led one trainer to open a school which reputedly incorporates both systems – beating the children with the material instead of a stick?

The quality of instruction by trainers who have not deviated from the Montessori philosophy remains good. Although the number of student teachers passing the international exam has declined in the last years, the drop is mostly due to the increase of enrolment of student teachers from disadvantaged backgrounds who have had less schooling than their better-off counterparts. These student teachers are important, however, to the overall objective of improving the quality of stimulation and education to pre-school children in their areas. A preparatory course will be launched in September 2004 to help these teachers to be more successful in the Montessori program.

Despite the many obstacles, a lot has been achieved. The real success story is that more than 10.000 children have now broken the cycle of bad learning and have attained self-esteem, confidence and problem-solving skills. Parents are now aware that there is an alternative to the traditional school system. This is reflected in the low drop-out rate of only 7 % of children in the Montessori schools.

This is encouraging and the Foundation will continue to reach more children by providing teachers who have successfully completed the training course to establish schools in their communities. The neces-

sary furniture and equipment – and in some cases remodeling or construction costs – will be given to help establish these schools. The Foundation will continue to monitor the quality of instruction by making regular technical support visits and providing concrete guidance on improvements to these schools.

Further efforts will also be made to improve the quality of instruction given to student teachers. Existing teachers' manuals will be updated and new ones developed in order to further increase the didactical ability of teachers and provide an effective and easily applicable teacher-training and working guide.

To be able to reach more teachers, a mobile training was started in 2002 – for teachers who would not normally have the possibility of coming to Port-au-Prince to be trained. This training offers the full course to teachers in a specified province, and then moves to another province. The course will move around in this way to different provinces training teachers who will then be able to improve the level of teaching skills in their areas.

Teachers from all provinces are invited to attend seminars that are given by the Foundation once a year during "les grandes vacances" (summer holidays). Special topic seminars are then offered. In one of these seminars teachers for example learned how to use the internet and send e-mails. Some now have their own e-mail addresses and can send e-mails and do research work at the small "One-computer-cyber-cafés" in their respective areas.

A great unsatisfied demand for high-quality schools in Haiti remains. To contribute towards the strengthening of the Haitian education system, the Foundation will continue its activities to improve teacher competency and provide quality education to children in at risk circumstances.

Carol Guy-James Barratt
Directress CENTRE MONTESSORI D'HAITI

To add to Carol's announcement from 2003, to create a new preparatory course:

This new one year (nine-month) course has indeed been developed and first introduced in fall 2004 by herself. Carol had realized that many students from very deprived surroundings needed more than a year to really become good Montessori teachers. The needed change in attitude from teacher-centered to child-centered behavior was difficult to overcome in only one year. Montessori teacher-students in the countryside had no experience in self-organized work. They had always been taught to learn by heart in their oral culture. Carol's new course helps to bridge the gap from traditional Haitian school with merely repetitive learning by heart to comprehension of at least the basics of Montessori's philosophy and some organizational skills. The new additional course ends with a "Certificat d'Aptitude Professionelle (CAP)", a "certificate of professional (pre-school teacher) qualification". This is not intended to compete with a full several year study sequence for highly qualified Early Childhood Educators, as they are offered for example in Finland. This course, however, paves the way to better results in the Montessori teacher-training in Haiti to make children benefit even more.

Carol has also written a separate textbook in French to support this training which is in preparation to be published by the Peter-Hesse-Foundation in Haiti as soon as possible for our CAP-courses. This new addition to her writings in the framework of the educational Haiti project is designed to allow students to gain the necessary skills needed to function effectively as teachers in a pre-school classroom. A major part of the course consists of planning age-appropriate activities for the pre-school curriculum as well as for classroom organization and administration. The course shall allow students to understand fundamentals of early childhood education.

The course encourages students to learn through guided experiences, rather than instructional sequences that require learning of certain content. Students shall construct their own knowledge, reasoning and problem-solving process rather than memorizing the "right answer" and regurgitating information without understanding its meaning. Successful students can then continue with our "traditional" second academic year to specialize in Montessori education.

Carol and André Roberfroid in Liancourt, Haiti, 3rd March, 2008

Foundation policy / Guidelines for work

1. The Foundation shall help the poorest of the poor to solve their own development problems.
2. Holistic mental, spiritual and physical as well as social, ecological, economical, cultural, technical and political development must be wanted, started and carried forward by the people themselves.
3. It is equally important to strengthen skills and opportunities for self-help as well as for helping others (charity).
4. Help must be directed to the smallest possible self-help structure (subsidiarity-principle).
5. Development goals must not be decided and pursued without those who need help. They must decide as partners in all planning and implementation.
6. Problem-solving paths of those who want to help themselves have priority. To avoid pseudo-modernistic erring, problem-solving paths must, however, be checked through dialogue.
7. Peoples' dignity, value systems and culture, their spiritual and religious beliefs as well as their human relationships must always be respected.
8. Logical and rational help, which is correct in our view, may be wrong. Logic and ratio only have assisting functions, as long and as much as they do not endanger religious/spiritual and other cultural values of those who are concerned.
9. Where traditional values block harmonious holistic development because of changes in framework-conditions, peoples' attitudes may only be addressed with the utmost care and responsibility.
10. Help to individuals or groups may only be given in a manner which avoids as much as possible social injustice towards those who do not receive help.

11. Help shall only be given where those responsible are personally reliable and honestly engaged, where their personal lifestyle is adequate and where they possess a minimum of problem-solving skills in the framework of the respective culture.
12. Those who are being helped must at least contribute their own engagement and must (wherever possible) make some adequate contribution.
13. All help must be limited in time. The recipients' self-help capacity must grow to achieve self-sufficiency. Their self-financing capacity must be furthered.
14. All interventions must be reflected and considered beyond the period of help.
15. All but one-time interventions must be conceived in a way that allows the partners or local organizations to carry them forward.
16. All technical assistance must be adapted to the future local maintenance-capacity and energy resources.
17. Where training is involved, skills and problem-solving-capacities have priority over mere transfer of knowledge.
18. Problem-solving experience must be shared with others to enable comparable solutions.
19. In cases of doubt, rural help has priority over urban help.
20. To avoid multiple assistance, the Foundation shall harmonize its actions with other organizations.

One new guideline was added in the course of the later learning process:

"The Foundation's learning and experience must be used for global consciousness-development."

Some project details and facts from 1986:

To prepare for the first year (nine-month) training in Cap Haitien in 1986, we had developed a basic document in English as basis for a later French leaflet. A reduced facsimile version of those seven pages is included hereafter. It starts with the goals and objectives of the "CENTRE MONTESSORI D'HAITI" – followed by some further programmatic details. Here are some selected extracts of this document (quotes in italics).

The HAITIEN MONTESSORI CENTRE is run by the MONTESSORI DIRECTRESS Carol Guy-James Barratt (Advanced MONTESSORI Diploma, London)

Long-term goal: improvement of didactics of basic education in Haiti – mainly for the benefit of underprivileged children. Goals and objectives on the way:

1. To enable 30 pre-school teachers per one year training program to successfully teach pre-school children (aged 3 to 5) using the MONTESSORI method.

2. To select the most capable of the 30 pre-school teachers per one year program for further training to become trainers.

3. To train as many teacher-trainers as possible (as capable) in two or three years to spread MONTESSORI teacher-training in Haiti.

4. At the end of two or three years, the MONTESSORI pre-school training center in Cap Haitien must be run only by Haitians.

Outlook: If – after the first year – broadening of the MONTESSORI principles into Primary school seems desirable, an extension of the training-center could be envisaged and planned.

Subject of the one year program will be a three- year MONTESSORI pre-school sequence for children entering the pre-school between the age of 2 1/2 and 3 years.

338

Studies include: The MONTESSORI – and other – philosophies of education. Theoretical and practical training in the use of the MONTESSORI didactical material and on its making. The use and the conception of adopted practical-life exercises and of environmental studies. The making of individual detailed teaching files. Case study of a child (physical, intellectual, social). Basics of school- and classroom-management.

Our own pre-school – to train the teachers: In order to be able to train the full three-year sequence in one year, 10 out of the 30 children in the training-center's own pre-school should be old enough to reach primary school age after the one-year program. Some new children (2 1/2– 3 years old) could be accepted per term from the second year on.

The learning goals for the children: When the children reach primary-school age (between 5 and 6) they shall be able to think intelligently and have developed confidence and independence. They shall be able to count to 10, to identify the numerals 1 to 10, to know quantities 1 to 10, to know the meaning of 0 (zero) and to distinguish between odd and even numbers. Those capable shall be introduced to the decimal system. They shall also be able to recognize the letters of the alphabet, read and write at least some three-letter-words and write their names. They will have received a sensorial introduction to geometry, algebra and geography and will have acquired an awareness of their natural environment (plants, animals etc.)

This was followed by a typical pre-school schedule (from 8 to 12 hours) and a full page on Maria Montessori, her life and her views about children, on how they learn as well as on the importance of order in the classroom. This general introduction concludes: *"The MONTESSORI method ideally combines individual and social learning of useful abilities and positive attitudes. The method is being successfully applied world-wide in most different cultural and social environments."* Those illustrations followed:

MONTESSORI-Material

Original didactical material (imported from Europe) to be used in the one-year program. At least part of the material can (and should) later be reproduced in Haiti.

SENSORIAL

1. Cylinders
Purpose: Visual perception of differences in dimension. Co-ordination of movement, small muscle control, dexterity. Hand and eye co-ordination.

2. Pink Tower

3. Broad Stair

4. Red Rods

5. Knobless Cylinders

Purpose: Visual and muscular perception of dimension.
Co-ordination of movement.
Hand and eye co-ordination.

6. Colour Boxes
Purpose: Refinement of perception of colour. Awakening of a conscious awareness of colours in the environment. Development of the forming of mental order. A preparation for future art work.

7. Rough and Smooth Boards
Purpose: Refinement of the tactile senses. Awakening of conscious awareness of the texture of surfaces.
Indirect preparation for writing.

8. Stereognostic Material
Purpose: Development of the stereognostic sense (the sense by which we recognize size and shape in space)

9. The Sound Boxes
Purpose: To train the ear.
To interest the child in sounds.

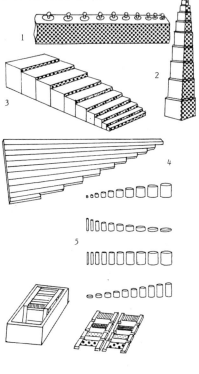

340

10. **Insets for Design**
    Purpose: To prepare the hand for writing.

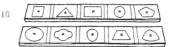

11. **Sandpaper letters**
    Purpose: To recognize forms by touch and sight,
    To know the phonetic sounds of all letters
    of the alphabet. To gain muscular memory
    of the form of letters through touch.
    Understanding of the composition of words.

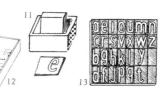

12. **Sand Tray**
    Purpose: Preparation for writing.

13. **Large Movable Alphabet**
    Purpose: Analysis of words as a preparation
    for reading, writing, spelling and alerting
    the child to the sequence of sounds

NUMBER WORK

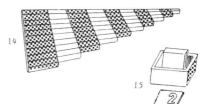

14. **Number Rods**
    Purpose: To learn the names of 1 to 10,
    and to associate the names with the quantities.

15. **Sandpaper Numerals**
    Purpose: To learn the names 1 to 10 and to
    associate them with the spoken name.

16. **Spindle Boxes**
    Purpose: To introduce "zero". To make the
    association between the figures 0 to 9 and
    their corresponding quantities.

17. **Number Cards + Counters**
    Purpose: To make the association between the
    figures and their corresponding quantities of
    the numbers 1 to 10. To give the visual
    impression of odd and even numbers.

18. **Golden Beads**
    Purpose: To help in the understanding
    of the decimal system.

One thousand · One hundred · One ten · One unit

19. **Numeral Cards**
    Purpose: Presentation of the written
    symbols for the decimal system.

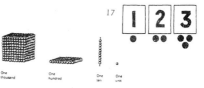

20. **Short Bead Stair**
    Purpose: Preparation for the Séguin Boards
    used later for simple addition and subtraction.

21. **The Séguin Boards A + B** - Purpose:
    A To learn the names and sequences
    of the numbers 11 - 19.
    To associate the names with the quantities.
    To make the association of the names
    11 - 19 with the written numeral.
    B To learn the names and sequences
    of the numbers 10 - 99.
    To associate the names with the quantities.
    To make the association of the names
    10 - 19 with the written symbol.

red
green
pink
yellow
light blue
brown
white
purple
dark blue

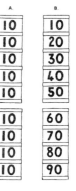

341

EARLY GEOMETRY + ALGEBRA

22. **The Geometric Solids**
Purpose: To stimulate the stereognostic sense. To indirectly prepare the child for geometry. To teach the names and to associate them with their corresponding solid.

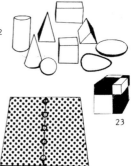

22

23. **The Binomial Cube** (a puzzle)
Purpose: To develop the child's perception of differences in proportion in 3 dimensions. To encourage the perception of a mathematical pattern. To indirectly prepare the child for algebra.

EARLY GEOGRAPHY

Puzzle maps of the world and of Haiti

PRACTICAL LIFE

24

23

24. **Dressing Frames**
Purpose: To teach the child to be independent in dressing himself. To help co-ordination of movement.

Other "Practical-life"-material, like mats, brooms etc. and percussion-instruments can be bought or made in Haiti. The practical-life exercises are adapted to Haitian culture.

Purpose of practical-life exercises in general: To help the child establish order. To help the child's ability to function using their own initiative in careing for, maintaining and upgrading the environment with special emphasis on agriculture. To develop the child's concentration. To develop motor perception and co-ordination of movement. To improve one self (inner need). To grow in independence. To prepare for sensorial development.

Course framework in the first year - starting October 8, 1986

- Mo - Fr. 8.00 to 12.00 h (4 hours) - from Nov. 3, 1986 with children

- Mo - Fr. afternoon: 14.00 to 17.00 h - 3 hours theory (without children)

- From Wednesday, Oct. 8, until Friday, Oct. 31, 1986 - in the mornings without children - student teachers work on assigned tasks, giving Carol Guy-James 4 weeks to organize the pre-school-work.

- From Nov. 3, 1986 some teacher-trainers will work with children in the morning hours - once (or twice) a week - while the others will work on assigned tasks or in their pre-schools.

- Term- and holiday periods according to Haitian law.

Dates to observe in the first year of the program in Cap Haitien:

1. Inscription of up to 30 paying teachers from Sept. 15 to Sept. 30, 1986
2. Meeting of 30 teacher-students with Carol Guy-James on Monday, Oct. 6, 1986
3. Inscription (selection) of 30 children from September 15 to 26, 1986
4. Pre-school to commence October 1, 1986
5. Dates of first trimester: 6.10.86 - 19.12.86
6. Dates of second trimester: 7.01.87 - 15.04.87
7. Dates of third trimester: 27.04.87 - 30.06.87

Course framework for the 2nd (and 3rd) year of the program:

Continuation of the one-year-program for 30 new student-teachers with the help of those capable students from the first year program who have qualified to become teacher-trainers themselves.
One or two years of such assistant-trainer-work will be needed after the first initial year to enable student-trainers to start their own teacher-training - respectively to continue training independently in the MONTESSORI pre-school-training-centre in Cap Haitien. Whether the centre can be operated by Haitian teacher-trainers after two or three years depends on the qualification of teacher-trainers recruited in the first year.

The last page was on admission and financial requirements, on the assessment as well as on the types of diplomas and on Carol Guy-James herself. Informing on financial requirements was important, even though all students of the first year were considered "project-students", who did not even have to pay the subsidized fee, but only a small fee for some working material. Since those conditions and the information on the course assessment are relevant to get the picture of the whole system, as it was originally conceived, those passages are quoted here.

On financial requirements in 1986:

The purpose of the project being mainly development-orientated, the admission-fee for teacher-trainees is subsidized. The fee per month is $ 10,-, payable at the beginning of each month. The full course lasting nine months, the total fee amounts to $ 90,- plus $ 10,- examination fee = $ 100,-. Teacher-trainees will need to spend only $ 5,- to $10,- for working material at the beginning of the course. Textbooks are only needed from the second year onward for those participants who will continue to become teacher-trainers. All teachers-trainees will be required to make their own teaching file under guidance of Ms Carol Guy-James. Due to the main purpose of the program, applicants will be judged mainly by their development-motivation rather than by their formal academic achievements. The organizers reserve the right of admission. The fee for children in the pre-school will also be $ 10,- per month – due at the beginning of each month.

The assessment of the one-year course is done in accordance with international MONTESSORI standards. The HAITIAN MONTESSORI CENTER aims at harmonizing the assessment with the CARIBBEAN MONTESSORI SOCIETY. Three diplomas and a certificate are awarded according to (50%) work done during the course and (50%) a final examination:

343

1. *MONTESSORI DIRECTRESS (DIRECTOR) – qualifying for the opening and running of a MONTESSORI pre-school,*
2. *MONTESSORI TEACHER – qualifying for teaching in a MONTESSORI pre-school,*
3. *MONTESSORI ASSISTANT – qualifying for assisting – but not solely teaching – in a MONTESSORI class,*
4. *Certificate of participation – not normally qualifying for MONTESSORI teaching.*

Precondition for any of those degrees is a participation in at least 90% of the program. The degree of MONTESSORI DIRECTRESS (or DIRECTOR) automatically qualifies the student-teacher for further training to become a MONTESSORI teacher-trainer.

Instead of Carol's original short c.v. from 1986, here is how we introduce her today in the context of her training manuals:

Carol Guy-James Barratt, born in Trinidad, started her professional career working with delinquent youths at the St Michaels School for Boys in Diego Martin. She was introduced to Montessori education by Sheila John of the Happyvale Montessori School, where she worked for 2 1/2 years before leaving Trinidad for formal training at the St Nicholas Training Center for the Montessori Method of Education in London, and then at the London Montessori College. In 1985, she traveled to Haiti and started working with the Peter-Hesse-Foundation to train Montessori teachers and promote early childhood education. As Founding Directrice of the CENTRE MONTESSORI D'HAITI, Carol has dedicated herself to improving the skills of Haitian teachers for child-centered education and training a growing cadre of professionals using the Montessori method. This small project had grown to a network of schools and teacher training centers throughout Haiti. She has also trained teachers in schools in Senegal and South Africa. Her work in early childhood

344

education was recognized by a nomination for the Right Livelihood Award in 1998. Carol has lived in several countries in Africa, Europe and the Caribbean and traveled extensively. She combined her artistic and professional pursuits when she was invited to design the Early Childhood Exhibit in the Basics Needs Pavilion for the World Expo2000 in Hanover. She is continuing her work to improve the standard of education for under-served children.

It is obvious that we started with the hope that it could be possible to limit Carol's engagement in Haiti to only a few years and that it would be possible to train sufficiently qualified trainers from inside our system relatively fast. But that proved to be an illusion. First of all, there were not enough "DIRECTRESSES" (or "DIRECTORS") with sufficient motivation to invest their own time with only limited income possibilities. Out of more than 700 young Haitians, who by now have gone through our yearly training, only 84 were qualified enough to get a "DIRECTRESS" or "DIRECTOR" degree. After the first training year, only one student became "DIRECTRESS": the wife of Père Bruno, the director of the "Collège du St. Esprit" in Cap Haitien.

Those international degree levels were given only after a second examination by a recognized "imported" Montessorian. In all the first years, up to 2003, it was Carol's original Montessori teacher from Trinidad, Mrs. Sheila John, vice-president of the CARIBBEAN MONTESSORI SOCIETY. She was trained by the "Association Montessori Internationale – AMI" and owns a Montessori pre-school in Port of Spain, Trinidad. Sheila John engraved Montessori in Carol's heart. This gentle, but very strict and quality-demanding lady came flying in from Trinidad every summer – from 1987 until 2003 (except during the 10th year, when the training had to be interrupted for a quality review of the system). All candidates, who had reached a "TEACHER's" degree in what we called our "national" exams, were offered the chance of a second examination by Mrs. Sheila John. We always considered the quality aspect of our model to be vital for success and therefore had to be very restrictive in awarding the degree which we consider to be on an internationally acceptable level.

In 2004, Mrs. Sheila John unfortunately was not capable any more to come and do the second exams in Haiti for health reasons. We had to look for a qualified alternative. He or she had to speak French, be free and willing to travel to Haiti. With intensive research and a lot of luck, we found the ideal Montessori professional: a German, Erwin Resch, who not only had the formal qualifications, but was perfect in French, basically free and motivated to help. Like in the case of Mrs. John, we never had money enough to fully pay for such services. We could only afford to refund expenses. Erwin Resch was not only a highly qualified, strict, but gentle Montessorian during his examination

346

work, he also proved to be a spirited writer and left us an impressive report in German on his voluntary mission in Haiti. (A few copies are still available in print on special request from the Peter-Hesse-Foundation but also reproduced on our German website www.solidarity.org in the section *"Veröffentlichungen"*).

Since 2005, the security situation in Haiti had deteriorated to a degree that made it impossible to safely travel to and in Haiti. Even Carol could not be there often and long enough to safeguard the necessary quality of the teaching work herself. Written exams were still formulated by Carol, but executed by our remaining faithful trainers in two affiliated training centers. Since 2005, however, there were no candidates sufficiently qualified to be potential "DIRECTRESSES" or "DIRECTORS". This led to new "joint ventures" in those later years – but let us first turn to some earlier visions and actions on the learning path.

Status of Foundation projects in 2008
as reported by Carol Guy-James Barratt in July 2008:

53 school projects received help from the Foundation
36 are known to still function in 2008,
18 function well as Montessori pre-schools,
17 function – but more or less slipped back to traditional pre-schools.
2 of those schools have again changed administration and are coming back to the Montessori method (the Foundation is working with them to determine what is possible).
1 more school is functioning – but we do not know how.
3 schools are located far away and we do not have enough contact to know, how they work.
11 schools are closed – for known and understandable reasons.
3 relatively new schools are also potentially good projects – but they were waiting to receive their didactical material during 2008 from this years material shipment.

Most of the 36 functioning schools (Montessori and non-Montessori) doubled or tripled in size. The number of children in each school vary from an average of 30 to 300 children.
The schools that continue to function as Montessori schools have either a sufficient number of Montessori trained teachers or non-Montessori trained teachers who participate in in-service training and can maintain the Montessori method even with the increased number of children.

The two main reasons that caused schools to resort to traditional teaching is the employment of non-Montessori teachers, and changes in the administration of the school.

This is especially so in religious schools where the nuns or priest in charge are assigned to a particular school for specified time only. When they leave, their work is not always continued by their successor. Two schools returned to the traditional method because they were neglected by the director, who however opened a successful private Montessori school.

There are three schools that still function (information gained by word of mouth), but have no contact with the Foundation, and visits to these schools are impossible for various reasons. The method used by these schools cannot be determined.

Out of the 11 schools that closed, 3 did so because they were affected by the political situation, 3 because the owners left the country, 1 (no. 31) for fear that a voodoo hex was placed on the school, 1 because the responsible person removed all the furniture and materials and started a private school in another area, and 4 others for various personal reasons of the directors/directresses.

Contact with 3 schools has been completely lost. These schools are located in parts of the country that are not easily assessable or unsafe to travel.

02 DEMONSTRATION PRE-SCHOOL – PETIONVILLE
    Closed. This was the pre-school that was attached to the CENTRE MONTESSORI D'HAITI when it functioned as a Peter-Hesse-Foundation project, before the center became a Haitian owned and run school.

03 CENTRE MONTESSORI D'HAITI
    Transferred the training of teachers which was formerly carried out by our own CENTRE to Haitian ownership (see 08).

06 LA PRECIEUSE – LA PLEINE
Functions as a Montessori pre-school and a traditional primary school. Formerly Montessori teacher training site. Currently training teachers in traditional method.

07 CENTRE MONTESSORI – RUELLE WAAG
Functions as Montessori pre-school. Former Montessori teacher training site.

08 CENTRE DE FORMATION – RUE CLEMONT, P-au-P.
Functions as the main Montessori teacher training center. This training center replaced our own CENTRE MONTES-SORI D'HAITI, the training center formerly run by the Peter-Hesse-Foundation. It functions in close collaboration with the Peter-Hesse-Foundation although it is Haitian owned.

09 CENTRE DES FORMATION MOBILE
Functions as the Foundation's temporary teacher-training program by training teachers in different towns or villages for a training cycle. The Foundation launched this mobile training program to reach potential teachers in rural areas who are unable to come to Port-au-Prince to attend the teacher-training course. The Foundation does this by allocating a trainer to a town or village outside of the capital to train a promotion of teachers. The trainer then moves on to another location after having trained a pool of teachers in that town or village. The mobile training takes place parallel to the training in Port-au-Prince and follows the same curriculum. Students sit the same exams issued by the Foundation.
Teachers were trained at several locations Cap Haitien, Ruelle Waag in Port-au-Prince, La Pleine, Liancourt, Jeremie and Ti Place Cazeau*.

* The responsible person of Ti Place Cazeau still runs a clandestine Montessori teacher training center. The relationship between the Foundation and the school became strained because the owner did not agree with the results of the exams given by the Foundation (their teachers had very low results and were not adequately trained). Things became even more strained when the center decided instead to have their own training and give their own diplomas.

10 ST- ESPRIT – CAP HAITIEN

Functions as a traditional pre-school, this school reverted to the traditional method because of changes in administration. There were 4 different priests, since the inception of the school, each of them had his own idea as to how it should be run.

11 ST-LUC – TROU DU NORD

Functions as a traditional pre-school. This school is under the auspices of the Priest in Cap Haitien (see 10).

14 CENTRE MONTESSORI – DELATTE

Lost touch with this school since it is difficult to access and is only reachable by passing through unsafe areas.

15 ST-ETIENNE – LIMONADE

Functions as a traditional pre-school. This school is under the auspices of the Priest in Cap Haitien (see 10).

16 KIRO – LA CHAPELLE

Closed when the priest responsible for the school was transferred to another diocese.

17 LEKOL LAKAY – AVE. POUPELARD

Functions as a traditional pre-school with some Montessori input. This is because of the increase in the amount of children enrolled and the employment of non-Montessori trained teachers.

18 NOTRE DAME – ILE DE LA TORTUE
Functions.

19 LEKOL ST LWIS – FURCY KENSCOFF
Functions as a pre-school, method unknown. The person responsible for the school was replaced. Contact was discontinued because of differences in opinion in the quality of teaching between the Foundation and the new person.

21 LEKOL DES PETITS – PLEIN DU NORD
Closed mainly for superstitious reasons.

22 TERRE DES HOMMES – LES CAYES
Functions as a traditional pre-school due to differences in pedagogic opinion.

23 MAISON DE SILOE – SANTO, CROIX DES BOUQUETS
Functions as Montessori pre-school and traditional primary school.

24 TRUE SONS OF DUMAY – DUMAY
Closed because the person responsible for the school removed all the furniture and materials and opened a private Montessori school somewhere else.

25 ECOLE LOLOTTE – THOMASSIN
Closed because the directrice immigrated to France.

26 COEURS JOYEUX – RAQUETTE
Functions as a traditional pre-school The director neglected the school and there were problems with stolen and lost materials. He however opened a for-profit Montessori school in another location (same director as 27).

27 COEURS JOYEUX – CARREFOUR
Functions as a traditional pre-school The director neglected the school and there were many problems with stolen and lost materials. He however opened a for-profit Montessori school in another location (same director as 26).

28 MARELLE – CAP-HAITIEN
Functions as a traditional pre-school. Lots of problems between the directrice of the school and the priest who owns the building. Also problems between some members of the community and the directrice, including destruction of materials.

29 LEKOL BAHAI – ANIS ZUNUZI CROIX DES BOUQUETS
Functions as a pre-school with some Montessori input.

30 TI MOUN SE LIMYE – MIRAGOANE
Closed, the director of the school moved the materials to the pre-school in GELEE and increased the amount of children enrolled there (see 32).

31 ECOLE MARIE SOLEIL – MIREBALAIS
Functions as a traditional pre-school. This is because of the increase in the amount of children enrolled and the employment of non-Montessori trained teachers.

32 TIMOUN SE LIMYE – GELEE
Functions as a Montessori pre-school.

34 EXTERNAT ST-JOSEPH – FT LIBERTY
Functions as a traditional pre-school. The nun who previously ran the school was replaced and the new nun who preferred to have twice as many children in one classroom,

took in 60 children. She also felt that children did not need toys at school (this is how she referred to the Montessori materials).

35 NOTRE DAME – PORT-DE-PAIX
Functions as a traditional pre-school. The priest responsible was not convinced about the Montessori method and the teacher was incompetent.

36 LES PETITS POUPONS – ST-LOUIS DU NORD
Lost touch with this school since it is difficult to access and is only reachable by passing through unsafe areas.

37 JERRY'S KINDERGARDEN – CITE ETERNAL
Closed because owner migrated to Miami.

38 TIMOUN SE LIMYE – CROIX DEPREZ
Functions as a Montessori pre-school.

39 INSTITUTE MONFORT – P-A-P. RUE ST MARTIN
Functions as a traditional pre-school. School for the deaf. Traditional teachers outnumber trained Montessori teachers and too many children enrolled.

40 LA MAISON DES ENFANTS – DUFORT
Lost touch with this school since it difficult to access and is only reachable by passing through unsafe areas.

41 ECOLE MARIE SOLEIL – FOND MICHEL
Closed due to problems with the ownership of the building.

42 LA FANMI SELAVI – P-A-P. RUE CAMILLE LEON
Closed for political reasons.

44 LA FANMI SELAVI – RUE CAMILLE LEON, P-A-P.
Closed for political reasons.

45 LA PETITE ECOLE MONTESSORI – MARIANI
Functions as a Montessori pre-school.

46 LEKOL MONTESSORI – DOMPTE
Functions as a traditional pre-school.

47 L'ARC- EN-CIEL – BOUTILLIERS
Functions as a traditional pre-school.

48 KINGDOM KINDERGARDEN – HINCHE
Functions as a traditional pre-school because too many children are enrolled and due to the employment of non-Montessori trained teachers.

49 PETIT NAVIRE– BEREAU
Functions as a Montessori pre-school.

50 LA MAISON DES ENFANTS – LEOGANE
Functions as a Montessori pre-school.

51 KINDER NOTHILFE – CARACOLIE, JEREMIE
Functions as a Montessori pre-school.

52 PEPINIERE MARIA MONTESSORI– CARREFOUR
Functions as a traditional pre-school. Change in ownership.

53 LIANCOURT
Functions as a Montessori pre-school.

55 PETIT NAVIRE – MAIS GATE
Functions as a Montessori pre-school.

54 LA JOIE DES ENFANTS – TABARRE
Functions as a Montessori pre-school.

56 ECOLE MONTESSORI DE FRECINEAU – ST MARC
Closed for political reasons.

57 LES AMIS LA SANTE – CANGE
Functions as a traditional pre-school because too many children are enrolled and due to the employment of non-Montessori trained teachers.

58 CARMEL KINDERGATEN – KENSCOFF
Functions as a Montessori pre-school.

59 LES PETITS MINOUX – TI GOAVE
Functions as a Montessori pre-school.

60 ECOLE MUSPAN – TI PLACE CAZEAU
Functions as a Montessori pre-school.

61 LA MAISON DES ENFANTS MONTESSORI – CASTERA
Functions as a Montessori pre-school.

62 ECOLE DUMARSAIS ESTIME – MEYER
? – Implementing Montessori is a possibility in the future. This school is run by a German missionary. Three teachers have been trained for this school. The problem so far is that the room set aside for the school is totally inadequate. During my last visit there were 110 children to 3 teachers. A space in the adjoining church where several primary school classes are held is to set aside for thee Montessori class.

63 MICHAEL KAASCH – CARREFOUR FEUILLES
Functions as a Montessori pre-school and traditional primary school.

64 PRIMARY SCHOOL – LIANCOURT
Functions as a primary school with Montessori approach.

65 MAKANDAL – JEREMIE
Functions as a Montessori pre-school.

356

Financial overview

Yearly spending in and for the Foundation's projects from its creation on 7 December 1983 and during the initial 3 years in US $ or in EUR(O) ("€") – from 2002, the creation of the European currency EUR, which was originally rather close to the value of the US Dollar.

Years		Short indications where the money was being spent:
1981–83	$ 35.000	Sewing machine project + various bottleneck opening activities in Haiti.
1984	$ 13.000	Food for Ste. Suzanne pre-school + start of Port Margot Haiti-initiative.
1985	$ 17.000	Learning activities, Montessori test and dental work in Ste. Suzanne.
1986	$ 42.000	Enlarging in Ste. Suzanne and Port Margot. Start of Montessori training.
1987	$ 55.000	Investing Ste. Suzanne + move of Montessori training to Port-au-Prince.
1988	$ 110.000	$ 31.000 from BMZ* for carpenter proj. + purchase wood in Dominica.
1989	$ 122.000	$ 51.000 from BMZ* for building a training center on bishop's roof-top.
1990	$ 72.000	Doubling + intensifying of Montessori training through double capacity.
1991	$ 58.000	New pre-schools and start of fishermen project on island La Tortue.
1992	$ 108.000	Growing Montessori project + purchase of jeep for distant interventions.

1993	$ 114.000	Concentrating on opening school projects + providing of material.
1994	$ 53.000	Further growth of new and existing Montessori pre-school projects.
1995	$ 61.000	Intense training and move to new small center after end of roof-top.
1996	$ 84.000	Montessori material + training summer camp "10 years of Montessori".
1997	$ 64.000	Hurting rent for training site. Therefore purchase of land for future site.
1998	$ 61.000	Steadily more pre-schools + financial help for EDUTAC, South Africa.
1999	$ 52.000	"Normal" Montessori training and opening of new pre-school projects.
2000	$ 61.000	New co-operating training centers + cost of retraining needs by Carol.
2001	$ 68.000	Last year in rented training site + for more Montessori material needs.
2002	€ 56.000	Starting of semi-independent training site + for Montessori material.
2003	€ 30.000	Restrained spending to save for building training center on own land.
2004	€ 48.000	Difficult spending for projects due to growing political unrest.
2005	€ 59.000	Minimal normalization, but enduring problems to reach distant projects.
2006	€ 51.000	Worsening security situation not allowing growth of projects as planned.

| 2007 | € 111.000 | Continuing insecurity; printing of training manuals in French + English. |
| 2008 | € +100.000 | Gradual normalization of political situation in Haiti allows continued investments there + start of new Montessori project in Côte d'Ivoire. |

The budget of the Peter-Hesse-Foundation was supported from the early years by a varying group of up to about one hundred friends and since several years by a yearly Christmas public collecting activity of children of Peter Hesse's German home town Düsseldorf for children of the world. The total support from outside the Foundation and beyond Peter Hesse's own yearly donations turned around an average of 40 % of the yearly budget. In 1988 and 1989, the German Ministry for Development* (BMZ) supported two larger projects of the Foundation. The Foundation had never tried to actively acquire supporting funds from the public. This was considered to cost too much time and effort which could be better used in the direct project work and for political initiatives in the field of ONE world development.

From the very beginning, most administrative expenses in Germany were either fully (or later at least to a large extent) carried by Peter Hesse privately. The Foundation was originally created with a minimal capital of DM 200.000 (+ 2 donations of DM 5.000), amounting to roughly US $ 100.000 or (originally) 100.000 EUR. From 1 January 2007, the capital was enlarged to 300.000 EUR (now about US $ 430.000) and will be increased to one million EURO at the end of 2008 from the private savings of Peter Hesse. Further capital increases are projected in the will of Peter and Isa Hesse. The Peter-Hesse-Foundation shall finally be integrated in the German Agro Action ("Deutsche Welthungerhilfe"), preserving its purpose and its name.

INVESTING IN OUR CHILDREN'S FUTURE

FROM
Early
Child
DEVELOPMENT

TO
Human
DEVELOPMENT

THE WORLD BANK

EDITED BY MARY EMING YOUNG

1. Haiti: Montessori-Based Teacher Training and Preschools

The Montessori Preschool Project provides high-quality, internationally recognized teacher training. Through a scholarship scheme, individuals with limited economic resources are financially supported to become certified preschool teachers and to open their own preschools. The project was created and is supported by the Peter-Hesse Foundation, Solidarity in Partnership for One World, a nonprofit organization registered in Germany and Haiti. Peter Hesse started the foundation in 1981 for the purpose of sustaining small self-help projects for poor people in Haiti. Initially, the foundation focused on 2-day seminars on project management for self-help groups and on alleviation of small financial bottlenecks, mostly for rural initiatives. In 1984, the foundation changed its emphasis to early childhood care and development, which led to creation of the foundation's first teacher training center (in 1986), the Centre Montessori d'Haiti.

Mission

The Montessori Preschool Project aims to influence Haiti's education sector, at public and private levels, by demonstrating that high-quality early childhood education is possible—even with limited resources—if the quality and length of teacher training are adequate. The mission of the Montessori program is to give poor children a better chance to develop themselves early enough through quality teacher training and creation of community-based preschools. The training of qualified teachers translates directly into increased local capacity to provide early stimulation and education programs of good quality to children ages 2.5–5 years.

Cultural Context

Haiti's culture is based heavily on oral communication. Teachers are accustomed to memorizing and reciting teaching material, but have difficulty applying this knowledge in the classroom. To improve application, most of the Montessori training course is presented through oral instruction in Creole, the local language. In addition, the project adapted the curriculum to the needs of student teachers in Haiti, adding substantial practice time to help them transfer theory into practice. The student teachers must complete supervised internships, create didactical material, and be able to adapt everyday objects as teaching tools. Haitian teachers compensate for a shortage of books and materials by developing their own lessons, teaching materials, and visual aids.

Methodology and Approach

Montessori education embraces a child-centered philosophy that emphasizes individuals' learning paths and the capabilities of each child. Children can access different kinds of materials freely and are encouraged to learn at their own pace. The freedom for purposeful activity allows children to develop not only their intellectual faculties, but also their powers of deliberation, intuition, independence, and self-discipline, as well as the social awareness and behavior needed to function in the world. Teachers and children are taught mutual respect and nonaggressive behavior; competition is strictly avoided.

In the Montessori approach, didactical materials present knowledge to children in an orderly way so that their intellect can classify the information into an organized system of thought. This process of working with the material exercises a child's intellect constantly and expands the child's mental abilities. The effectiveness of the material derives from the thoughtfully planned manner of its presentation, which flows from:

- Concepts presented in isolation (which reduces the confusion of receiving too many ideas at once), to
- Appreciation of various difficulties in isolation, from easiest to most difficult (for young children, from concrete to abstract), to
- Use of a graduated series of self-teaching materials suited to the various stages of a child's development, to
- Incorporation of body movement (occupation) for specific purposes (i.e., combining movement and mental concentration).

363

More than 50 percent of the didactical material for Montessori preschools, including most reading material, is produced locally. Teachers make most of the material at the beginning of the academic year. In addition, one basic set of imported Montessori teaching materials, which costs approximately US$1,000, is provided to each new preschool. Because the Montessori teaching material benefits the child's cognitive development even when a teacher does not fully understand the didactical background, teachers who do not completely comprehend the Montessori pedagogy can become effective teachers. From training in the Montessori teaching method, people from poor communities and with relatively low levels of education have become certified teachers.

Children attending Montessori preschools range in age from 2.5–5 years and, in exceptional cases, 6 years. Classes are not divided by age groups, and children are invited to learn from each other and to interact across ages. Older children learn to take pride in helping weaker and smaller children and, thereby, enhance their social skills.

Implementation

Montessori student teachers complete a 9-month training course, a final examination, and two 6-week internships in an affiliated Montessori school. They can receive three types of diplomas: assistant's diploma, national teacher diploma, and international Montessori directress/director diploma. All student teachers are examined and given their diploma by the Centre Montessori d'Haiti. To obtain the international diploma, students must pass all parts (written, oral demonstration, practical) of the national examination conducted by the Centre Montessori d'Haiti, demonstrate a complete understanding of the Montessori philosophy, and pass a second examination conducted by an outside, internationally recognized specialist. About 20 percent of all Montessori-trained student teachers have obtained the international Montessori directress/director diploma, which certifies them as Montessori teachers entitled to teach and open schools in Haiti and around the world. After teaching for 1 year, they can also become assistant student teacher trainers in one of Haiti's Montessori training centers.

About 50 percent of all Montessori student teachers are scholarship students who sign a contract with the Centre Montessori d'Haiti which obliges them to teach for 3 years in a poor community after they complete their training. Most teachers return to their own locale to establish a school, and most extend their commitment beyond the initial 3-year agreement.

All Montessori project preschools throughout Haiti are strongly linked by their common structures, teaching philosophy, and administrative organization. Each summer break, the teachers gather for a 3-week workshop to share experiences and enrich their teaching skills. During 1996–97, the Centre Montessori d'Haiti interrupted its teacher training courses to strengthen the Montessori preschool structure across Haiti and to conduct evaluations. Also in 1996, seventy-five Haitian Montessori teachers established the Association Montessori d'Haiti (AMOH), a professional teachers group.

Evolution

The Montessori Preschool Project in Haiti began in 1986. Since then, forty-three Montessori preschools have been established, and forty-one are still operating, having persisted in Haiti's turbulent years of political instability. They provide services, in sixty preschool classes, for about 2,000 children each year from poor communities.

Sustainability and increasing local teaching capacity are essential aspects of the project. When it began, one Montessori training center, with a preschool class of twenty-five children, trained twenty teachers in the first 9-month course. Both the center and the class were directed by expatriates. Under the leadership of a London-trained Montessori specialist from Trinidad, the capacity of the center soon grew to an annual average of forty students, mostly women. Recently, two additional training centers were established with financial support from the Peter-Hesse Foundation and are linked closely to the original center. With all three centers, the Montessori project currently has the capacity to train sixty teachers each year.

365

The forty-one operating Montessori preschools include one for children with human immunodeficiency virus infection, one for deaf children, and two attached to an orphanage. Since the project began, an average of three new preschools open each year. Over the years, only one preschool has ceased operation, and one has returned to Haiti's traditional system of rote learning. Classes remain "small" (thirty children per class), compared with the traditional Haitian classrooms of sixty children. To date, 450 teachers have been trained; 297 have received national teacher diplomas, and 83 have received international teaching diplomas. The increase in local capacity to train qualified teachers translates directly into increased capacity to provide high-quality stimulation and education programs for preschool-aged children. The children stay in the Montessori schools an average of 2 to 3 years. Of the 2,000 children enrolled each year, only about 10 percent drop out. About 660 children graduate each year, and more than 80 percent continue on to primary school. Parents do not seem to favor enrollment of boys over girls at the preschool level, which helps to increase the number of girls going on to primary school.

Financial Support

The average annual financial support for the Montessori Preschool Project has been US$100,000 or less. Often far less has been available, but funding has always been sufficient to support the project. Financing is secured privately by the founder and approximately fifty individual donors per year. The German government occasionally assists with small grants to cover exceptional needs. The United Nations Development Programme (UNDP) and the German Development Service (DED) have financed a U.N. volunteer in past years.

The foundation's funding supports overall project coordination and supervision and scholarship students who later teach in schools for disadvantaged children in poor communities. In addition, each new preschool receives US$3,000–$4,000 in startup funds which are used to purchase a basic set of Montessori teaching material, help with school construction and administrative organization, and

366

procure technical advice. Montessori graduates are encouraged, and financially supported, to open Montessori preschools for children at risk if the local community provides support to enable the school to become sustainable in the long term.

Other financial resources are limited, but sufficient to sustain the preschools and are secured through school fees and community in-kind contributions (e.g., providing a building). The Montessori training centers raise financial contributions from the regular fees paid by student teachers who are not on scholarship. The two recently established training centers are paying back startup funds to the project by providing scholarships for a number of student teachers each year.

Principles of Success

The success of the Montessori Preschool Project can be attributed to the following characteristics.

- *Driven by Demand.* The Montessori Preschool Project started small and has expanded in a sustainable manner.
- *Community-based.* Schools are opened only when requested by a community and when community involvement proves to be reliable.
- *Teacher Ownership.* Teachers privately own the schools and are accountable for financing, student performance, and school reputation.
- *Financially Sustainable.* Schools and training centers become financially independent after approximately 1 year.
- *Culturally Relevant.* The project builds on indigenous cultural patterns, and the teaching methods are adapted to the local language (Creole) and oral culture.
- *Well-defined Selection Criteria.* Selection criteria for student teachers are clearly defined, and scholarship students are screened carefully to ensure their future commitment to rural communities.

367

- *Low-income Employment Opportunities.* The project provides employment opportunities for low-income individuals. Poor students who have completed secondary education can become qualified and certified teachers and are supported to open their own preschools.
- *Economically Inclusive.* The program brings together teachers and children from different economic backgrounds. The combination of poor and rich students helps the schools become financially sustainable and achieve a good reputation.
- *Successful Teaching Method.* The Montessori approach builds self-esteem, confidence, problem-solving skills, and positive life attitudes.

Outlook

The Montessori Preschool Project is making strides in going to scale, program evaluation, and advocacy and visibility.

Going to Scale

Haiti continues to have a great unsatisfied demand for high-quality preschools. With the two new Montessori training centers, training capacity has increased from twenty to sixty teachers per academic year. This increase is expected to have long-term spill-over effects as new teachers open new preschools in poor communities.

To improve the educational standard in Haiti, better teacher training is needed at all school levels. The Peter-Hesse Foundation proposes to establish a resource center to provide assistance and professional development for teachers of preschool and primary school. To improve their skills in teaching and curriculum development, teachers using the center would be able to participate in continuing education and special-topic seminars with professional education experts. They would have professional assistance to access print and electronic media materials, do research, and review didactical materials for specific classroom needs. To reach working teachers, the center would be available to any teacher from the public or private sector and would remain open during off-work times (e.g., Saturdays, vacation periods).

Program Evaluation

In addition to its own 1996–97 evaluation, the Centre Montessori d'Haiti is pursuing an independent external evaluation of the project's effect on the educational outcomes of poor children and the professional development of proficient preschool teachers.

Advocacy and Visibility

Promoting high-quality early child development and education as a priority in development politics, in Germany and internationally, is an important part of the foundation's activities. For broader visibility, the foundation registered as an NGO and is represented in several childcare networks and at international early child development and U.N. conferences. The foundation's "Three Suggestions for One World Development" was selected as input from NGOs to the U.N. World Summit for Social Development, held in March 1995. The Montessori Preschool Project was also internationally selected for presentation at EXPO 2000 in Hannover, Germany.

Source: *"From Early Child Development to Human Development"*, edited by Mary Eming Young, the World Bank, Washington, D.C., USA, 2002.

We, Carol an I were happy about the ***project evaluation*** by the World Bank in 2002 – along with four much larger early childhood initiatives, who were also present in Haiti on a limited scale, but with much more money per project. Our main strength is not financial, but the involvement and the quality training of our mostly female teachers. Our strength lies in the Montessori concept, but mainly in the people themselves, in our teachers and in the parents, who see, how well their children develop.

Peter-Hesse-Stiftung   für EINE Welt

November 15, 1990

Follow-up to the Jomtien "World Conference on Education for All" in March 1990

Project-proposal to the organizers - **UNDP, UNESCO, UNICEF, World Bank** - of the Jomtien-Conference "Meeting Basic Learning Needs":

As required in the "World Declaration on Education for All", this is a concrete proposal for action to promote (**the goal**):

Qualified early childhood education (mainly) **in the "3rd world"**
- wherever "natural" stimulation by the traditional (family-) environment is not given to the child during the 3 years before primary school age and
- wherever the respective authorities accept such promotion.

Why ?
Self-initiative and self-help being prime factors for self-development in and of the "3rd world" in the framework of the respective culture, the capability of using ones head for thinking and problem-solving (instead of just repeating) is most important. Such capabilities, learning scills, as well as basic positive attitudes can best be learned/implanted at pre-school age. This age is also the best time to promote and safeguard the childs natural creativity and spiritual potential.

Wherever learning traditions are being lost or their static character is not helping to further the necessary mental flexibility to cope with inevitable change in ONE future world, systematic mental stimulation is needed - adapted to the childs natural learning behaviour **and** to the cultural environment.

More detailed objectives:

The proposed promotional action for pre-school-education shall:

1. give scientific/professional "weight" to the necessity of high quality systematic pre-school education for those governments and institutions who do not believe in it yet;

2. help to stimulate the allocation of funds for pre-school-education in the "3rd world",

3. compare and evaluate existing didactical pre-school methods (like MONTESSORI),

4. produce recommendations, which didactical method(s) is/are most suitable in which "3rd world" framework.

. 5. initiate the production of optimized didactical pre-school material and teacher-training for its application - for pre-school projects in "3rd world" countries.

Büro der Peter-Hesse-Stiftung: Otto-Hahn-Str.2, D-4006 Erkrath, Tel. (0211) 2509440, Fax 2509461, Telex 8586603 kufa d

Allgemeine selbstandige Stiftung im Sinne des § 2. Abs. 1 StiftG NW vom 21. Juli 1977 — genehmigt am 7. Dezember 1983 vom Innenminister NRW
Konto 3 156 080, Commerzbank Düsseldorf (BLZ 300 400 00), Stiftungssatzung § 1 und § 2 Abs. 1: Die Peter-Hesse-Stiftung hat ihren Sitz in 4000 Düsseldorf 13, Im Diepental 16
Die Stiftung verfolgt ausschließlich und unmittelbar gemeinnützige und mildtätige Zwecke im Sinne des Abschnittes „Steuerbegünstigte Zwecke" der Abgabenordnung.

Steps to reach those objectives:

1. Listing of **key-specialists** on early childhood education - worldwide

2. Proposing to initiate informal small **national working groups** in each country where such specialists can be found to accept this honorary task.

3. **International meeting** of didactical specialists for early childhood education - delegated by their respective national working groups. (Qualification and experience of participants should be more important than their "position".)

   Working method of the meeting should be as practical and "down to reality" as possible - using most of the time for practical comparisons and evaluation of existing and working methods.

4. Optimizing **didactical material** as much as international consensus can be reached.

5. Initiating **pre-school projects** in those "3rd world"-countries willing to participate.

The Organizers (UNDP, UNESCO, UNICEF and World Bank) could/should support the initial steps financially only in a limited way. Private initiative should be encouraged. Cost of initial national contacts and the international meeting should be carried by the participating specialists to the greatest possible extent (this would secure their continuing motivation). Pilot projects and optimizing work should be supported by the organizers by providing didactical material at least for the initial phases.

Why do I **propose** this initiative ? I found in my own development-projects in Haiti (since 1981) as well as through numerous visits and discussions in other "3rd world"-countries (mainly in Africa) that a lack of learning ability caused by lack of early stimulation of the minds and by repetitive school-didactics is a serious handicap for future learning and for problem-solving ability. On the other hand practical experience with positive results of MONTESSORI pre-school training in Haiti (see next page) as well as further investigations into the relevant reality in other "3rd world"-countries have convinced me that more and **better** pre-school activities could bring an important improvement of the "3rd world" capability to learn selfhelp scills. I believe that **real development must come from "down" and inside.** Governments and the international community must help to create the framework-conditions.

Once a problem-solving path is found, I/we must walk on it - to **ONE future world.**

Peter Hesse

Curriculum vitae – Peter Hesse

Born on April 5, 1937 in Port Chester, New York, from German parents. (Was) moved to Germany at 3 months of age.

Unusual family situation during world war II. After the war and a primary school year in Geneva: Schule Schloss SALEM (private country school) + one year Phillips Academy ANDOVER, Massachusetts, USA.

Studies in Business Administration and Economics, University of Munich, Germany. After end of formal studies ("Diplom-Kaufmann" 1963) further training in Germany and England to become marketing and management trainer – parallel to practical learning in family business "Schmincke" artists' color factory.

Until 1970 marketing and management trainer in German industry and in educational institutions – parallel to marketing work in "Schmincke" company and conceptual work on management subjects. Publication of "Management System" (circular management models). Seminar specialization in GRID group dynamics and SYNECTICS creativity training.

1966–1968 Regional president of Germany's Young-Presidents'-Organization (Bundesverband Junger Unternehmer – BJU) – (main activity: testing of new/modern management-seminars).

1969 Founder of "Komitee für Managementbildung in Europa" Committee for Management Education in Europe – a group of 163 mostly young professionals trying to modernize formal management education in Europe, mainly in Germany – resulting in the development of a Management Education Concept (4 stages: school / university / postgraduate / lifelong).

1971–1998 President of "Schmincke" family business. (1999 retired to consultant status).

1974 Co-founder of "Deutsche Management Gesellschaft" (German Management Society).

1974 (until 1983) Trainer in "fair dialectics", group activities and political subjects for the Christian Democratic (CDU) party of Germany in Düsseldorf.

1975/76 Candidate for Federal Parliament in the Christian Democratic party (narrow miss). Since that time various political CDU posts, engagements and initiatives on a local and national level, especially in the field of ONE-world development.

Since 1984 Member of the Federal CDU Development Commission – since 2003 including human rights. Re-appointed in 2008 after Germany's formation of a coalition government. ("CDU Bundesfachausschuss Entwicklungszusammenarbeit und Menschenrechte")

1978–1987 Chairman of regional employers' association of the chemical industry.

Since 1978 member of the board of the regional umbrella organization of all major employers' associations ("Unternehmerschaft Düsseldorf").

1993 Vice-President.

2001 until April 2003 President.

Since 1981 poverty-fighting activities in Haiti. Initially seminars in project management, later mainly Early Childhood Development through Montessori teacher training and opening of Montessori pre-schools for poor children.

1983 Establishment of the "Peter-Hesse-Foundation SOLIDARITY IN PARTNERSHIP for ONE world". 1988 formal creation of a sister organization in Haiti (same name).

1988 Co-creation of German association "ONE world for ALL" (EINE WELT FÜR ALLE).

Since 1988 part-time (half of year) in family business (due to growing social engagement).

1989 First "mystical" experiences (guiding messages received in meditative states of mind).

Since 1990 global activity for consciousness-building / promoting early and basic education.

Since 1991 Honorary Consul of Iceland in Düsseldorf, NRW.

1992 Foundation: "INITIATIVE PRE-SCHOOL EDUCATION for children in ONE world".

1993–1998 Member of SOCIAL VENTURE NETWORK EUROPE.

1994–2001 elected chairman of "PARITÄT International", a network of German NGOs, working in ONE-world development.

Since 1995 active participation in international conferences like

– UN Social Summit in Copenhagen (publication of 3 "SUGGESTIONS FOR ONE WORLD DEVELOMENT")

– UNICEF and IFCW Children's Conferences

– UN-Mid-Decade-Review EDUCATION FOR ALL, Amman, Jordan

– STATE OF THE WORLD FORUM, San Francisco (organizing and convening roundtables on global education in 1995 and 1996).

1996 Five-bypass heart operation – followed by decision to (soon) quit the family business and concentrate on ONE-world work.

1997 Hiring of a young successor for the "Schmincke" family business – and beginning to work on first German book following 60th birthday.

End of 1998 hand-over of the presidency of the "Schmincke" artist's color factory.

Since 1998 Member of the INSTITUTE OF NOETIC SCIENCES (IONS), California, USA

1999 Initiating regional Düsseldorf/Neuss IONS Community Group: "NE-D-IONS", since 2006 transferred to Duisburg "DU-D-IONS".

1999 Publication of book in German "Von der Vision zur Wirklichkeit", (From Vision to Reality)

2000 Concentration on international work – mainly for the promotion of high quality EARLY CHILDHOOD DEVELOPMENT/EDUCATION – mainly through work with

– The World Bank, Washington, DC (Introduction of Haiti Montessori project into the World Bank-Conference "INVESTING IN OUR CHILDRENS' FUTURE",

– UNOPS (United Nations Office for Project Services) Conference AID & TRADE, N.Y.

– EXPO 2000 – as a registered project "EARLY CHILDHOOD EDUCATION" of the World Exposition, Germany, displayed in the EXPO "basic needs" thematic area.

– EXPO 2000 Global Dialogues on Fighting Poverty and on Building Learning Societies.

Since 4 May 2000: "NGO in SPECIAL CONSULTATIVE STATUS with the Economic and Social Council of the United Nations – ECOSOC". Since later in 2000 member of CONGO.

Since 2001 International conferences – mainly for ECD (Early Childhood Development). German representative of the WORLD FORUM ON EARLY CARE AND EDUCATION.

2003 Co-writing and publishing German book "On the way to a Jesus of today".

Since 2002 yearly participation in the "World Social Forum" in Porto Alegre, Brasil (2004 in Mumbai, India, 2007 in Nairobi, Kenya) – including offering workshops on a UN reform vision and on the Global Marshall Plan since 2003.

2003 "Creative Member" of the Club of Budapest (2005 recipient of the "Change-the-World-Award"). Engagement in the "Global Marshall Plan Initiative" for a peaceful "world in balance" and in NGO work for a transparent, democratic and participatory reform of the UN.

2004–2006 IFCW representative to the United Nations in Geneva and Vienna.

2005 move to second home in Seynod/Annecy, France, 40 minutes from the United Nations, Geneva, to improve UN presence and working conditions for "ONE world in diversity".

2006 125-years Schmincke & Co. + 25 years Haiti engagement (book by German journalist). Editor of "SOLIDARITÄT die ankommt!" (Solidarity which fulfils its purpose) for the Global Marshall Plan Initiative. Participation in the ADEA-Biennale in Gabon (a meeting of African Education Ministers).

2007 Start working on first English book "VISION WORKS".

2008 Member of "Associaton Montessori Internationale (AMI)" and of CIVICUS. Participation in the ADEA-Biennale in Maputo, Mozambique.
Publication of book "VISION WORKS".

376

Reader Group Guide

1. Over breakfast, Peter Hesse and his wife Isa came up with the title of this book, Vision Works. Does this title work for you? Why or why not?

2. Peter refers to his involvement in global development as an "awakening" that happened gradually. Do you think such awakenings take time, or do they happen overnight for some? In your life, have you ever experienced such an awakening?

3. Pastor Otto, from Salem castle, had a life slogan: "DENNOCH." Peter adopts "Dennoch" as his motto too, and Bernd Dreesman refers to Peter as the "Dennoch-type." Peter says the German word carries "emotional power and constructive anger." How do you understand this word and its driving force in his life? Do you have a sense of DENNOCH in your life?

4. Peter went to Haiti for the Cadence music. He did not plan to do development work, but what he experienced in Haiti prompted him to change his plans, and later to alter his career path. Where and when have you experienced something that has prompted you to change your plans in a way that you would not have anticipated?

5. People react differently to seeing human misery. Bernd Dreesmann says when Peter saw "the miserable condition of the children—badly nourished, shabby and with no chance to even receive a minimum of education," Peter's response was, "I cannot bear this." Peter's strong emotions prompt him to action. What is something in the world you cannot bear, which might prompt you to action?

6. Peter admits becoming more skeptical about his own "good ideas" even if they were "theoretically sound and logical."

He realized his ideas had to be vetted with Miot Jean Francois, his Haitian friend and teacher. From your experience, name some "good ideas" that did not work, because they did not address local concerns or a local culture? Name some that embraced local partnership?

7. A number of initiatives did not work out as envisioned like the sewing machines, the Port Margot micro-credit loans, child sponsorship, etc. These setbacks were learning experiences for him. He did not give up in spite of them. What do you think kept him going, kept him working on Haitian projects even after these incidences? Would you have continued?

8. There is a section of this book entitled, "the difficulty of true partnership." Name a few qualities you think are needed in a true partnership between people?

9. The people of Ste. Suzanne wanted Peter's foundation to "do something" for their children, and Carol Guy-James Barratt started the Montessori vision. Carol agreed to work in Haiti for at least two years, which later became 20. She was the right person at the right time for this valuable work. Have you ever been the right person at the right time?

10. Maria Montessori worked with children in the slums outside of Rome. Would you have guessed the Montessori method would work in Haiti? Why or why not?

11. How do you see Peter's spiritual journey feeding his work in political, business, and global development circles? Did anything about his spiritual journey resonate with your own?

12. Have you ever been politically involved? Who are your favorite political figures? Why? How did your political involvement turn out? What did you learn from it?

13. Many leaders talk about the guiding messages in their lives. In March 1989, Peter felt he got the guiding message, "Das

Ganze muss durch Lernen wachsen" or "The whole (all) must grow through learning." He got additional messages as well. Do you believe in these sorts of messages? Have you ever gotten a guiding message in your life? Is there a guiding message for your life?

14. Who do you see as visionaries in the world today? People working in any arena who are creating effective change in either political, religious, social, or business circles? What are they doing that is different?

15. Peter mentions other development models and efforts he values like the Micro-Credit Grameen Bank and the Global Marshall Plan. Can you name examples of projects or efforts that you have come to value?

16. What do you think of the U.N. Millennium Development Goals? The Global Marshall Plan Initiative? The 10 Global Compact Principles? Do you think they are, or can be, effective?

17. Peter says, "We need a new integral vision of a peaceful, fair and just balanced world organization as a result of a new think tank." He mentions the need for reforms in global institutions. Do you think there should be global oversight of nations? If yes, what do you think might work? What does work now?

18. This book talks about both micro and macro changes. Where do you think the most effective change happens, on a micro or macro level? Where do you feel most comfortable working, at a micro, mezzo, or macro level? Why?

19. What would you like to ask Peter Hesse about his life, this book, or about his work in Haiti and beyond?

20. Was there a story or incident in Vision Works that stood out for you?

Recommended Reading:

* *Global Marshall Plan A Planetary Contract: For a Worldwide Eco-Social Market Economy* by Franz Josef Radermacher
* *Mountains Beyond Mountains: The Quest of Dr. Paul Farmer, a Man Who Would Cure the World* by Tracy Kidder
* *Three Cups of Tea: One Man's Mission to Promote Peace...One School at a Time* by Greg Mortenson and David Oliver
* *Banker To The Poor: Micro-Lending and the Battle Against World Poverty* by Muhammad Yunus
* *The End of Poverty: Economic Possibilities for Our Time* by Jeffrey Sachs
* *Maria Montessori: Her Life and Work* by E. M. Standing
* *How to Raise An Amazing Child the Montessori Way* by Tim Seldin
* *Krik? Krak!* By Edwidge Danticat

Contributor's Footnote:

When I first met him, Peter Hesse struck me right away as a person of conviction. He is a force for good in this world, and I feel both honored and grateful to know him. For Peter, spiritual matters need to be grounded in physical action. He is passionate about fair international initiatives and practices. Poet Rainer Maria Rilke said, "build the great arch of unimagined bridges." Peter Hesse has sought to do that with his life. Our hope is that this Reading Group Guide will encourage dialogue, bridge-building, and bridge-builders.

Peace,
Rev. Susan Baller-Shepard, editor of www.spiritualbookclub.com